LEARNING THEOLOGY

through the

CHURCH'S WORSHIP

An Introduction to Christian Belief

Dennis Okholm

Baker Academic

a division of Baker Publishing Group
Grand Rapids, Michigan

Published by Baker Academic
a division of Baker Publishing Group
PO Box 6287, Grand Rapids, MI 49516-6287
www.bakeracademic.com

Printed in the United States of America

Library of Congress Cataloging-in-Publication Data
Names: Okholm, Dennis L., author.
Title: Learning theology through the church's worship : an introduction to Christian belief / Dennis Okholm.
Description: Grand Rapids, MI : Baker Academic, a division of Baker Publishing Group, [2018] | Includes bibliographical references and index.
Identifiers: LCCN 2018023370 | ISBN 9781540960016 (paper : alk. paper)
Subjects: LCSH: Theology, Doctrinal—Popular works.
Classification: LCC BT77 .O275 2018 | DDC 230—dc23
LC record available at https://lccn.loc.gov/2018023370

Material from chapter 2 originally appeared in a slightly different version in Dennis L. Okholm, "I Don't Think We're in Kansas Anymore, Toto! Postmodernism in Our Everyday Lives," *Theology Matters* 5, no. 4 (July/August 1999): 1–7. Used by permission.

18 19 20 21 22 23 24   7 6 5 4 3 2 1

"Theology and worship belong together. What we do together in public worship arises out of and then further forms our particular visions of who God is, the kind of salvation that is offered to us in Jesus Christ, and the nature of the Holy Spirit's work in the world. Ideas, practices, convictions, and perceptions all work together. Thanks to Dennis Okholm for inviting students to see so many of the connections! This book promises to deepen our engagement in worship, to encourage us in our life of faith, and to invite us to further reflection and learning."

—**John D. Witvliet**, Calvin Institute of Christian Worship, Calvin College and Calvin Theological Seminary

"Okholm pens this book with the admirable goal and heartfelt hope that it will enable the reader 'to see how the church's doctrine often arose out of worship and, conversely, how its worship reflects its doctrine.' My kudos! Mission accomplished! As a biblical studies instructor, I appreciate the thorough and thoughtful interface of Scripture with careful and informed theological reflection. As a worship studies instructor, I welcome an approach that puts the history and practice of Christian liturgy in conversation with systematic theology. I especially commend Okholm's pastoral concern and spiritual sensitivity in recognizing that prayer and the work of theology always belong together. Okholm offers a most helpful model for the integration of biblical theology, theology proper, and worship studies. I enthusiastically recommend the book for pastors, teachers, students—all Christian worshipers."

—**Andrew E. Hill**, Wheaton College and the Robert E. Webber Institute for Worship Studies

"An amazing ride! Okholm has brought prayer and worship together with orthodox and historical theology around a liturgical outline in a truly engaging way. This book has rare breadth, and where needed, serious depth—all aimed at showing how praying and worshiping shape followers of Jesus in true belief and fruitful practice."

—**Todd Hunter**, Anglican bishop; founder, Churches for the Sake of Others

"A pestilent dichotomy between doctrine and worship has infected Christian thought, making the doctrines of the Trinity, the atonement, and creation among many others seem foreign to the church's life and worship. Reading *Learning Theology through the Church's Worship* will heal you of the disease. In this book, Okholm introduces us to the rich beauty of our doctrine, performed every time we come together in worship. Reading this book will lead you to profound hallelujahs!"

—**Brian Lugioyo**, Azusa Pacific University

To my granddaughters,
Clara Woods and Elanor Wren,
who have been singing the doxology
from the day they could toddle.
May they never stop singing it,
knowing that the church's praise is always
one generation away from extinction.

Contents

Acknowledgments, Admissions, and Aspirations

When my Wheaton College colleague Timothy Phillips died nearly two decades ago, I promised him I would write the systematic theology that he and I envisioned. Since that time I have been on a journey studying liturgy and its relationship to theology. So in one sense I have kept my promise, though in a technical sense this is not the book that we envisioned.

It *is* the result of teaching theology to college and graduate students for the past thirty-five years. And so I must apologize ahead of time to those who deserve credit if there are phrases or discussions that seem borrowed. It is not my intention to pretend that all that follows is original with me. Some of what I teach has been lodged in my mind by those who have taught me in person or in books. I have tried to cite sources at all times, but I am sure there are those unconscious borrowings that have lost any memory of their origins.

One debt I *do* consciously owe is to Geoffrey Wainwright's *Doxology: The Praise of God in Worship, Doctrine and Life; A Systematic Theology.* Wainwright's knowledge of the church's liturgy is encyclopedic, and I am no match. But what he did in that book to bring theology and liturgy together is what inspired this book. Because Wainwright assumes so much of the reader (which is not a deficiency of his book, but a deficiency in the church's catechesis), I have used the book in small seminars of honors students who could ask me to elaborate on terms and concepts that Wainwright discusses. But I wanted to do something in the same spirit that would be accessible to students who had little or no previous knowledge of theology, liturgy, or both. Hence, this book.

I also wanted to write a student's first introduction to theology that would be *interesting*. I recommended to a millennial colleague a favorite introductory theology book I have used for years, but she recoiled from my suggestion because she found the book to be boring. Most systematic theology textbooks *are* dry and boring. That's not necessarily bad; it's just that they are not meant for the novice. They are important and necessary for the theology major and the "professional" theologian. So this book will just be an introduction for the uninitiated, and along the way I hope the student sees the value and relevance of theology. One of my joys in over three decades of college teaching has been getting non-theology students excited about the necessity and relevance of good theology for our lives. If that happens to some who read this book, then my joy will be increased.

Two more items deserve mention: Occasionally the book rehearses the context of the historical debates that lie behind our theology because I don't want anyone to think that the church's doctrines just dropped out of heaven. Rather, the theology that resulted from these debates contributes to an ongoing conversation among those who believe and worship. While I cannot avoid theological terminology (since learning a language is necessary for understanding subject matter more deeply), the text does keep in mind the theological newbie, so I have tried to provide definitions along the way.

Since this is a humble introduction, it is my hope that professors will supplement this text with whatever they think students need in addition. I have always supplemented my intro texts with the most recent trade books on specific topics (such as James Cone's *The Cross and the Lynching Tree*) and with brief introductory books for specific traditions (such as Kallistos Ware's *The Orthodox Way*). I am also hoping that this book will pique the curiosity of students who want to go further and deeper—who ask for advice about reading a past or present systematic theology or finding resources on liturgy. Some sample assignments at the end of the book aim to inspire relevant explorations of the doctrines discussed in hopes that this will encourage further study.

It is time to return worship to its proper close proximity to theology. As the fourth-century monk Evagrius once said, "A theologian is one who prays, and one who prays is a theologian." For too long and in too many theology textbooks, worship has been virtually ignored. Hopefully this book makes a small contribution to correct that oversight.

Preface

How to Read This Book

In the spirit of full disclosure and by way of orientation—especially since all theology is contextual—you should know where the author is located and why he has written this book.

As might be the case with you, the reader, I was completely unfamiliar with the history of Christian worship while I was being reared in communities of faith during my youth and college days. It was only when I took a course on worship from a Christian Reformed Church pastor at an Evangelical Free Church seminary that I first encountered the rich legacy of the church's worship. I had been shaped by Pentecostals and Baptists who did a great job of teaching me the Bible and Christian discipleship, but what was completely foreign to me and seemed inauthentic at the time were the actions and words of those "other churches" that wore robes, lit candles, had people come forward for communion, marched in and out, read prayers, and all the rest of what the church had been doing in worship for centuries. But when I began to study the heritage of the Christian Faith of which I was a part, I realized that there was much more to Christianity than I had ever known. What I learned led me on a journey to the Presbyterian Church, where I remained for three decades before making one more move, this time to the Anglicans.

Some of you have a very different history, perhaps having been *lifelong* participants in churches whose worship you recognized in my description of robes, candles, and such. (You might even have grown weary of it, and if you have, I hope this book reenergizes your participation in the liturgy.) Others of you share my background in what are sometimes referred to as nonliturgical churches, and you still find yourself in that context. If that is the case, I will have to convince you in chapters 1 and 2 that worship must not be separated from theology if we are going to act in a world we see through a Christian lens. And if I am successful, then we are off to a very significant exploration of how worship, theology, and life intersect as we work through the church's doctrines.

Whichever Christian community claims you, my hope is that this book will help you to see how the church's doctrine often arose out of its worship and, conversely, how its worship reflects its doctrine. (For instance, if you really want to know what someone believes, listen to her prayers and observe how she worships.) The book is even laid out as if it were a traditional Christian liturgy. (We'll discuss the meaning of the word *liturgy* later.) Beginning with the first chapter, the structure of the Christian liturgy (sometimes referred to as the *ordo* or "order") shapes the design of this text, beginning with the "gathering" and ending with the "dismissal." This will serve as a constant reminder that theology and worship should not be separated.

If you take a look at the table of contents, you will see that each chapter's title identifies where we are in the order of worship as well as what doctrine we will be considering. Sometimes the word or phrase that refers to our location in the liturgy may be unfamiliar, but not to worry: it will be explained in the chapter. In all but the chapter on the sacraments, an excerpt from the liturgy itself accompanies each chapter title or appears in the first paragraph or two. As you work your way through a chapter, it will become clear why we are discussing a particular doctrine in the context of one aspect of the worship service. Within each chapter, where it is appropriate, historical and theological connections will be made between the doctrine discussed and the church's liturgy. Many of the examples in this text will be drawn from resources like the Anglican *Book of Common Prayer*,[1] but the goal is to relate theology to aspects of Christian worship that belong to the historical church's practices throughout history and across denominational lines.

Hopefully this will be a unique experience for you, since this book differs from other introductions to theology. There are many good ones that introduce the doctrines, and some of those explicitly connect those doctrines to the life of the Christian. We will take it one step further and relate worship to doctrine and life.

Whatever your history with the church's worship has been, you and I must keep in mind that we cannot be formed into people who see the world a

---

1. The *Book of Common Prayer* was first composed by Thomas Cranmer in 1544 during the English Reformation. It has been revised several times since then and shapes the worship of churches in the Anglican (Church of England) communion today, which includes the Episcopal Church.

certain way unless we are first changed by God's grace. As sinners who want
to be the authors of our own story, we do not desire to see the world the way
God has established it and as God intends it to become. And so we need the
regenerating work of the Holy Spirit, especially because of the way sin affects
our minds and dispositions such that we do not even *desire* to see reality as
God sees it or appreciate the need for a Spirit-filled, Spirit-gifted, Spirit-led
worshiping community. Only as we are so enabled by God's Spirit can we
begin the process of seeing the world as Christ sees it, as if it were to us second
nature. And then we can follow Paul's admonition to "Let this same mind be
in you that was in Christ Jesus" (Phil. 2:5). Only then can we come to know
Christ by sharing in the power of his resurrection and becoming like him in
his death (Phil. 3:10).

And so we begin by considering how it is that we are shaped into the kinds
of people who have the mind of Christ. We begin with a prayer of Thomas
Aquinas:

> Creator of all things,
> true source of light and wisdom, lofty origin of all being,
> graciously let a ray of your brilliance
> penetrate into the darkness of my understanding
> and take from me the double darkness in which I have been born,
> an obscurity of both sin and ignorance.
> Give me a sharp sense of understanding,
> a retentive memory,
> and the ability to grasp things correctly and fundamentally.
> Grant me the talent of being exact in my explanations,
> and the ability to express myself with thoroughness and charm.
> Point out the beginning, direct the progress,
> and help in the completion;
> through Christ our Lord. Amen.[2]

---

2. St. Thomas Aquinas, translation from *Day by Day: The Notre Dame Prayer Book for Students*, ed. Thomas McNally, CSC, and William G. Storey, DMS, rev. ed. (Notre Dame, IN: Ave Maria Press, 2004), 60.

1

Liturgical Ophthalmology, or Why Christian Theology and Ethics Begin and End with Worship

We Enter by "Gathering"

Your eye is the lamp of your body. If your eye is healthy, your whole body is full of light; but if it is not healthy, your body is full of darkness. Therefore consider whether the light in you is not darkness. If then your whole body is full of light, with no part of it in darkness, it will be as full of light as when a lamp gives you light with its rays.

—Luke 11:34–36

The God Christians worship is known through initiation into the practices of a tradition that are necessary to know how rightly to name God.

—Stanley Hauerwas, In Good Company[1]

When I was four years old my parents took me to the ophthalmologist, suspecting that my vision wasn't up to par. I remember that the doctor

1. Stanley Hauerwas, *In Good Company: The Church as Polis* (Notre Dame, IN: University of Notre Dame Press, 1997), 158.

and my parents took me over to the window, pointed toward something, and asked if I could see "that flag." I tried and tried, but I couldn't see what they were talking about. That led to a forty-seven-year series of increasingly thicker glasses until I got my eyes lasered to correct my nearsightedness—all so that I could *see* what I was *looking at*. I needed thick lenses to *see* what only those with good eyesight could see.

The consequences of uncorrected vision can be significant. In one episode of *Seinfeld*, George loses his glasses, yet, through squinting eyes, he thinks he sees Jerry's girlfriend kissing another man across the street. Jerry is suspicious and accuses his girlfriend on two occasions before they eventually break up. Of course, George was mistaken, something he learns when he again thinks he sees Jerry's girlfriend kissing another man until he puts on his new glasses and actually sees a policewoman nuzzling her horse.

Centuries before my ophthalmology appointment and any episodes of *Seinfeld*, John Calvin drew out the theological significance of these anecdotes with a wonderful analogy: "Just as old or bleary-eyed men and those with weak vision, if you thrust before them a most beautiful volume, even if they recognize it to be some sort of writing, yet can scarcely construe two words, but with the aid of spectacles will begin to read distinctly; so Scripture, gathering up the otherwise confused knowledge of God in our minds, having dispersed our dullness, clearly shows us the true God."[2] The point is this: We do not *see* merely by *looking*. We do not *see* reality the way God created it and is in the process of redeeming it merely by *looking* at our lives and the world. Seeing requires correction—in this case, correction made possible by God's revelation in the incarnation, in Scripture, and in Christ's church.

If seeing were merely a matter of looking, then the centurion's assessment of the crucified Jesus—that "truly this man was God's Son" (Matt. 27:54)—would have been shared by the entire Roman garrison that day. If seeing were merely looking, then Paul would be wrong to say that the same cross that is foolishness to the Greeks and a stumbling block to the Jews is the saving power of God to those who believe (1 Cor. 1:18–25). If seeing were merely looking, then Jesus would not have asked his host, Simon the Pharisee, "Do you *see* this woman?" since Simon was *looking* at her; yet apparently he *saw* not a woman, but merely a prostitute (Luke 7:44), and his reactions to the situation were based on what he *saw*.

Anyone who has suffered from an ailment like myopia knows what Simon was experiencing: how and what you see has a lot to do with how you act.

2. John Calvin, *Institutes of the Christian Religion*, ed. John T. McNeill, trans. Ford Lewis Battles (Philadelphia: Westminster John Knox, 1960), 1.6.1.

In fact, a number of theologians have taken up Iris Murdoch's pithy remark: "You can only act in the world you can see." If that is true, then what we need to realize is that the way a Christian acts has less to do with determining right from wrong, and more to do with seeing the world *Christianly*.

And it's not only acting that flows from what we see. We *become* what we see. Hopefully that truth will become more obvious the further we get into our discussion.

Learning to See the World Christianly

Let's start with what should be self-evident: seeing is always from a perspective. There is no view from nowhere. If I witness an accident that takes place in a busy intersection, I can recount what took place from my vantage point on one corner, while another person on the opposite corner will recount what took place from *her* perspective. Both of us may provide accurate accounts of what took place, but there will be variations between our accounts due to our different perspectives. We interpret reality from *somewhere*; we cannot do it from *nowhere*.

While that should be obvious, it is not always admitted in our modernist milieu. The modernist assumption is that neutrality and complete objectivity are not only possible, but desirable. The claim is that we should look at the world without presuppositions or assumptions or culturally shaped perspectives because our modern Western scientific way of looking at the world is the only way any self-respecting, rational human being *would* look at the world. The Declaration of Independence makes this claim: "We hold these Truths to be *self-evident*, that all Men are created equal," even though the author of this statement had African slaves, and women would not be allowed to vote in this "equal" society for nearly 150 years after these words were written. Presumably to any "right-thinking rational" person, this statement about males of European origin was true. Even some zealous defenders of Christian apologetics and morality argue with unbelievers under the assumption that if the non-Christian disagrees, it is only because the other person is being irrational. Modernists who make these assumptions need to be brought up to speed by what I once heard Dallas Seminary's Howard Hendricks say, "You can't teach a person to walk before they're born."

If we really hear what the apostle Paul is saying in 1 Corinthians about perceptions of the cross, then we should realize that the biblical story—the true story of the world—does not make its appeal to some supposed universal rational assessment for legitimation. Augustine knew this when he articulated what most of his peers held: "faith seeks understanding." Centuries later, Anselm would be explicit as well, though he meant something slightly different by "understanding": "I believe in order to understand. And I believe that if I do not believe, then I cannot understand."

In his book *The Spirit of Early Christian Thought*, Robert Wilken narrates how early Christians did not rely so much on demonstration or argument or proof, as the philosophers did, but on witnesses to what happened; as he puts it, they were concerned with "the ability to *see* what is disclosed in events and the readiness to trust the words of those who testify to them."[3] And he shows how much of this was accomplished through the church's liturgy,[4] as we will demonstrate below.

But first we need to establish how the perspective from which we see as Christians is developed.

Communities cultivate perspective. They shape the way we see the world. For instance, consider why you believe that everything that surrounds you is composed of atomic and subatomic particles that you have never seen, or that the earth is spinning even though to all appearances it seems that the sun rises rather than that the earth turns each morning, or that our planet is orbiting the sun at an incredible speed, which you do not feel. *Traditioned* scientific and educational communities that you *trusted* taught you to see and experience the world in these counterintuitive ways to the point that you would consider someone a fool or "uneducated" who did not see things this way.

Of course, adopting this perspective of things required you to learn a language. You learned about protons, electrons, and neutrons rather than simply referring to "little things that make up atoms." You even had to learn the words *atom, earth, planet, sun, orbit*, and so on. And the more you mastered the language, the more embedded in the community and its view of the world you became.

So, what we see and how we interpret and articulate what we see has much to do with being part of a language-using community—a linguistic culture. In

3. Robert Louis Wilken, *The Spirit of Early Christian Thought* (New Haven: Yale University Press, 2003), 7 (italics added).

4. The word that Christians use to speak of worship is *liturgy*. It is often misunderstood (etymologically) as "work of the people (*laos*)." It comes from the Greek word *leitourgia*, which comes from the Greek *leitos* (public) and *ergon* (work). In other words, it is a secular Greek word for public work done on behalf of the people by another person or group appointed to the task. In the New Testament the primary use of the term refers to Christ himself: Hebrews 8:2 designates him as our *leitourgos*. In other words, we join a liturgy already in progress—the Son, our high priest, renders worship to the Father, and we participate in that worship as we offer ourselves to Christ. See Maxwell E. Johnson, *Praying and Believing in Early Christianity: The Interplay between Christian Worship and Doctrine* (Collegeville, MN: Liturgical Press, 2013), xi–xii.

fact, language operates as the filter through which we experience the world. Early on, perhaps with the help of *Sesame Street*, you learned to call "the one that is not like the others" a "triangle." Later, when painting the interior walls of your house, you learned that white isn't just white, but eggshell white, seashell white, ivory, and cosmic latte.

In the book *The Giver* by Lois Lowry, Jonas couldn't understand what he was perceiving when he looked at Fiona's hair until the Giver gave him the word *red*. Once he had a word to interpret his experience, he began to see the color associated with the word—something that had been lost because the dystopian community in which he was reared had intentionally changed the language and altered the perception of reality.

These interpretive communities are known by the language they use. For example, if you heard "Play ball," you would associate that with baseball. "Start your engines" would conjure up images of a speedway. If you heard the phrase "Let us pray," you would surmise you were in some Christian worship context.

But only those who have been reared in a specific community know the language more deeply because they have been shaped by a particular community's language to describe and understand and even participate in its concerns and activities. For instance, if I have entered more deeply into the baseball community, I will know that the initials ERA do not stand for "Equal Rights Amendment," but for a statistic that will be important in the baseball community's assessment of a pitcher's abilities. To know the words "I believe in God the Father Almighty" and to really appreciate the meaning of those words, I might likely have been catechized and reared in the Christian community.

To be part of a community that shapes the way I see the world and respond to it, then, requires that I learn, understand, and function with the language of that community. Though they will understand if I naively order a small latte, when I become integrated into the Starbucks community I will eventually find myself ordering a "Tall." When I become more sophisticated and more thirsty, I will tout the word "Venti" and receive a twenty-ounce hot drink or a twenty-four-ounce cold drink, even if I don't know the exact translation of the word "Venti." And if I want to become a priest at Starbucks, I will have to learn the liturgical language that only a few parishioners know, such as "iced single Venti Mocha no whip" or "double tall skinny cappuccino, extra dry" followed by the person's name as they are called forward to the altar to receive the cup. There are even websites and videos to train the neophyte; think of them as new membership classes for Starbucks.

This communal training to see the world a certain way happens both intentionally and unintentionally. When my family learned that I had not only nearsightedness but also astigmatism, my mother was told to train my eyes by daily having me follow the slowly rotating movements of the head of a hatpin. That was intentional. But we are being trained every day, usually without our intentional involvement, to see the world as consumers in a capitalist economy with its advertisements, news reports, and excursions to the mall. One corporate manager put it this way: "Corporate branding is really about worldwide beliefs management."[5] This involves what James K. A. Smith calls competing "liturgies"—ritual practices of deep significance.[6] Furthermore, because we are members of at least these two communities—the consumerist and the Christian—we are often afflicted with "double vision" over against the single focus on the kingdom that Jesus insists upon in Matthew 6:33. Or, worse, like my monovision LASIKed–eyes that permit me to move back and forth between near and distant foci because one eye is immediately and unconsciously dominant over the other depending on the circumstance, often the consumerist eye is dominant over the Christian.

So we need to be even more intentional about training ourselves to see Christianly. Jesus put it this way in Matthew 6: your heart is where your treasure is. The order is important: what you treasure, that is, what you worship—what you invest your time, money, and energy in pursuing—is what will shape your heart. We not only become what we see. We become what we *worship*.

This is where the church community comes in. It is in the church that we learn the language and engage in the practices or rituals that will train us to see reality as disciples of the crucified, risen, and ascended Christ. This happens especially as we rehearse the biblical narrative, particularly that part of the narrative centered on Christ. Our moral conceptions depend on the way that this ecclesiastical language–using community shapes the way we as moral people see the world by recounting and reliving the story into which we have been baptized. Our worship—our liturgy—plays a central role at this point, centered in the Eucharist (the Lord's Supper or communion).

To illustrate, in his book *Christianity Rediscovered*, the American Roman Catholic priest Vincent Donovan tells the story of being sent in the late 1960s to evangelize the Masai people of Tanzania. He describes how a series of communities came to grasp the significance of the Eucharist (communion) and how the regular practice of the liturgy informed and shaped their common life—how the liturgy changed the way they *saw* everything. But at first it wasn't easy. Here is what he wrote:

5. Quoted in William T. Cavanaugh, *Being Consumed* (Grand Rapids: Eerdmans, 2008), 47.
6. James K. A. Smith, *Desiring the Kingdom: Worship, Worldview, and Cultural Formation* (Grand Rapids: Baker Academic, 2009).

Masai men had never eaten in the presence of Masai women. In their minds, the status and condition of women were such that the very presence of women at the time of eating was enough to pollute any food that was present. . . . How then was the Eucharist possible? If ever there was a need for the Eucharist as a salvific sign of unity, it was here. . . . Here, in the Eucharist, we were at the heart of the unchanging gospel that I was passing on to them. They were free to accept the gospel or reject it, but if they accepted it, they were accepting the truth that in the Eucharist . . . "there is neither slave nor free, neither Jew nor Greek, neither male nor female."[7]

They came to accept it. It radically changed their lives. Because of the liturgy—the Eucharist—the men now *saw* the women in a new way and, as a result, treated them differently.

When we sing and internalize a praise song or hymn, we are being shaped to see the world Christianly. For example, singing the hymn "This Is My Father's World" reminds us that, in spite of the temptation to find our identity in the community of a political party or nation, we believe that "though the wrong seems oft so strong, *God* is the *Ruler* yet." Our responses to events that are reported in the news or that we encounter in our everyday lives come to be shaped by this reminder in our liturgy.

Listening to Scripture read in worship—whether from stories of Jesus's encounters with people in the Gospel accounts or a reminder from Genesis or 1 John that we are all made in the image of God—shapes the way we see and therefore respond to a homeless person rummaging around in a trash can, a welfare recipient, an immigrant, or even the worst of sinners for whom Jesus Christ died.

Nathan Mitchell put it this way: "Christian liturgy begins as ritual practice but ends as ethical performance."[8] Our lives should correspond to what we articulate in our worship such that our works verify or authenticate our sermon engagement, praying, and singing. This is as old as the Hebrew prophets (see Amos 5:21–24) and Paul's Letter to the Corinthians (see 1 Cor. 11:17–34). The relationship between how we worship, what we believe, and how we live is nicely summarized by Maxwell Johnson: "Christians act morally or ethically because of what they believe, and what they believe is continually shaped by worship, by how they are formed by the words and acts of worship, by the divine encounter with the God of grace and love mediated in the liturgy via its spoken words, texts, acts, gestures, and sacramental signs."[9]

7. Vincent Donovan, *Christianity Rediscovered* (Maryknoll, NY: Orbis, 2003), 91.
8. Quoted in M. Johnson, *Praying and Believing*, 95.
9. M. Johnson, *Praying and Believing*, 98.

And if our lives do not match our words and acts in worship, perhaps it is not because the liturgy is at fault, but because it is not really *Christian* worship that is shaping us. To paraphrase Paul, who scolded those who cut in front of the line at the *agapē* (love) meal that included communion, "When you come together, it is not really to eat the Lord's supper" (1 Cor. 11:20). And as N. T. Wright articulates Paul's analysis of the human situation in the first chapter of his Letter to the Romans, "The primary human problem . . . is not 'sin,' but 'ungodliness.' It is a failure not primarily of behavior (though that follows), but of *worship*. Worship the wrong divinity, and instead of reflecting God's wise order into the world you will reflect and then produce a distortion: something out of joint, something 'unjust.'"[10]

When we are baptized, we are initiated and immersed into a community that is attempting to live into and be shaped by God's story. And we commit ourselves to learning this story with the church, embracing it, and letting it get into us as we continually rehearse it. The church calendar functions as one of the means by which we remember this baptized identity. Every day I catch myself glancing at the calendar from *Touchstone* magazine that hangs in our kitchen by the refrigerator. I am looking to see who in my church family—my first family—is to be remembered today. Often it is not someone whose name I recognize, but, thankfully, their work, their mission, their martyrdom—their participation in this same story—is not forgotten, and I learn more about the way I should live as one who shares their vision of life.

This is what it means to "tradition" the faith. We maintain the tradition—hand on what we have received—through liturgy and lectionary (a two- or three-year sequence of biblical readings) and church calendar, because we are people of space and time, and the church is an embodied, time-sequenced, historical community that participates in what G. K. Chesterton once called the "democracy of the dead."[11]

As Stanley Hauerwas and Sam Wells remind us, "Theologians like Augustine and Aquinas never forget that their task was to help Christians remember that their lives are shaped by story-determined practices that make all that they do and do not intelligible."[12] And what makes our words and behavior intelligible is the story that we hear in the Word and rehearse in the sacraments in our praise and worship of God.

10. N. T. Wright, *The Day the Revolution Began: Reconsidering the Meaning of Jesus's Crucifixion* (San Francisco: HarperOne, 2016), 268.

11. From "The Ethics of Elfland," chap. 4 of *Orthodoxy* (New York: John Lane Company, 1908), 85.

12. Stanley Hauerwas and Samuel Wells, eds., *The Blackwell Companion to Christian Ethics* (Malden, MA: Blackwell, 2004, 2006), 46.

Figure 1
The Church Year Calendar

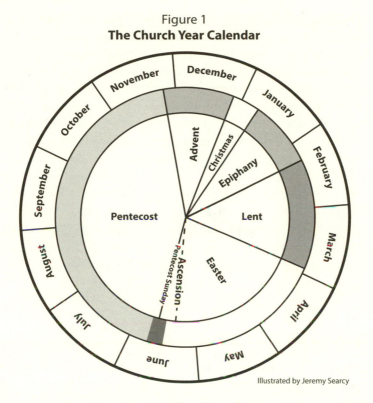

Illustrated by Jeremy Searcy

Hauerwas summarizes these last few thoughts even better:

> Practically speaking, what the church asks of people is difficult *to do* by oneself
> . . . what the church asks of people is difficult *to see* by oneself. Christian ethics
> arise, in great part, out of something Christians claim to have seen that the
> world has not seen, namely, the creation of a people, a family, a colony that is
> a living witness that Jesus Christ is Lord. Tradition, as we use the term here,
> is a complex, lively argument about what happened in Jesus that has been car-
> ried on, across the generations, by a concrete body of people called the church.
> Fidelity to this tradition, this story, is the most invigorating challenge of the
> adventure begun in our baptism and the toughest job of Christian ethics.[13]

And this "tough job" falls on the church. But how does the church accomplish
this when the world finds our lived Christianity unintelligible because it is
looking at us from the perspective of different stories given ultimacy in their
lives? How do grace-enlivened people of the church stay on track?

13. Stanley Hauerwas and William Willimon, *Resident Aliens: Life in the Christian Colony*
(Nashville: Abingdon, 1989), 72 (italics original).

If you've ever mowed a lawn or plowed a field, you know that it is difficult if not impossible to keep a straight line if you only look at what is immediately ahead of you. The trick is to keep your eye on the distant goal—the end of the mowed path or plowed row. It is the same with those who belong to Christ's church: in order to maintain a rightly focused and single vision, we center our attention on a *telos*—the goal of the kingdom of God that is already here but not yet fulfilled. Those of us who sit through the biblical narratives during the Easter Vigil (the Saturday evening liturgy before Easter Sunday) reenter the story of God's promise and provisions for this coming kingdom. And when we celebrate the Eucharist we not only look backward to Jesus's Last Supper with the Twelve before his crucifixion, but we also look forward to the eschatological banquet of the Lamb. In fact, in the Eucharist we actually experience in the present these two events at opposite ends of the chronology. (More about this will come in chap. 11.)

Again, here we find ourselves at odds with those shaped by a different story, for the *telos*—the end goal or purpose—depends on the story. And the dominant story in our culture is liberal democracy. Now, on the one hand, we appreciate the narrative of our nation driven by the perspective of philosophical architects such as John Locke, for it makes it possible for us who are being shaped by the biblical story to live out that story with little interference. But, on the other hand, the problem with our liberal democracy is that we in the West have no agreement on the *telos*. In fact, we relish the individualism that allows each person to define her own *telos* as long as the means to achieve it do not interfere with others in the pursuit of their own chosen *telos*. But, as we have said, the church is defined by the *telos* of the story that is centered in the establishment of God's kingdom.

Furthermore, we hold that this story is the only true story of the world— the only correct interpretation of reality that explains why we see the world the way we do and act in it as we do. The kingdom requires certain characteristics that must be cultivated—such as the description of kingdom people in the Sermon on the Mount. To cultivate those characteristics requires discipline, but also a community of memory—both of which we have already mentioned. It is not possible to develop the character traits of humility and patience and love outside the community that is centered on the worship of the God revealed in Jesus Christ, whose life, death, and resurrection define these characteristics.

So we are the people who seek this kingdom. (By the way, a "seeker church" should not be a church that *attracts* people to *it*, but a church that seeks the kingdom [Matt. 6:33] and that seeks people to invite into the kingdom who are usually not in the church building.) We seek because, before we are knowers, we are desirers, lovers. (Note the prevalent images of hungering, thirsting, seeking, and the like in Jesus's teachings. Even the word *know* is sometimes connected with sexual desire in the biblical narrative.)

We often make a huge miscalculation in thinking that if we just give people the right cerebral information, they will become deeply committed followers of Christ.[14] Instead, as whole embodied people who are both thinkers and desirers, we are to be shaped into certain kinds of people who, like Jesus, exhibit the fruit of the Spirit, love our neighbor, pray for our enemies, bless our persecutors, and care for orphans and widows. And, as we have been saying all along, that shaping comes by participating in the storied community centered on the narrative of Scripture and in the liturgy that replays the narrative in action. Then, as people so changed and so shaped, we tell and live the story within our world's prevailing story of a plurality of *teloi*.

So what is this biblical narrative that shapes the storied community called church?

The Story into Which We Are Called

The Bible unfurls one grand story. It is the true story of God and the overarching narrative of the world. It deals with God's purposes for a world God created, sustains, and is in the process of restoring. It is into this story that the church is called to participate.

Just as a person's history might help a psychologist better understand an episode in a person's life, so the parts of the Bible are correctly understood only when they are placed in the context of the whole biblical narrative. Unfortunately, what often happens is that another narrative supersedes the biblical narrative such that "Bible bits" get absorbed into that other story and, because they are taken out of context, the bits get misused and misunderstood. For example, 2 Chronicles 7:14 has to do with Solomon and the establishment of the temple in Jerusalem; the "my people" in this verse is referring to the Jews with whom God made a covenant. But often this verse gets superimposed on an American flag and misused as if citizens of the USA were the "my people" to which the verse refers. The danger is exacerbated when the association justifies an American ideology or action. When we do this, we are giving more authority to the nation's narrative than to God's written Word. Robert Louis Wilken graphically made the point: "Without a grasp of the plot that holds everything together, the Bible is as vacuous as a mosaic in which the tiles have been arbitrarily rearranged without reference

---

14. This is a point forcefully made by J. Smith in *Desiring the Kingdom*.

to the original design."[15] When this happens in sermons, passages get treated as moralisms, lessons for "Everyman" (see *VeggieTales*), or psychological helps.[16]

This does not mean the Bible does not contain directives for how we should live our lives. But how we are to act and what we should decide only make sense if we know what story we're in.[17] This comes out beautifully in the movie *Sweetland*, which features a quote by Don Snyder at the beginning of the movie: "Let us hope that we are all preceded in this world by a love story." The film is about a Minnesota farmer who is tempted by a developer's significant monetary offer for his land; his final decision is made in the context of his remembrance of the story of his father and immigrant mother, whose farm he inherited.

Another movie that communicates the narrative context for the moral life is *Stranger than Fiction*. Harold Crick (played by Will Ferrell) is upset when he learns that his story—including his imminent death—is being written by a novelist (played by Emma Thompson). But after reading and understanding the story and after accepting the assessment of a literary critic (played by Dustin Hoffman), Harold is able and willing to die.

The biblical story is not about my happiness or my success. It's about fitting into the history that God is writing concerning the establishment of God's kingdom on earth as it is in heaven—even if fitting into God's story includes my death. In the end, I can only answer the question, What am I to do? If I can answer the prior question, in what story do I find myself?[18]

This, again, is why liturgy plays such an important role in our moral life. For example, cycling through the three-year lectionary of Bible readings reminds us of the entire biblical narrative, especially as it is tied to the church

---

15. Wilken, *Early Christian Thought*, 68.

16. A good example of this is the book on marriage *Love and Respect* by Emerson Eggerichs (Nashville: Nelson, 2004). Taken from one verse in Ephesians 5 (v. 33), psychological principles get spun out differentiating how husbands should *love* their wives, while wives are to *respect* their husbands. Seen in the larger context of Ephesians, let alone the entire biblical narrative (to which Paul *is* referring in Ephesians 1–2), the relation of husbands and wives is *primarily* about serving Christ's church and the kingdom of God, with happiness in marriage a by-product. That focus is missing in most Christian books on marriage. (Though see that focus played out in Trevecca Okholm, *Kingdom Family: Re-Envisioning God's Plan for Marriage and Family* [Eugene, OR: Cascade, 2012]).

17. This point is developed well in *The Drama of Scripture: Finding Our Place in the Biblical Story*, by Craig G. Bartholomew and Michael W. Goheen (Grand Rapids: Baker Academic, 2004). Also see Stanley Hauerwas, *The Peaceable Kingdom: A Primer in Christian Ethics* (Notre Dame, IN: University of Notre Dame Press, 1983). I am especially indebted to Bartholomew and Goheen for some of the concepts developed in this chapter.

18. This is the point Alasdair MacIntyre makes in *After Virtue: A Study in Moral Theory*, 3rd ed. (Notre Dame, IN: University of Notre Dame Press, 2007).

calendar, so that by the time the cycle is complete, we have reentered God's story in ways that shape our entire being. In fact, though the church year after year wends its way from the Jewish expectation of a Messiah (Advent) to the experience of the church in the book of Acts (so-called Ordinary Time), the circle is not a mere repetition, as Philip Pfatteicher reminds us:

> When we begin the year once more, we are not the same people as we were when we began the cycle the year before. The world has changed, and we have changed with it. New experiences must be incorporated in the recurring cycle. . . . The Church's year is a circle, but it is not an endless round. It has a goal, an end, a purpose as we move from slavery to the Promised Land, from exile to return, "from this world to that which is to come.". . . As the Church progresses through the circle year after year, it leads ever higher, spiraling ever up the mountain, for this journey is going somewhere, moving always to a higher level, toward the final goal.[19]

Craig Bartholomew and Michael Goheen,[20] along with suggestions made by N. T. Wright, help us to see the biblical narrative as a play in six acts and how that narrative dictates the way we live.

In act one, God creates his kingdom (Gen. 1–2). But by the second act his creatures have rebelled (Gen. 3–11). So God promises to restore the kingdom and bless all nations through Israel—the progeny of Abraham with whom he makes this covenant—a covenant that actually goes back to the promise God made in Genesis 3:15 that Eve's seed would crush the serpent's head. Some theologians have called this initial promise in Genesis 3 the *protoevangelion* or first announcement of the gospel—of the coming of Jesus Christ.[21]

God extended the promise of Genesis 3:15 in the story of Noah and the flood. But it really gets its impetus in act three—the story of Abraham that begins in Genesis 12 and continues with Israel's history throughout the Old Testament.

However, Israel is sent into exile for failing to keep the conditions of the covenant (see Deut. 1–28). Thus, redemption of the creation and reestablishment of God's kingdom must be accomplished by the only faithful Israelite—the God-man, the Messiah (King), Jesus. This is act four, told to us in the four Gospel accounts.

19. Philip H. Pfatteicher, *Journey into the Heart of God: Living the Liturgical Year* (New York: Oxford University Press, 2013), 344.

20. See Bartholomew and Goheen, *Drama of Scripture*.

21. Philip Pfatteicher (*Journey*, 68) notes that Johann Heinrich Wicher (nineteenth century) invented the Advent wreath for a boys' home he founded, and he had the promise in Genesis 3:15 recited by the children as the candle was lit for the first Sunday in Advent.

The preview of the kingdom coming in all of its fullness is portrayed in act five, as the church carries out its mission of living and telling the news of the king and the kingdom, inviting folks to join in; Acts and the Epistles are the script.

Finally, the play concludes with act six, when the king returns, the kingdom is fully restored, and the redemption of creation is complete—essentially the book of Revelation.

So where do we fit into this six-act play? Wright asks us to imagine the following scenario.[22] We are members of a Shakespearian acting troop. We have mastered the plays of Shakespeare. Recently a previously unknown six-act play has been found, but the fifth act is incomplete and the sixth is somewhat vague. Nevertheless, because we are imbued with Shakespeare and because we have rehearsed over and over (like a three-year cycle in a lectionary and church calendar) this particular play, when we get to the incomplete fifth act, no one in the audience can tell that it is unfinished because we improvise in a way that fits what *is* available to us. In like manner, we Christians know full well the first four acts, what is available of the fifth, and the gist of the sixth. And so we improvise, living out our lives in a way that corresponds to the conclusion God has determined and toward which the end of the drama is moving. We have been so shaped by the story that those who observe our thoughts and behaviors have no idea that we are improvising during the fifth act.

We were called and baptized to live within God's story—a story about God's mission to restore the creation. It is the true story of the whole world. It is God's story of our world, and God expects us to appropriate this story for ourselves. We do this in worship, especially when we participate in the *anaphora* (literally, "offering")—the ancient prayer of thanksgiving that has been central to the church's eucharistic liturgy to this day (see the box titled "Part of the *Anaphora* from *The Book of Common Prayer*" for an excerpt). It has a "distinct narrative structure," which Robert Louis Wilken says "follows biblical precedent. . . . The liturgy kept intact the biblical narrative, and by recounting the story of Israel and Christ in ritual form it confirmed Christian belief that God's fullest revelation came through historical events."[23] So, in every baptism and every communion service, the church's liturgy educates us and reminds us of the story in which we, as Christians, are living our lives.

Understanding that we are baptized into this story calls into question the ease of so casually referring to salvation with phrases such as "Jesus came

22. N. T. Wright uses this model (of five acts in his case) in several of his writings.
23. Wilken, *Early Christian Thought*, 33.

Table 1
The Acts in the Biblical Drama

"Before the foundations of the world" (Eph. 1:4)	ACT 1 Gen. 1–2	ACT 2 Gen. 3	ACT 3 Old Testament	ACT 4 Gospels	ACT 5 Acts & New Testament Epistles	ACT 6 Revelation
Our lives are preceded by a love story.	CREATION	THE FALL	ISRAEL	JESUS CHRIST	THE CHURCH	KINGDOM OF GOD
	Mandate: "Fill the earth" as God's image-bearers (Gen. 1:26–28).	Genesis 3:15—the "Protoevangelium" as the first announcement of the coming of a Redeemer—Eve's seed, Mary's child.	Genesis 12—God's covenant with Abraham for the sake of the world.	The only faithful Israelite takes on Israel's punishment so the covenant can go forward.	The body of Christ takes it to the ends of the earth (Acts 1:8). *We are here in the story!*	The re-creation of the fallen cosmos—a renewed heaven and earth.

into my life" and "I accepted Jesus into my heart." These statements subtly hint that we may still be in control, asking Jesus to come into *our* story. Also, even though Paul often uses the phrase "Christ in us" (thereby making our phrases acceptable), he more often uses the phrase "we are in Christ." In other words, what if *we* more often referred to our salvation with phrases like, "I have been accepted into Jesus's life, death, and resurrection" and "I have been baptized into God's story—into Jesus's death and resurrection"? The Christian claims not to be merely copying Jesus Christ as a model, like copying a rock star or sports figure, though "putting on Christ" might mean that sometimes the Christian acts like Christ even if she does not yet understand why (Rom. 13:11–14). Nor does one just accept the values of Jesus Christ (as with nineteenth-century liberalism). And neither is this simply following a code of conduct or set of rules for living a respectable moral life. We are not talking about a self-help or self-improvement program that merely "baptizes" insights from psychology with Christian jargon. We have been talking about sharing Christ's life in an organic way, just as a vine is attached to its branch, just as we are one with Christ and each other as the Son and the Father are one (John 15:1–17 and 17:20–24).

This is precisely what the church's liturgy calls us to. So how does the church's eucharistic liturgy with its narrative structure help participants align

---

Part of the *Anaphora* from *The Book of Common Prayer*

Holy and gracious Father: In your infi-   mercy, sent Jesus Christ, your only and
nite love you made us for yourself; and,   eternal Son, to share our human nature,
when we had fallen into sin and become   to live and die as one of us, to reconcile
subject to evil and death, you, in your   us to you, the God and Father of all.

---

their lives with all that God is up to? To answer that, we need to get a general overview of this liturgy.

The Structure and Significance of Christian Worship for Theology

From its early Christian origins the church established a pattern for the order of liturgy (referred to as the *ordo*). The first half of worship was designated the "Liturgy of the Word," while the second half was the "Liturgy of the Eucharist." All were invited to participate in the first half, but those who were yet to be baptized were dismissed before the second half in order to be trained (or catechized) in the Faith.

Catechesis means "instruction" in Greek. By the fourth century this catechesis might have taken two to three years before the catechumen (learner) was baptized on Holy Saturday (the night before Easter Sunday). During Lent (the weeks before Easter) those to be baptized underwent the "scrutinies"—examinations, exorcisms, and prayers—and, before baptism, the "handing over" of the creed (*traditio symboli*) to the catechumens so that they would "hand it back" (*redditio*) by repeating what they had memorized.[24] As time went on, catechisms, such as Martin Luther's, included instruction organized around the Apostles' Creed (what Christians believe), the Ten Commandments (how Christians live), and the Lord's Prayer (how Christians worship).

The Liturgy of the Word, in which all participated, began with the gathering, calling the people to worship. This might involve a greeting (such as "The Lord be with you"), a prayer of preparation, and a collect (a prayer prayed by the priest[25] that "collects" the thoughts of the people and expresses the theme of the day). As Simon Chan develops it, gathering means the church comes from the world to be church—to be the new creation.[26] This is a "grand

---

24. See Pfatteicher, *Journey*, 142.
25. Note that *priest* is a shortened form of the Greek word *presbyteros*, which is usually translated "elder."
26. See Simon Chan, *Liturgical Theology* (Downers Grove, IL: InterVarsity, 2006), 130–34.

entrance," as Edith Humphrey calls it: the church enters into a space, time, and fellowship that is larger than what it sees.[27] But this then situates the church between the call to gather and the dismissal at the end of worship when the church reenters the world that is yet to be fully redeemed. It becomes a reminder to the church that we live between the "already" and the "not yet" of the kingdom. This is especially prominent in Eastern Orthodox worship,[28] since the liturgy and the sanctuary are meant to represent heaven. For a few hours the church experiences its true reality and a reality that is yet to come. Alexander Schmemann captures this so well:

> It is not an escape from the world, rather it is the arrival at a vantage point from which we can see more deeply into the reality of the world.
>
> The journey begins when Christians leave their homes and beds. They leave, indeed, their life in this present and concrete world, and whether they have to drive fifteen miles or walk a few blocks, a sacramental act is already taking place, an act which is the very condition of everything else that is to happen. For they are now on their way to *constitute the Church*, or to be more exact, to be transformed into the Church of God. . . . And now they have been called to "come together in one place," to bring their lives, their very "world" with them and to be more than what they were: a *new* community with a new life. . . . The purpose is to *fulfill the Church*, and that means to make present the One to whom all things are at their *end*, and all things are at their *beginning*.[29]

The Liturgy of the Word continued with the reading of Scripture. The Scripture for the day might involve more than one passage. In fact, as the lectionary evolved, the Scripture that was read included a passage from the Old Testament, a New Testament Epistle, and the Gospels, with a psalm or portion of a psalm. After the readings, a homily or sermon explained what had been read. Typically the recitation of the creed (Apostles' or Nicene) followed as the church's response to the written and preached Word—kind of a "pledge of allegiance" to the One who has just, once again, made himself known in Scripture and sermon. Intercessions (prayers for the concerns of the church and the world) would often follow.

27. See Edith M. Humphrey, *Grand Entrance: Worship on Earth as in Heaven* (Grand Rapids: Brazos, 2011).

28. The Christian church is divided into three communities: Eastern Orthodox (which includes communions such as Greek Orthodox, Russian Orthodox, Coptic, etc.), Roman Catholic, and Protestant (which is further divided into Lutheran, Reformed, Anabaptist, and Anglican camps).

29. Alexander Schmemann, *For the Life of the World* (Crestwood, NY: St. Vladimir's Seminary Press, 1973), 27 (italics original).

The Liturgy of the Eucharist or the Table began with the church's offerings, including the presentation of the bread and wine to be used in the Eucharist.[30] This was followed by prayers (such as asking God to set apart this common bread and wine for this holy purpose), the Lord's Prayer (a prayer that only the baptized could pray, since it begins with the address "Our Father"; see Gal. 4:6), the exchange of peace (the first words with which the resurrected Jesus greeted his disciples; see John 20:19, 21), and communion. The service concluded with a dismissal (from which we get the word *Mass*) that sent the worshipers back out into the world as witnesses of what they had heard, seen, and tasted in worship.

Table 2
The Order of Worship

The Liturgy of the Word		The Liturgy of the Eucharist	
Gathering	The Word	Eucharist	Dismissal
God welcomes us into God's presence.	We hear the Word of God read (Scripture) and preached (sermon).	We join in the prayers and communion.	We are sent back into the world in love and service.

A chart comparing all the details of the liturgy in the Roman Catholic and Eastern Orthodox liturgies is found in Fernando Arzolo Jr., *Exploring Worship: Catholic, Evangelical, and Orthodox Perspectives* (Eugene, OR: Wipf and Stock, 2011), 50–51.

Where Are We Going from Here?

As we work our way through essential Christian beliefs, we will pay close attention to the ways that these beliefs have been generated out of and expressed in the community that has been shaped by its language and rituals—language and rituals that ultimately go back to their founder, Jesus Christ.[31] The first Christian confession of faith, "Jesus is Lord," was both a declaration used in worship and an assertion of doctrine. It also reflected the life of those who made that claim. Here we begin our exploration of what it means to believe and worship and live as disciples of Jesus Christ.

30. *Eucharist* is another word for communion. It comes from the Greek *eucharistos*, meaning "thanksgiving," as in the words of the biblical text that "the Lord Jesus on the night when he was betrayed took a loaf of bread, and when he had given thanks, he broke it" (1 Cor. 11:23–24).
31. We must also remember that Jesus was a Jew, as were the first disciples and the earliest New Testament church. So some of the language and rituals have been influenced by Jewish practices, not to mention the Hellenistic (Greek) and Roman culture in which the church developed.

2

What Is Christian Theology?

We Pray the "Collect" of the Day

Almighty God, which dost make the minds of all faithful men to be of one will; grant unto thy people, that they may love the thing, which thou commandest, and desire, that which thou dost promise; that among the sundry and manifold changes of the world, our hearts may surely there be fixed, where true joys are to be found; through Christ our Lord.

—*from* The Collects of Thomas Cranmer[1]

Centuries ago Prosper of Aquitaine (ca. 390–455) coined a phrase that has become commonplace. Its abbreviated form is *lex orandi, lex credendi*: "the law of praying [is] the law of believing." More accurately, he wrote *ut legem credendi lex statuat supplicandi*, "that the law of supplicating [i.e., praying] may constitute the law of believing." In a nutshell, Prosper was saying that "praying and worshiping shape believing."

There have been two arenas of disagreement regarding Prosper's mantra.

1. C. Frederick Barbee and Paul F. M. Zahl, *The Collects of Thomas Cranmer* (Grand Rapids: Eerdmans, 1999), 58.

First, there are those who argue for a bottom-up approach and those who argue for a top-down approach.[2] Those in the first camp are oriented more ecclesiocentrically; that is, they hold that the church's beliefs arise out of the worship of the community. Those in the second camp approach the matter more theocentrically or Christocentrically; that is, they emphasize God's agency, initiative, and self-communication in the liturgy. Most likely both dynamics shape Christian theology, comparable to the orthodox understanding of Christ as both *fully* human *and fully* divine, as we shall discuss in a future chapter. Keeping in mind both approaches helps us avoid either an adoptionist or a docetic understanding of the relation between the liturgy and the development of Christian doctrine. ("Adoptionist" and "docetic" will be explained in a future chapter—specifically chapter 5 if you want to look ahead.)

Second, some, like Aidan Kavanagh, insist that Prosper's statement is to be taken in a unidirectional manner. In other words, Kavanagh would have liturgy determine theology.[3] Geoffrey Wainwright suggests that this reflects a more Roman Catholic emphasis over against a Protestant position that favors doctrinal control over worship. Wainwright favors a bidirectional approach so that liturgy (the law of praying) shapes theology (the law of believing), just as theology shapes liturgy.[4] This seems to get it right and to reflect more accurately what really goes on in the church's life. In fact, Prosper himself probably never considered liturgy to be the *only* source of doctrine, but *a* source of doctrine and theology since the experience of worship *is* formative for the faith and life of disciples of Christ in the church.[5]

Praying and Believing

Since we have already introduced one term of this binary—*liturgy*—now we need to clarify what we mean by the other term: *theology*.

Etymologically, theology is "the study of or words about God." And since, in the Christian Faith, God is definitively revealed in Jesus Christ, to study

2. See Maxwell E. Johnson, *Praying and Believing in Early Christianity: The Interplay between Christian Worship and Doctrine* (Collegeville, MN: Liturgical Press, 2013), x–xiii. He places Alexander Schmemann, Aidan Kavanagh, and others in the first group; Paul Bradshaw, Pope Benedict XVI, and others in the second.

3. See Aidan Kavanagh, *On Liturgical Theology* (Collegeville, MN: Liturgical Press, 1992).

4. See Geoffrey Wainwright, *Doxology: The Praise of God in Worship, Doctrine and Life; A Systematic Theology* (New York: Oxford University Press, 1980), chaps. 7 and 8. M. Johnson concurs with this bidirectional approach in *Praying and Believing*, 13–16.

5. M. Johnson, *Praying and Believing*, 22.

Christ is to study God. Furthermore, because Jesus is the "truth and life way," theology is a quest for the truth about God, ourselves, and the world.[6]

But we need to say more about the *task* of Christian theology than this. The first thing we must say about the task of theology is that prayer and theological work always belong together. This is the most important application of the *lex orandi, lex credendi* relationship. On this point Karl Barth was insistent: "The first and basic act of theological work is *prayer*. . . . In its totality it is peculiar and characteristic of theology that it can be performed only in the act of prayer."[7]

The worshiping psalmist knew this relationship between prayer and theology. For example, we can see it played out in Psalm 27. The psalmist begins with a theological statement: "The LORD is my light and my salvation; / whom shall I fear? / The LORD is the stronghold of my life: / of whom shall I be afraid?" (v. 1). This leads the psalmist to make his supplication in verses 7–9: "Hear, O LORD, when I cry aloud, / be gracious to me and answer me! / 'Come,' my heart says, 'seek his face!' / Your face, LORD, do I seek. / Do not hide your face from me."

Another way to put this is to say that what we speak *about* God (if even we can speak "about" God[8]) and how we speak *to* God are reciprocally related. Even more to the point, our theological speech must be a response to God's prior Word to us. Again, Barth says it crisply:

> Human thought and speech cannot be *about* God, but must be directed *toward* God, called into action by the divine thought and speech directed to men, and following and corresponding to this work of God. . . . True and proper language concerning God will always be a response to God, which overtly or covertly, explicitly or implicitly, thinks and speaks of God exclusively in the second person. And this means that theological work must really and truly take place in the form of a liturgical act, as invocation of God, and as prayer.[9]

If the theologian does not perform theological acts in a posture of prayer—open toward and by heaven—then the theologian will end up alone in her work. It would be something like this: imagine two people are engaged in a conversation about a friend's recent problems in a relationship, analyzing who might be at fault in the relationship, why the relationship has gone south, and

6. Shirley Guthrie, *Christian Doctrine*, rev. ed. (Louisville: Westminster John Knox, 1994), 10.
7. Karl Barth, *Evangelical Theology: An Introduction* (Grand Rapids: Eerdmans, 1963), 160.
8. Our sisters and brothers in the Eastern Christian tradition would warn us to be very cautious at this point. Their approach is *apophatic*—that is, they insist that what we can say *about* God is precisely what *cannot* be said about God.
9. Barth, *Evangelical Theology*, 164.

making suggestions about how the friend might or might not be coping. All the while their friend is sitting with them but being ignored *as if she were not present*, even though she could provide the details necessary for understanding the problematic relationship. Talking about someone but never communicating with her personally, even when she is present, is a good way of limiting your "relationship" with that person to merely *your ideas* about that person.

Correctly understood, engaging in theological work or speaking to another about God *as if* God were absent is to break the third commandment (Exod. 20:7). To "take the Lord's name in vain," as the commandment is often quoted (KJV, NKJV, RSV, NASB), does not meant to swear. Since in the Hebrew mind one's name cannot be dissociated from one's person, to take God's name in vain is to treat God's name as empty of meaningful content—to use God's name as if God were not present or was of no consequence (see NRSV: "make wrongful use of . . . misuse"). It is something like what I encountered at a baseball playoff game when I asked a man sitting next to me why he was singing the prayer "God Bless America" if he didn't believe in God (as he had informed me). Not only was he engaging in a patriotic act with words that ultimately meant nothing, but he was also imploring a "God" he did not believe existed because he was not really thinking about the words he was singing.

And that brings us to what ought to be a guiding principle as we begin our theological work: We are to think about God prayerfully and to pray to God thoughtfully. If we do not maintain this connection, our thinking about God will become stale and academic, while our praying will become trite, empty, and, eventually, nonexistent. Austin Farrer put it more forcefully: "No dogma deserves its place unless it is prayable, and no Christian deserves his dogmas who does not pray them."[10]

There are at least two *practical* reasons for doing theology in the context of prayer.

First, theological insight can be generated by the activity of praying. This is another way of understanding *lex orandi, lex credendi.*

The model for this could be the Lord's Prayer as it was used (and is still used) for catechetical instruction in the early church, as the newly baptized learned what was involved in being a Christian. The prayer was parsed into its words and phrases so that a catechumen (one who is taught) would be able to memorize answers to questions, such as Martin Luther's wonderful catechetical response to the question, What is meant by "daily bread"? "Everything included in the necessities and nourishment for our bodies, such as food, drink,

10. Austin Farrer, *Lord, I Believe: Suggestions for Turning the Creed into Prayer*, 3rd ed. (Cambridge, MA: Cowley, 1989), 10.

clothing, shoes, house, farm, fields, livestock, money, property, an upright spouse, upright children, upright members of the household, upright and faithful rulers, good government, good weather, peace, health, decency, honor, good friends, faithful neighbors, and the like [in case he missed anything!]."[11]

In other words, when we pray this petition in the Lord's Prayer, we come to a theological understanding of God's providential care for his creation, without which we would have no bread at all. Those who had been catechized would now pray this prayer with an understanding of the theological significance of each word and phrase.

A second practical reason for keeping theology and prayer together is that a person's prayers reveal what he believes about God and God's relation to the world. In fact, if you want to know what someone *really* believes about God and God's relation to the world, don't first ask him for a statement of faith; listen to his prayers. Maxwell Johnson puts it this way: "While not the only criterion for doing so, one can—or *should* be able to—read theology, belief, and doctrines in any given church by means of what its liturgies pray, say, sing, and direct."[12] What a church believes is reflected and expressed in its worship (just as its worship had a role to play in the formation, development, and expression of the church's beliefs).[13]

This is illustrated by the disciples' request of Jesus that he teach them how to pray, "as John taught his disciples" (Luke 11:1). What is going on here is that a rabbi would teach his disciples to pray in a manner that reflected the theology of the one they followed. If you were to hear one of John's disciples praying, you would know that person was a disciple of John. So Jesus's disciples are asking, "How does one who believes as you want your disciples to believe express those beliefs in prayer?" Indeed, a Christian who begins prayer with the address "Our Father" has already revealed something about her conception of God.

Beyond the practical reasons for doing theology as a prayerful liturgical act, there are *theological* reasons for doing so.

First, doing theology in the context of prayer assists us in keeping a proper perspective on our theological work. It reminds the theologian who she is in relation to God. God is God, and we are not! The proper perspective, then,

11. "The Small Catechism," in *The Book of Concord: The Confessions of the Evangelical Lutheran Church*, ed. Robert Kolb and Timothy J. Wengert, trans. Charles Arand, Eric Gritsch, Robert Kolb, William Russell, James Schaaf, Jane Strohl, and Timothy J. Wengert (Minneapolis: Fortress, 2000), 357. Note that catechisms were not only used in the early church, but they also especially proliferated during the Protestant and Catholic Reformations.

12. M. Johnson, *Praying and Believing*, x.

13. M. Johnson, *Praying and Believing*, 21–23.

is one of humility. John Calvin remarked that if you asked him about the precepts of the Christian religion, "first, second, third, and always I would answer, 'Humility.'"[14]

Second, theology as a liturgical act should keep us from constructing idols of our ideas about God. In prayer the Spirit will challenge our human ideas, since our theology must be judged by God. One way in which this happens is to see if our theological claims and assertions are prayable—the kind of thing that Farrer was talking about in the above quote. For example, if a person believes that *all* things are ordained by God, then in his prayers he should be able to thank God for famines, rapes, the Holocaust, 9/11, and all other human atrocities. But, in fact, thanking God *in* all circumstances, which the apostle Paul commands us to do (1 Thess. 5:18), is quite different from thanking God *for* all things. The former is prayable, while most (but not all)[15] find the latter difficult to pray.

Third, if prayer is the liturgical act in which thinking about God is performed, then the theologian must always be in a posture of listening to God before speaking. Barth reminds us that "our theological work should be a *response* to God's Word," since "God is not an 'It,' but a 'He.'"[16]

Fourth, if we situate our theological work within the context of prayerful worship, we will be reminded that effective theology—that is, theology that enables life to flourish the way that God intended—must be dependent on God's grace from beginning to end (as articulated by Thomas Aquinas's prayer with which this book began). That dependence is best expressed in prayer, something the German word for "prayer"—*Gebet*—handily communicates, since it means "ask."

Defining the Theological Task

Many definitions of the theological task have been articulated. It could be as simple as "the study of God according to rules." It could be as sophisticated as Donald Bloesch's comprehensive description: "an intelligible and articulate

14. John Calvin, *Institutes of the Christian Religion*, ed. John T. McNeill, trans. Ford Lewis Battles (Philadelphia: Westminster John Knox, 1960), 2.2.11.

15. Is thanking God *for* events like 9/11 implied in the repeated refrain of the praise song "Blessed Be Your Name": "You give and take away / my heart will choose to say / Lord, blessed be Your name"? (by Beth Redman and Matt Redman, © Capitol Christian Music Group).

16. Barth, *Evangelical Theology*, 163–64. Obviously, by using the pronoun "He" Barth was not suggesting that God is male. He was insisting that God is subject, not an object that we can manipulate, and it is difficult to express this in the English language (a translation in this case) without using gender-specific pronouns referring to the one God.

explication of the message of Scripture on the basis of an experience of the Lord of Scripture for the purpose of greater obedience to him."[17]

Keeping in mind the liturgical framework for all theological work, I propose this definition of the task of theology, though it is always open to revision and refinement: Theology is a (a) *human* (b) *response to the revelation of God*, done (c) *within and for the Christian church*, which engages in (d) *critical reflection for responsible talk* about God.

(a) Theology is a *human* discipline. This means that theology is contextual: it cannot be divorced from the theologian's personal, social, cultural, and religious experiences. It is always important for a theologian (and the one receiving the theologian) to know who she is and from where she is coming. There is no view from nowhere, and that applies to theology as much as it does to any other aspect of human thought. Additionally, because theology is a human endeavor, we must remember not only that it is limited and finite, but also that a theology is not to be confused with God's Word.

(b) Theology is a *response* to God's *prior* Word to us that, following Barth, comes in a "threefold form": Christ (God's Word in person); Scripture (God's Word written); and the church's proclamation (God's Word preached and made visible in the sacraments). We will revisit this threefold form of God's Word, but for now it is sufficient to emphasize that the focus in each case is on God's action toward us in Jesus Christ.

(c) Worship, even while an individual experience, is always contextualized in the corporate life of the *church*, Christ's body.[18] (Note the plural pronouns in the Lord's Prayer.) And so, those who do theology must always be conscious of the corporate context in two ways.

First, theology is done *within* the church. This involves a distinction between the "primary" conversation and the "secondary" conversation.[19] The theologian's primary conversation is with God's Word in Scripture—hearing, understanding, and applying the biblical text. But

17. Donald Bloesch, *A Theology of Word and Spirit: Authority and Method in Theology* (Downers Grove, IL: InterVarsity, 1992), 129.

18. Simon Chan observes that "there is a tendency to treat daily prayers as 'private devotions,' divorced from the corporate prayer of the church, although this was not the case in the past. . . . They were originally part and parcel of the church's liturgical life. We are spiritually nourished by being in the church—a branch of the vine, a member of the body. To divorce private prayer from liturgical prayer is to cut the branch from the vine. We need to see our own quiet times as joined with the corporate prayer of the church. They are not just 'my private prayers' but belong to the whole church." *Liturgical Theology* (Downers Grove, IL: InterVarsity, 2006), 161.

19. See Barth, *Evangelical Theology*, 173–75.

the secondary conversation is the communal discussion that is had by all who have been engaged in the primary conversation—including those who have long since joined the Church Triumphant (those Christians who have died). It is the history, both past and present, of primary conversations with the text. The theologian is a member of a very large "discipleship small group" that consists of his contemporaries as well as the likes of Augustine, Calvin, Hildegard of Bingen, and many others. As Barth put it, "To study theology means not so much to examine exhaustively the work of earlier students of theology as to become *their* fellow students [of God's self-revelation]."[20]

To be clear, the primary conversation has to do with the *source* and *norm* of theology—Scripture. We need the secondary conversation for clearer *understanding* of Scripture, especially because it is easy for us to be mistaken in our understanding of Scripture if we remain alone with the text.

Second, theology is done *for* the church (and, consequently, for the world). This involves another distinction, this one between first-order discourse and second-order discourse. The former consists of the language used in the church's liturgical life—the creeds, preaching, prayers, and so forth. The latter is critical to make sure the human church's first-order discourse remains faithful to God's revelation in Christ and in Scripture. It involves *criticism* and *correction* of our talk about God, using the revelation of the Word in Scripture as our norm. This recalls what we have said about the two-way street between *orandi* and *credendi*.

Early in his pastoral career Karl Barth became disillusioned with the theologians who had trained him for his preaching. They had become university-centered rather than church-centered. So later, as William Hordern narrates, "as a theologian, Barth remained convinced that the only excuse for a theologian is that he should be a servant and critic of the preacher. When theologians ignore the task of the preacher, they end up mumbling about ideas that already are popular in the modern world."[21] Years later, Donald Bloesch concurred: theology is to be done "in the service of the church's proclamation of the gospel"; it is "for the purpose of equipping the church in its apostolic task of preaching and teaching."[22]

20. Barth, *Evangelical Theology*, 173 (italics original).
21. William Hordern, *A Layman's Guide to Protestant Theology*, rev. ed. (New York: Macmillan, 1968), 131.
22. Bloesch, *Theology of Word and Spirit*, 124, 134.

Of course, this makes demands on the theologian who joins the church in its worship. After a piano concert that I thoroughly enjoyed, I shared my enthusiasm with a colleague who taught keyboard performance at our college. His response was less sanguine since he had noticed several mistakes that my untrained ear had not noticed. So it is with the theologian in the pew: her participation in the liturgy will not always be as "enjoyable" as the less-informed layperson's sitting next to her, since her role is to serve the church as a critic of its first-order discourse.

(d) Finally, theology involves *critical reflection for responsible talk* about God. Another way of articulating this claim is to say that theology is a science with a never-ending task.

Theology is a science in the sense that it is intelligible (not gobbledygook), logical (though often according to its own sui generis logic, since a science is defined by its object of study and this "object" is a one-of-a-kind God), critical, and working with precise and technical language. It is an intellectually rigorous discipline comparable to other intellectual disciplines, though Thomas Aquinas correctly noted that its axioms are revealed and not available to the natural mind (see 1 Cor. 2:14–16). As Bloesch put it, "We are called to bring our thoughts into conformity to the will of God, and this involves disciplined reflection upon the Word of God."[23]

Since theology serves those who lead the church in its liturgy, pastoral care, and preaching, the concern for responsible talk about God (that is necessary for a flourishing life) is extremely important. Stanley Hauerwas once said that we would never tolerate a doctor who was not diligent in his study of medicine since our biological life depends on it, while folks in the church readily tolerate an ill-trained pastor, despite the fact that their spiritual lives depend on it.

Dallas Willard made a similar point:

> We vigorously reject shallow thinking and erroneous conceptualization on the part of a computer analyst or a bridge designer or a brain surgeon. For some strange reason, though, we find it easy to put our minds away when it comes to religion, when it comes to bringing the same type of care to our faith as we would to other subjects. But in reality, we need to be even *more* careful with our religious teachers and theologians. The

---

23. Bloesch, *Theology of Word and Spirit*, 112.

religion teacher's subject matter is . . . much more important [than other subject matter].[24]

We should mention here that, as a discipline, theology must be in dialogue with other disciplines and sciences. For example, how one understands the theological claims arising out of Genesis 1 must be in conversation with the disciplines of geology and anthropology. One's theological musings about the problem of evil should include conversation with the disciplines of political science, philosophy, biology, and others.

Along these lines, it is important that theology be *relevant* while remaining *faithful* to what God has revealed. Those who veer too far in the former direction we might label "liberal"; that is, the culture or the academic disciplines set the agenda. Those who veer too far in the latter direction we might label "fundamentalist"; that is, their allegiance to "the blood, the Book, and the Blessed Hope" (as one country preacher put it) clouds awareness of their own cultural formation, and they remain irresponsive to the life situations into which their theology must speak. Barth is famously quoted as saying that a good theologian must have a Bible in one hand and a newspaper in the other. (I would add that she must also have a foot planted in the academy and a foot planted in the church.)

All that we have said about the task of theology should sound daunting. This is not Saturday night Sunday school preparation. In fact, theology involves work that is never ending, especially since it *is* the study of God. It's like running around in my backyard with a straight pin in my hand trying to capture a butterfly. God will not be "captured" by our theology. We seek to understand, but we never quite have it. Or, to apply the Reformed tradition's mantra regarding the church, theology is always reforming and being reformed.

These days, those who engage the theological task have become more specialized, as is the case in any discipline today. So it would be good to quickly list areas of theology that are more narrowly defined.

1. *Fundamental* theology has to do with clarifying the foundations, such as the terms we use. Also, this area of study discusses the conditions necessary for the possibility of receiving revelation and the methods theologians employ to unpack received revelation.

24. Dallas Willard, *The Spirit of the Disciplines: Understanding How God Changes Lives* (San Francisco: Harper & Row, 1990), 33 (italics original).

2. *Biblical* theology carries out something like the "primary conversation" we have discussed. The biblical theologian clarifies and outlines basic themes and narratives of the two Testaments, identifies theologies within the Bible (such as Pauline theology), investigates the relation between the Old and New Testaments, considers canonical questions, establishes hermeneutical principles, and studies the cultural and social settings of biblical material.

3. *Historical* theology engages in something like the "secondary conversation." This specialty traces the development of doctrines and the theological history of the church. It studies the theology of major figures and movements, as well as the relation of church and society throughout history.

4. *Systematic* theology builds on the previous specialties to set out an orderly, methodical, comprehensive, and integrative presentation of the biblical narrative and teachings of the Christian church for the theologian's contemporaries. Sometimes this is referred to as "dogmatics"— the articulation of the church's teachings or "dogma" that holds authority over those who claim to belong to the Christian church.

5. *Moral* theology, sometimes referred to as theological ethics, develops an ethic based on biblical foundations in dialogue with philosophical ethics and other disciplines. It investigates the relation between theological claims and the life conduct stipulated by those who make these claims.

6. *Practical* theology explores the theological underpinnings of the church's practices (such as preaching, liturgy, and pastoral counseling). It derives its content from biblical exegesis and church dogmatics, but its form comes from the "moment." Barth described it best when he said that it has to do with the way in which God's Word may be served by human words.[25]

7. *Apologetics*. Not all would include apologetics in a list of theological specializations, but that is precisely where it should be located if it is to be a legitimate enterprise. In other words, apologetics should be developed within the orb of church dogmatics. As Donald Bloesch rightly pointed out, the best defense of the faith is good theology, especially as one leads those who make secular claims to ask the right questions— "questions that are hidden from sinful humanity until the moment of revelation."[26]

25. Barth, *Evangelical Theology*, 182. Barth describes these areas of theology, except for the first and last on our list.
26. Bloesch, *Theology of Word and Spirit*, 128.

What Is the Cultural Context?

In many churches, when the people gather for worship, they often begin with a prayer for purity and a collect (prayer) for the day. The former reminds us who we are, especially in relation to the holy God we worship, and why we have come together:

> Almighty God, to whom all hearts are open, all desires known, and from whom no secrets are hidden: cleanse the thoughts of our hearts by the inspiration of your Holy Spirit, that we may perfectly love you, and worthily magnify your holy name; through Christ our Lord. Amen.[27]

The collect reminds us what time it is in the church's calendar—a different time zone from the one we were in before we entered the sanctuary. Harmon Smith nicely indicates the significance of these gathering rituals and why they are a "moral act": "In one way or another, all of the Christian liturgies with which I am familiar take account, either from the very outset or quite soon thereafter, of the fact that we are gathered out of many places into this one place and out of many diverse loyalties to focus singly on the one God who is made known to us in Jesus Christ."[28]

We need this reorientation when we gather. In part, we need this because our existence in the world cannot be denied. Aidan Kavanagh said it well: "Since Christian worship swims in creation as a fish swims in water, theology has no option but to accept the created world as a necessary component of every equation and conclusion it produces."[29] In worship we are gathered in from the world, and after the liturgy has finished, we are sent back out into the world. Bumper stickers that tout the phrase "Not of this world" are only half right (and quote only half of the biblical statement). In worship we are reminded that, although we are not of this world, we are, nonetheless, *in* this world. And the Christian theologian must remind herself that theology is always done as one who is both in *and* not of the world.

This reorientation correlates with what we said about being *both* faithful *and* relevant. Bloesch succinctly states how the theologian must go about his task with these two orientations in mind:

27. This is a prayer that goes back to at least the eleventh century in the Western (Latin) church before it was incorporated in Anglican worship by Thomas Cranmer in the sixteenth century. Among other places, it can be found in the *Book of Common Prayer* used in Episcopal churches.

28. Harmon L. Smith, *Where Two or Three Are Gathered: Liturgy and the Moral Life* (Eugene, OR: Wipf and Stock, 1995), 72.

29. Kavanagh, *Liturgical Theology*, 4.

[Theology is] the systematic reflection within a particular culture on the self-revelation of God in Jesus Christ as attested in Holy Scripture and witnessed to in the tradition of the catholic church. . . . Theology in this sense is both biblical and contextual. Its norm is Scripture, but its field or arena of action is the cultural context in which we find ourselves. It is engaged in reflection not on abstract divinity or on concrete humanity but on the Word made flesh, the divine in the human. . . . Theology in the evangelical sense is the faithful interpretation of the biblical message to the time in which we live.[30]

So, how should we describe the "time in which we live"?

In the popular idiom, we live in "postmodernity." There are debates about how appropriate this term is in locating our cultural position, and, frankly, the term has been tossed around to the point that it has almost become innocuous.[31] But the term does help us in one respect, since the prefix *post-* means that to one extent or another (and that is also debated) our culture is not as ensconced in modernity as it once was. We are not in the Kansas of modernity anymore—at least not in the same zip code.

Modernism takes us back to the Enlightenment, lodged primarily in the eighteenth century, but stretching from seventeenth-century Descartes through Kant to Hegel and the Romantics in the nineteenth century.

This period followed the premodern period of "superstition," blood fanaticism, and religious wars, all based on the excesses and prejudicial commitments of particular religious traditions (such as various forms of Protestantism and Roman Catholicism). Folks like Descartes and Kant attempted to establish culture and life on a universal objective foundation that is beyond dispute, that all human beings can agree on, and that gives us certainty about truth and reality. Only then, it was thought, can we live in peace and make progress as the dignified humans we are.

In the modern project one need not and should not rely on particular religious traditions and specific historic communities to know the truth. The human individual's reason can know ultimate reality and the absolute truth

30. Bloesch, *Theology of Word and Spirit*, 114–15. Also see a similar point made by Vincent Bacote, "Theological Method in Black and White: Does Race Matter at All?," in *The Gospel in Black and White: Theological Resources for Racial Reconciliation*, ed. Dennis Okholm (Downers Grove, IL: InterVarsity, 1997), chap. 4.

31. Though the term's origins are debated, it appears as early as the 1930s. But the consensus seems to be that its current use began in the 1970s. See Thomas Docherty, "Postmodern Theory: Lyotard, Baudrillard and Others," in *Twentieth Century Continental Philosophy*, ed. Todd May (Englewood Cliffs, NJ: Prentice Hall, 1996), 474. Also see Stanley J. Grenz, "Star Trek and the Next Generation: Postmodernism and the Future of Evangelical Theology," in *The Challenge of Postmodernism: An Evangelical Engagement*, ed. David S. Dockery, 2nd ed. (Grand Rapids: Baker Academic, 2001), 75–89.

that transcends all cultures, all times, and all places. Such ultimates and absolutes are just there waiting to be discovered. Such confidence is enshrined in the familiar line from our Declaration of Independence: "We hold these Truths to be *self-evident*, that all Men are created equal." Through confidence in Reason (not just an individual's rational capacity, but a universal rationality that we all share), humans can understand the cosmos, establish social peace, and improve living conditions. This was especially important historically in the aftermath of Europe's bloody Thirty Years' War, which was fought over religious convictions. The Peace of Westphalia in 1648 ended wars *of* religion, but also heralded a culture of wars *on* religion with its appeal to ahistorical and acultural Reason.

Behind this confidence lay a relationship between the individual human person and the universe that was put forth by Galileo, Descartes, and others: namely, there is the thinking human—a spectator—on the one hand, and the nonthinking, machinelike universe outside of the human, waiting to be known by objective observation and also pliable to human technology.

Except for a rationalistic deistic unitarianism, modernism relegated confessional religion to the private world, since it was thought to be a matter of opinion or tradition. Deism gained the status of a religion to which all reasonable folks could and should subscribe: it required only belief in a creator who set in motion a machine of a universe, programmed with moral instructions accessible to the thinking person, for which he would be held accountable in some afterlife. Miracles were not needed; the machine worked quite nicely on its own. Moreover, in any case, no rational person could take seriously the miracles recorded in the Bible. As a child of such Enlightenment thinking, Thomas Jefferson clipped stories of Jesus's miracles out of his copy of the Gospel accounts, but lauded Christ's moral teachings.

Until recently, this modernist perspective held sway in the West, with only minor disruptions from time to time. But then a new paradigm (often referred to as "postmodernism" or "late modernism") entered popular culture. (The first time I saw the word *postmodern* in popular culture was in an advertisement for the movie *Pulp Fiction* in 1994.) Perhaps our cultural situation could best be labeled "postmodernity with a modernist hangover." So what are some of the characteristics of this culture in which we now do theology?

No longer is truth "out there" waiting to be discovered. All knowledge is system-dependent and culturally bound. There is no neutral, timeless, self-evident foundational truth available to anyone that gives us absolute certainty about anything. The Augustinian dictum "All truth is God's truth" has come to mean "Everybody's truth is God's truth." It all depends on how one looks at it. There is no view from nowhere. As scholars ranging from Thomas Kuhn to Parker Palmer to Lesslie Newbigin point out, even the scientist is not some neutral intellect unlocking secrets from the stuff she studies; she brings with her to her studies a certain perspective that colors her interpretation and even her observation of the data.[32] This is what Charles Taylor means by "secular": "a situation of fundamental contestability when it comes to belief, a sense that rival stories are always at the door offering a very different account of the world." We live in a world of contested meanings.[33]

Not only has reason been demoted from its role as the unbiased discoverer of objective truth, but it turns out that reason is not all it was cracked up to be. Enlightened reason and the knowledge it brought are not an uncompromised good. Wars have *not* stopped, and knowledge of the atom allows us to cook not only our food, but whole cities as well.

This cultural shift leaves us with reason that is molded by its social location. How and what human beings know is affected by their ethnicity, gender, socioeconomic group, and so on. Furthermore, the Galileo/Cartesian depiction of the knower who stands aloof from the object of knowledge she observes is simply naive. Knowledge comes through a relationship with the object of knowledge, whether the object is a person or molecules.[34] The knower should also be fully engaged; that is, knowledge comes through holistic means—not just through reason, but also through emotions, intuition, embodiment.

A good example of this phenomenon occurred one evening as my wife and I visited our son's high school classes on the annual "curriculum night." In his math class the teacher wrote a problem on the board and asked the parents to solve it. Those who got the answer right were asked how they arrived at the answer. When he came to one woman, she responded, "It just *felt* right." That response probably won't go over well if she challenges her bank's account of her assets.

What contributed to these shifts?

Intellectual factors play a role. Individuals and schools of thought in philosophy and literary criticism account for some of the genesis of what is

32. Thomas Kuhn, *The Structure of Scientific Revolutions*, 2nd ed. (Chicago: University of Chicago Press, 1970); Parker Palmer, *To Know as We Are Known* (San Francisco: HarperCollins, 1983); Lesslie Newbigin, *Foolishness to the Greeks: The Gospel and Western Culture* (Grand Rapids: Eerdmans, 1986), chap. 4.

33. See James K. A. Smith, *How (Not) to Be Secular* (Grand Rapids: Eerdmans, 2014), 10; see 21–23. Smith's book is an accessible distillation of Taylor's opus of more than nine hundred pages, *A Secular Age* (Cambridge, MA: Belknap, 2007).

34. See the account of the scientific research of Nobel Prize winner Barbara McClintock in Evelyn Fox Keller, *A Feeling for the Organism: The Life and Work of Barbara McClintock* (New York: W. H. Freeman, 1983).

now popularly described as postmodernism. The influences of past thinkers such as Nietzsche and Freud must be considered. But more to the point are Jean-François Lyotard, Michel Foucault, Jacques Derrida, Richard Rorty, and Stanley Fish. As a school, deconstructionism is also important. Some of this reading is rough going for the novice, but there are some handy summaries.[35]

Cultural factors cannot be ignored. For example, the ongoing technological revolution has shrunk the world but expanded our awareness. It was rare for someone from the United States to have traveled to an African or Asian country where life and thought radically differed; today it takes only hours on a comfortable jet to find oneself disoriented in Khartoum or Delhi. Add to this the information explosion through a web that is worldwide. The world that felt so comfortable, so manageable, is now overwhelming and often unfamiliar. Perhaps this in part accounts for the rapid cultural change we seem to be experiencing. Enlightenment universal, acultural reason begins to look quaint at best—at the worst, an illusion.

Perhaps the most profound cultural change is the proliferation of choice. Here the paradigmatic icons include such things as DVR and cable television and streaming. It wasn't that long ago that television watching forced unification: we had to watch what all others wanted to watch at the time the networks determined, at their speed, and with their accompanying commercials. Now the individual can watch what he wants, when he wants, and at any speed he desires, with or without commercials. It is even better using Netflix, HuluPlus, and any number of websites that provide the viewer with a seemingly infinite number of choices. Perhaps most revealing is the grocery store: we have gone from a few hundred product choices a century ago to tens of thousands in the twenty-first century. The cereal aisle alone is enough proof. This proliferation of choice led Alan Ehrenhalt to lament: "Too many of the things we do in our lives, large and small, have come to resemble channel surfing, marked by a numbing and seemingly endless progression from one option to the next, all without the benefit of a chart, logistical or moral, because there are simply too many choices and no one to help sort them out. We have nothing to insulate ourselves against the perpetual temptation to try one more choice, rather than to live with what is on the screen in front of us."[36]

---

35. One rather enjoyable way to get at deconstructionism and its implications for Christian theology is to read John Caputo, *What Would Jesus Deconstruct? The Good News of Postmodernism for the Church* (Grand Rapids: Baker Academic, 2007). For a positive interpretation of postmodernism for the church's life, see James K. A. Smith, *Who's Afraid of Postmodernism: Taking Derrida, Lyotard, and Foucault to Church* (Grand Rapids: Baker Academic, 2006).

36. Alan Ehrenhalt, *The Lost City: Discovering the Forgotten Virtues of Community in the Chicago of the 1950s* (New York: Basic Books, 1995), 272.

The shift to a postmodern paradigm has been made easier in the United States by the *breakdown of a Constantinian alliance* between the culture and Christianity.[37] The Christian paradigm no longer serves as the prevailing religious or moral view in the United States today, and it probably never will again. This is obvious. In the 1950s it was American to be "Christian" and "Christian" to be American. To the chagrin of today's right-wing Christians, the sign that now reads "Happy Holidays" would have read "Merry Christmas" only a few decades ago.

Given these factors and more, modernity's claim to ground life in universally accessible and defensible common knowledge turns out to be illusory. No longer is there a universal rational point of view, a universal morality, or a universal religious truth. What is left? To answer that, we turn to a description of the postmodern state in which we have landed.

First, the dismissal of a universal point of view means rejecting master narratives (or metanarratives). That is, overarching narratives that define reality or history for all people at all times *and are self-legitimated* are not acceptable. This includes our twenty-first-century scientific worldview. To claim the existence of such a narrative appears oppressive, yet we can't help it—we need to construct a master narrative to make sense of an otherwise blind, deaf, and mute cosmos. The Christian claims that the biblical story *is* the true story of the world, but the Christian should not claim that this is self-legitimated. It is a particular point of view from the Christian horizon—one into which a person is baptized and liturgically trained, as we discussed in the previous chapter.[38]

Second, in place of a master narrative, the autonomous self plays a central role. By "autonomous" we are not ignoring the fact that the self is shaped by a community. That is to say, the way we use the term *autonomy* here does not mean "self-constructed." The phenomenon of the "selfie" is iconic, such as when spectators at the Tour de France step into the path of cyclists in order to get a selfie with oncoming bikers in the background; all that matters to the person taking the snapshot—all that is central—is the person taking the snapshot. So the self becomes the source of truth and reality. Nothing else should interfere. As Roger Lundin pointed out, we live in "an age that believes

37. "Constantinian alliance" is an allusion to Emperor Constantine's promotion and protection of Christianity in the Roman Empire in 312–13. Before that, the empire had persecuted Christians; now began a synthesis of church and state that rose to a crescendo in Europe in the eleventh century before it began to slowly disintegrate. The European invasion of North America began a similar synthesis or alliance.

38. See James K. A. Smith, *Desiring the Kingdom: Worship, Worldview, and Cultural Formation* (Grand Rapids: Baker Academic, 2009).

that freedom will make you true."[39] All selves are autonomous. Our world is a fragmented, chaotic, arbitrary amalgamation of multiple selves; functionally, even our understanding of the church is that of a collection of individuals. Gone is the Enlightenment's claim that there is a universal human nature, a universal humanity, a universal self. Marketers know this (even those who become consultants for churches!): niche marketing is the order of the day. We can end up with a purely self-sufficient humanism with no final goals—no *telos* beyond human flourishing.[40]

If each self is autonomous to construct its own reality and truth, then we must respect others the way they define themselves. Postmodernism carries an acute awareness of the Other. Again, this results from the fact that there is no metanarrative, no universal way of interpreting things. Each December equal respect must be paid to Hanukkah, Christmas, and Kwanzaa. And so we live by the dictum of "political correctness" and use "PC language," all buttressed by the supreme virtues of niceness, tolerance, and civility. All selves have an equal voice and, more importantly, all are considered equally valid. As Derrida has suggested, the primary form of postmodern discourse is the collage.

Third, this brings us to the power of language. If our lives together are fragmented into a plurality of views, and if meaning and truth are not "out there" waiting to be discovered, then "truth" or "reality" are social constructions created by groups that share a common tradition or perspective expressed with a common language—collectives of like-minded selves. But some of these groups manage to gain a privileged status, silencing or marginalizing the views of others and insisting that their interpretation of reality and truth is the only true one. Even concepts such as "rational" and "justice" are up for grabs.[41] But those who pretentiously define the terms for everyone else are the "victors." The entire cultural and social history of the "victims" is ignored, denied, or brought into line with the dominant narrative of the victor. The victim is a deviant or simply wrong. So knowledge of reality is not the discovery of what is waiting to be grasped in the same way by everyone. In the most radical senses of postmodernism, reality has to do with who has the power. For example, do we call what gestates in the womb of a pregnant woman a "fetus" or a "baby"? Is the termination of the pregnancy "abortion" or "murder"? We create reality with words that we use for pragmatic purposes.

39. Roger Lundin, "The Pragmatics of Postmodernity," in *Christian Apologetics in the Postmodern World*, ed. Timothy R. Phillips and Dennis L. Okholm (Downers Grove, IL: InterVarsity, 1995), 38.

40. See J. Smith, *How (Not) to Be Secular*, 23, citing Taylor's *A Secular Age*, 18.

41. See Alasdair MacIntyre, *Whose Justice? Which Rationality?* (Notre Dame, IN: University of Notre Dame Press, 1989).

Language is used to tell stories that rearrange information and redescribe whatever worldview a person or group is constructing. Richard Rorty put it this way: "Anything can be made to look good or bad by being redescribed."[42] As we said toward the beginning of this book, language shapes the way we see. Once again we are reminded of the significance of the church's liturgical language in forming the disciple's perceptions of truth and reality.

Fourth, it should be obvious that the cultural-linguistic construction of reality has implications for morality. This is poignantly portrayed in Woody Allen's *Bullets over Broadway*. Several times in the movie scriptwriters insist, "An artist creates his own moral universe." The trouble is that the artist must then learn to live by the rules of the moral universe he has created.[43] The protagonist in the movie—a young scriptwriter who has sold out to a gangster-turned-producer and his "leading lady" girlfriend who cannot act—becomes entangled in a moral universe he creates in hopes of reversing his artistic failures. After compromising his craft, ruining his relationship with his steady, and learning of the homicidal elimination of the artistically challenged gangster's girlfriend, he finally rejects the fabricated moral universe and submits to the one that he found himself thrust into all along. In a final scene of reconciliation with his original girlfriend, he admits: "I know two things: I'm not an artist, and I love you. Now I'm free."

But one's own construction of reality is not always rejected in the end. In the Italian film *Big Night*, after two brothers realize that their supposed friend, neighbor, and competing restaurateur has ruined their business with a ruse, the competitor defiantly announces, "I am a businessman. I can be anything I want to be at any time." And in *Star Trek: Generations*, where virtual reality turns a spaceship hurling through the galaxy into a tall ship sailing through the high seas, there is no moral responsibility in the end: Captain Kirk can simply go back in time and replay an event in which he acted less than virtuous until he gets it the way he wants it. In the movie *The Matrix* we witness *both* the computerized construction of reality by machines and the attempt to sabotage such a construction by a small minority of quasi-religious human remnants.

Fifth, appealing to movies to make the previous point is apropos in this context, because images are important in the construction of reality, whether

42. Richard Rorty, *Contingency, Irony, and Solidarity* (Cambridge: Cambridge University Press, 1989), 7.
43. This is echoed by William Adama in *Battlestar Galactica*: "You cannot play God, then wash your hands of the things that you've created. Sooner or later, the day comes when you can't hide from the things that you've done anymore." Cited in Robert Joustra and Alissa Wilkinson, *How to Survive the Apocalypse: Zombies, Cylons, Faith, and Politics* (Grand Rapids: Eerdmans, 2016), 10.

one is courting sympathy in a murder trial, invading the territory of an enemy portrayed as another "Hitler," slipping in sound bites and irrepressible images in a political campaign, or capturing a family vacation on a GoPro. The trouble is that in something like the last example one often misses the underlying reality of relationships unfolding before one's eyes while trying to get it digitally correct so that it will play well on social media. That is the essential message in the movie *Reality Bites*: a young woman becomes so caught up in her attempt to construct a filmed image of her friends' daily lives and interactions that she finds herself unaware of the relationships in which she is embroiled with the objects of her movie.

Language and video do not convey what simply is, but rather fabricate "what really is." Perceptions *become* reality. The lines between fantasy and fact begin washing away. Pretty soon everything becomes a continuous interpretation of (and debate about) words. Words refer to words. Even the word *is* might be up for grabs, as former president Clinton reminded us!

Sixth, in the culture we have been describing, the important occupations are the manager and the therapist. The pragmatic person seeks to manage her experience and environment in the interests of a "manipulatable sense of well being."[44] *The* concern is self-improvement and a comfortableness with one's self over against the ethical ultimates and obligations imposed by "universal truth." Ironically, historically Anglican liturgy included what are called the "Comfortable Words"—not words to help one avoid moral imperatives, but words of God's forgiveness in light of the fact that in the liturgy one had just confessed falling short of ethical imperatives. (For example, one of the four Comfortable Words comes from 1 John 2:1: "My little children, I am writing these things to you so that you may not sin. But if anyone does sin, we have an advocate with the Father, Jesus Christ the righteous.") But even churches are caught up in the cultural shift. The pastor's chamber used to be referred to as a "study"; today it is more often called the pastor's "office." In fact, many churches have resorted to psychologizing the gospel to meet self-centered, consumer-oriented, media-induced "felt needs." Proof came in my mailbox one day: relatives sent a church's Easter-season brochure announcing its offerings. While it did not list a single Bible study or prayer group, it described courses on managing finances, getting through grief, coping with divorce, handling medical emergencies, anger management, and potty training.[45]

---

44. Lundin, "Pragmatics of Postmodernity," 31.

45. See Skye Jethani, *The Divine Commodity: Discovering a Faith beyond Consumer Christianity* (Grand Rapids: Zondervan, 2013).

Recommendations for Believing and Worshiping as Church

What implications for theology and the church's liturgical practices emerge when this is the cultural context in which the worshiping community articulates its beliefs?

First, the church must realize that the shift away from Enlightenment modernism has taken place.

Stanley Hauerwas and William Willimon indicted the contemporary church in their book *Resident Aliens* for blithely carrying on as if modernism and the American-Christian (Constantinian) metanarrative were still in place. While the indictment hit closer to home in 1989 when the book came out than it does in the undeniably pluralistic atmosphere we now breathe, the church still has a lot of catching up to do. For one of the authors, the shift took place as early as a Sunday evening in 1963, when the Fox Theater in Greeneville, South Carolina, opened for the first time on a Sunday: "On that night, Greeneville, South Carolina—the last pocket of resistance to secularity in the Western world—served notice that it would no longer be a prop for the church. There would be no free passes for the church, no more free rides. The Fox Theater went head to head with the church over who would provide the worldview for the young. That night in 1963, the Fox Theater won the opening skirmish."[46]

In other words, even the significance of "Sunday" is in contention among our cultural and linguistic communities. Over against the Fox Theater, Simon Chan reminds us that Sunday "is 'the original feast day' and 'the foundation and nucleus of the whole liturgical year.'" Early Christians called it the "Eighth Day"—the "distinguishing sign of the new covenant."[47] Now it has also become one of the heaviest shopping days of the week.

Second, the church should celebrate the overthrow of modernism's confidence in acultural reason. In sync with what we have said up to this point, the gospel is not something that can be known by everyone merely through human reason. Paul makes this clear in 1 Corinthians 1:18–2:16. In the modernist climate of the past, it may have been a wise strategy to approach people with rational arguments for the truth of Christianity and its morality, believing that any rational person who was not simply stubborn would accept the gospel as the only guide to belief and practice. We often defended our beliefs and practices in terms of some publicly acceptable criteria of truth. The trouble was that until postmodernism came along we did not readily recognize the fact that we had made reason the final arbiter of truth and morality. Along

---

46. Stanley Hauerwas and William H. Willimon, *Resident Aliens: Life in the Christian Colony* (Nashville: Abingdon, 1989), 15–16.
47. See Chan, *Liturgical Theology*, 127–28.

with that, we were so confident in human reason that we assumed we could achieve a rational certainty about Christian beliefs and practice.

As an unfortunate side effect of this approach, our articulation of Christian doctrine and our Christian practice looked a lot more like Western (specifically US) reasoning than Christian reasoning. So, for example, we reinterpreted the "hard sayings" of Jesus about turning the other cheek and a camel getting through the eye of a needle to fit a violence-prone consumerist culture. Even our idea of the Christian-sanctioned "traditional" family, which we took to be a timeless, acultural paradigm, really turned out to be a concept dictated more by late nineteenth-century and early twentieth-century industrial America. As Rodney Clapp argues, postmodernism gives the church an opportunity to recover the particular *Christian* understanding of the family.[48]

We have the opportunity to reclaim what has always been true in orthodox Christianity—namely, that the truth of Christianity and its morality is *not* accessible to mere reason. Once again, looking is not the same thing as seeing—seeing from a *specific* perspective. The Christian's perspective on God, humans, morality, and so forth is dictated by a very distinctive and particular point of view—that of Jesus Christ. The postmodern demotion of reason frees us to echo the insight of the apostle Paul that spiritual truths are only known by the spiritually minded; they cannot be known by the natural mind (1 Cor. 2:14–16). We must therefore take responsibility as the church to live out before a watching world a *distinctive* understanding of what it means to be "rational" and "moral"—an understanding not necessarily shared by all people, but one that is shaped by the liturgical practices of the cultural-linguistic community of Jesus Christ.

A caution is in order at this point. In accepting postmodernism's rejection of the modernist optimism about reason, we cannot slip to the other extreme and abandon all rational scrutiny, seeing Christianity as just one more option among equally valid religions. Many in today's culture would want us to do just that. But the claim that all religions are pointing to the same God and talking about the same salvation is itself an intolerant metanarrative—what Alister McGrath calls an "intellectual Stalinism": "The days when it was possible to regard Christianity [or any other particular religion] as simply a local manifestation of a universal category of 'religion' are long since passed, despite the fact that this view is maintained on life-support systems throughout religious study facilities in North America."[49]

48. See Rodney Clapp, *Families at the Crossroads: Beyond Tradition and Modern Options* (Downers Grove, IL: InterVarsity, 1993), chap. 2.

49. Alister McGrath, "A Particularist View: A Post-Enlightenment Approach," in *Four Views on Salvation in a Pluralistic World*, ed. Timothy R. Phillips and Dennis L. Okholm (Grand

This came home to me when I sat on a panel at the national headquarters of the Theosophical Society discussing the assigned topic, "Many Paths, One Reality," with a Buddhist monk, a Jain, and a Sikh. With a recitation of the Christian story I attempted to make it clear that we were not talking about the same God (if about any god at all), nor were we talking about the same concept of salvation; in fact, our views were often contradictory (such as the Christian and Buddhist assessments of human suffering). Still, the moderator, who was the society's president, summarized each presenter's religion with observations of similarities in order to remind the audience that, in the end, we were all speaking about the same reality. This led him to pontificate that what I had articulated about the Christian concept of resurrection was the same thing as the concept of reincarnation in other religions.

So, while we want to avoid either extreme with reference to reason, neither enthroning it and equipping it with universally accessible truths nor dismissing it as if it were *merely* a social construction, we can appreciate the fact that our cultural situation forces us to examine ourselves and ask whether we have construed Christianity in North American white terms. We must listen to other voices, since there is no single unified human voice, as modernism has advertised.

Third, the church must cultivate among its members the Christian narrative about God as Creator, about humans as fallen in sin, about Christ as the definitive revelation of God, about redemption as solely available in Christ, and about the coming renewal of the creation when God's reign is complete. In other words, the world does not call the church into question, forcing it to answer the world's agenda; the church calls the world into question with the master narrative of the gospel.[50] We are like the hero in a Walker Percy novel who is always a "bubble and a half off plumb"—we look strange to a world that has become comfortable with itself because we see the world in a different way, in the light of a defining story that embraces all time and all things (Eph. 1:3–23).

In part, the church's job through teaching and worship is to cultivate people who understand what they cannot and do not comprehend through mere human reason or intuition. The incarnation is not only God entering into our world as a *resident*, but entering into it as an *alien*. For example, Jesus spoke in parables to make his teachings clearer *and also* to hide his teachings. If the culture understands everything we do in worship, if the culture can make

---

Rapids: Zondervan, 1995), 206–8. McGrath is responding to John Hick's pluralistic treatment of religions with this remark.

50. See Hauerwas and Willimon, *Resident Aliens*, 19–24.

complete sense of our Christian practices, if the culture can understand our proclamation of a grace that cannot be earned, then we should be worried that we are not truly articulating the Christian narrative. The church lives its life and professes its faith and worships in a way incomprehensible apart from the God revealed in Jesus Christ. Our morality does *not* make sense outside of the church and Jesus's vision of life. To the watching and listening world, severed from the biblical narrative, our actions and words should look and sound like a foreign culture and foreign language.

By the way, learning a foreign language and its culture is much easier when we are children. The church *must* teach the Christian narrative to its children (and they *do* imbibe this especially when participating in the church's liturgy). That we are not doing such a good job is easily demonstrated. Ask church-bred high school youth to put the following events in the correct order:

> Judah is taken captive by Babylon.
> Moses leads God's people out of Egypt.
> David becomes king of Judah.
> Isaac is born.

Or, if you think the Old Testament is too tough, broaden the exam:

> The prophets speak to Israel and Judah.
> People speak in tongues on Pentecost.
> God makes promises to Abraham.
> Christ dies for our sins.

This should not be a tough quiz for kids who take AP exams in US and world history. The question is, Whose master story *are* our children learning best and fashioning their lives after? What single event is their interpretive key to understanding history—the Holocaust, the American Revolution, the death and resurrection of Jesus Christ, or 9/11? By teaching the story, language, and practice of the narrative centered in Christ and by cycling through the biblical story each liturgical year, we can help those in the church make sense of life; we can give them a sense of coherence in a fragmented, decentralized world.

Fourth, the Christian story is rooted in history and refers to real events, but communicating that history and reality can no longer be done as if people will accept our claims "if only they were rational in their thinking." In fact, we must first convince those in our postmodern culture that we have something that needs to be heard that cannot be heard anywhere else; *then*, we can suggest that it might ultimately be true. John Stackhouse Jr. put it this way: we must argue for the *plausibility* of Christianity before we argue the *credibility* of Christianity.[51] Using sociologist Peter Berger's categories, Lesslie Newbigin is right when he states that the only "plausibility structure" in place today is the insistence that there is no socially accepted plausibility structure. And the one who says otherwise is a "heretic."[52] In fact, with our political philosophy of liberal democracy, the only thing that we agree on is that we will agree not to have to agree. So we have much to do just to get folks in our culture to accept the *plausibility* that resurrections are possible, let alone that there is only one true story of the world. To do this the church must make the biblical story evident in all aspects of its life. Given the culture as we have described it, we must focus less (not *believe* less) on doctrinal confessions and focus more on a lived-out gospel. That has implications for our worship. Evangelicals have largely relied on the sermon to change people's lives, but in our cultural situation it may be liturgical practices, such as communion, that affect people more deeply.

Finally, the church will need to be an alternative culture—an alternative cultural-linguistic community. This is different from being a *counter*-culture. If all we do is counter the prevailing culture, then it is still the prevailing culture that sets the agenda. Many Christians in the United States spend most of their energy countering. But to be an alternative culture, as mentioned in chapter 1, is to live life differently with an agenda set by the gospel. It means we reside as aliens. As Shane Claiborne, Jonathan Wilson-Hartgrove, and Enuma Okoro remind us, it is liturgy that "does not negate culture but creates a new one"—even with a new "time zone" into which we enter.[53]

---

51. John G. Stackhouse Jr., "From Architecture to Argument: Historic Resources for Christian Apologetics," in *Christian Apologetics in the Postmodern World*, ed. Timothy R. Phillips and Dennis L. Okholm (Downers Grove, IL: InterVarsity, 1995), 39–55.

52. See Newbigin, *Foolishness to the Greeks*, 13–14. A "plausibility structure" is defined as "a social structure of ideas and practices that create the conditions determining what beliefs are plausible within the society in question" (10n1).

53. Shane Claiborne, Jonathan Wilson-Hartgrove, and Enuma Okoro, *Common Prayer: A Liturgy for Ordinary Radicals* (Grand Rapids: Zondervan, 2010), 12, 14.

3

What Are the Sources for and the Results of Doing Theology?

We Hear Scripture and Respond in the "Liturgy of the Word"

Reader: "The Word of the Lord."
Congregation: "Thanks be to God!"

If theology, as we have defined it, is a human response to divine revelation, then we must begin with an understanding of what "revelation" is and follow that with a consideration of the *theological* ways in which humans have responded. And so we move on to discuss the *sources* for doing theology and the *results* of doing theology.

Revelation: Special and General

Once the people have gathered to worship, they hear the Word of God. As we have mentioned, in more liturgical churches this often involves four readings: Old Testament, Psalm, New Testament Epistle, and Gospel. Readings from *both* the Old and the New Testaments remind the church that she is immersed in a story that spans the entire Bible—something the church had to insist upon when it tussled with Marcion, whose ideas we will encounter below.

God has been revealing this story for some time. In fact, God's revelation even precedes what is written. Theology often refers to this as "general revelation," to distinguish it from "special revelation."

Before we unpack these two categories, we should consider the meaning of the word they have in common—*revelation*. It is reminiscent of the last book in the New Testament, "The Revelation to John." The Greek word there is *apokalypsis*, and it connotes that something is "unveiled" that would otherwise have been a hidden mystery. In this case, that "hidden mystery" is the unseen, incomprehensible God.

In the Christian Faith this unveiling refers to God's *gift* of *self*-disclosure— what God discloses about God's self, the creation, and us. It is a gift because God is under no obligation to be self-revealing, especially since those whom God created have rebelled against the One who gave them existence. This is precisely why in the liturgy after Scripture is read and the reader concludes with the affirmation, "The Word of the Lord," the congregation responds, "Thanks be to God." Even more assertively, after the *Gospel* is read and the reader concludes with the words, "The Gospel of the Lord," the congregation responds, "Praise to you, Lord Christ."

Last millennium, in the college cafeteria, I met the woman who would become my wife. Two hours later I asked her to go out on a date—that same evening! We ordered milkshakes (as college students we spared no expense) and talked for two hours, effectively introducing ourselves to each other. When I escorted her back to her dorm, I asked if she would like to go out again the next weekend, suggesting two different outings—A and B— followed by C: "None of the above." Thanks be to God that she did not choose C. But she could have. She could have decided that after conversing with this guy for two hours she had no interest in letting him know anything more about her.

In the biblical story we get no further than the third chapter before the creatures rebel against the One who has been providing for them and "conversing" with them. And after that rebellion, the story could have ended there with a three-chapter Bible, but, fortunately, God did not give up on us. God did not choose "None of the above," but continued to disclose truths about who the Creator is and what the Creator expects from his human creatures, even to the point of redeeming the rebels. Thanks be to God! And that *is* the response in the liturgy after worshipers listen to Scripture and hear the reader announce, "The Word of the Lord." We cannot thank God enough that God continues to speak to us.

What liturgical readers are doing when they read Scripture fits one of the categories of revelation we have mentioned, the category of "special revelation." This has to do with the authoritative unveiling of truths about God that are inaccessible to human reason *itself* and are not *clearly* available to us through anything in creation.

This would certainly include God's special acts in human history, particularly those having to do with Israel. Here we must be careful, as we will point out later, because history can be ambiguous, and many—especially people groups and nations—have confused their own voice with the voice of God. So when we refer here to God's special acts in human history, we have in mind especially the ones narrated in Scripture. In fact, Scripture—what we refer to as both Old and New Testaments—is a significant source of special revelation.

What Scripture points us to is Jesus Christ, the embodied Word of God and God's definitive act of self-disclosure. Moreover, Christ is made known through the community for whom the Bible *is* Scripture and which continues to exist as his body—the church. Scripture, Jesus Christ, and the church, along with God's special acts in the history that is recorded in the Bible, are the sources that make up the category of "special revelation."

Something to notice about these sources is that they are all phenomena related to our humanity: human language, human flesh, human institution, and human history. In other words, God's self-disclosure is *mediated* through what is human. It all takes place on *our* level in earthly, human, worldly ways. It is what John Calvin referred to as God's "accommodation" to us: God speaks to us, said Calvin, like a nursemaid speaks to a baby with a lisp. From God's perspective, this definitive self-disclosure is just baby talk.[1]

Another way to speak of special revelation is to use Karl Barth's notion of the "threefold form of the Word of God." That is to say, God's Word comes to us in personal, written, and proclaimed forms because it comes to us in Jesus Christ, the Bible, and the church's preaching (and her sacraments or ordinances—visible expressions of the Word).

There is a certain order and priority among these three in that each must be tested by and be in conformity with the preceding one on the list. The Bible witnesses to Jesus Christ, and the church's proclamation must be faithful to the Bible. We can see this priority in the Christmas story as Matthew presents it in his Gospel account (chapter 2). The magi ("wise men") were pointed to the Christ child once they had learned from the chief priests and

---

1. John Calvin, *Institutes of the Christian Religion*, ed. John T. McNeill, trans. Ford Lewis Battles (Philadelphia: Westminster John Knox, 1960), 1.13.1.

Excerpts from the Eucharistic Prayer in the *Apostolic Constitutions* (ca. 380, Syria)

You not only created the world but also placed a human being in it as the inhabitant of the world, making this person the ornament of the world. . . . You gave them an immortal soul and a mortal body. . . . As to the soul, you gave it rational judgment, the ability to distinguish godliness and godlessness, between justice and injustice. . . . [But] people corrupted the natural law, either considering creation as making itself or honoring it more than was appropriate, making it equal to you, the God of all. . . . Holy is your only-begotten Son, our Lord and God, Jesus the Christ, who serves you in all things, you his God and Father, doing so in your varied creation and according to your fitting providence. He did not abandon the human race to perdition. . . . He, our Creator, in his goodness and according to your will, was made flesh.

Cited in Lawrence J. Johnson, *Worship in the Early Church: An Anthology of Historical Sources*, vol. 2 (Collegeville, MN: Liturgical Press, 2009).

scribes whom Herod consulted that, according to the prophet Micah in the Jewish Scriptures, the Christ would be found in Bethlehem. Scripture led them to Jesus Christ.

In turn, they were led to Scripture by their astrological calculations—by creation: celestial phenomena led them to Scripture, which led them to Christ. And that brings us to the other category of God's unveiling: general revelation, something to which even Scripture itself attests.

General revelation can be said to be the *natural* knowledge of God that we find in the structures of human existence, in nature, and in historical phenomena.

With "structures of human existence" we include human reason and our sense of morality, or what Calvin referred to as the "microcosm." For instance, Paul implies in Romans 2:1 that our sense of morality is "proof" that God exists. And throughout history philosophers have devised rational arguments to "prove" that God exists, such as the *cosmological* argument that tries to explain why something exists rather nothing; the *teleological* argument that insists there must be a divine designer to account for the order we see in the universe; the *ontological* argument, which argues that the cause of our idea of a most perfect being must be that being itself; and the *moral* argument (such as Immanuel Kant proposed), which maintains that there must be a source for our sense of morality and something or someone who ensures that we conform our lives to it.

Nature is another source of general revelation, or what Calvin called the "macrocosm" and the "theater of God's glory."[2] We really ought to say *creation* instead of nature, especially given the context of this topic. Scripture itself testifies to this source, such as in the first four verses of Psalm 19: "The heavens are telling the glory of God; / and the firmament proclaims his handiwork. / Day to day pours forth speech, / and night to night declares knowledge. / There is no speech, nor are there words; / their voice is not heard; / yet their voice goes out through all the earth, / and their words to the end of the world." In verse 7 the psalmist begins to talk about the law (part of God's covenant with Israel) and the "LORD" (the transliteration for the name *Yahweh* by which the covenant-making God identified himself to Israel in Exod. 3:14), so that the psalmist is really transitioning from general revelation (speaking of "God" or *El* in Hebrew) to special revelation (speaking of "LORD" or *Yahweh* in Hebrew).

The apostle Paul also appeals to this source of general revelation in Romans 1:20, insisting that "ever since the creation of the world his [God's] eternal power and divine nature, invisible though they are, have been understood and seen through the things he has made." Many people stop at that point, arguing that we have adequate knowledge of God through creation, but they need to read what comes before and after verse 20: Paul is arguing that we distort that natural knowledge of God due to our sin-warped lives, and we end up worshiping the creature rather than the Creator. And that is why we need special revelation as a corrective, which we will point out when we get to the Reformed view of the relation between special and general revelation.

Finally, historical phenomena, such as our personal experience and the existence of other religions, alert us to the fact that God is known in these general ways. Paul seemed to work with this assumption when he spoke before the Areopagus, appealing to a monument with the inscription "To an unknown god" (Acts 17:22–28). Paul equated this generic "God" with the God revealed in Jesus Christ, though how successful he was is uncertain, since Luke (the author of Acts) reports that only a few believed, and we never hear of a church established in Athens during Paul's ministry. Again, questions come to mind: How effective *is* general revelation for our knowledge of God? And what is the relationship between special and general revelation?

Before we tackle those questions, we should indicate that legitimate claims have been made for what we *can* know about God through general revelation. As even Scripture attests, we can know that God exists and that God is Creator

---

2. Calvin, *Institutes*, 1.5.8, and several other references in the *Institutes*.

(keeping in mind, as Herbert McCabe has pointed out, that the word *God* in this context is simply the answer to the question, "Why is there something rather than nothing?"[3]). One might also come to the conclusion that there is a divine being who designed and controls the cosmos—a divine being who might also judge the good and the bad in the end.

Since at least the time that Paul tried to relate general revelation to special revelation in his Mars Hill address, Christian thinkers have suggested models that represent different ways of juxtaposing the two. We will look at four representative types using labels that are in one sense characteristic of these types, but keeping in mind that they *are* being identified with labels (or, as one person put it, training wheels for the mind).[4]

1. The Enlightenment Model

In this view special revelation is measured, judged, and corrected by general revelation. That is, what we know about God through Scripture, for instance, is filtered through what we claim to know about God through our reason and experience. As was discussed in the previous chapter, during the Enlightenment some sought to be free of what they considered superstition in the Bible and church tradition so that all could come to *rational* conclusions about what to believe. This was true of the deists, who dismissed accounts of miracles (as any "rational" person would do), but accepted the kinds of moral teachings found in the Gospels, for instance. At best, special revelation is a *republication* of the original natural religion. We can see this in a progression of book titles that span from the late seventeenth to the early eighteenth centuries: John Locke's *Reasonableness of Christianity* to John Toland's *Christianity Not Mysterious* to Matthew Tindal's *Christianity as Old as Creation*. And you can hear echoes of this in the US Declaration of Independence: "We hold these Truths to be *self-evident*, that all Men are created equal, that they are endowed by their Creator with certain unalienable Rights." In other words, we are not holding these truths on the basis of Christian special revelation, but on the basis of a general understanding that all human beings possess. (Whether all humans *do* hold these truths or find them "self-evident" is another issue, as we discussed previously.) This model might also argue that it is "self-evident" that a person does not come back to life after being dead for three days,

3. Herbert McCabe, *God Matters* (New York: Continuum, 1987), 3–5.
4. Calling labels "training wheels for the mind" was something Richard Chase, a former president of Wheaton College, mentioned in an address.

let alone that axe heads float on water or that you can feed thousands of people with a bag of bread and fish.

2. The Thomistic Model

This view might be typical of those who follow in the wake of Thomas Aquinas, for whom general and special revelation occupy somewhat distinct spheres that are compatible with each other, or, as it has been said, "grace completes nature." What can be learned from human reason and experience, for instance, is that God exists. But what cannot be known from those sources is that this God who exists is a Triune God—Father, Son, and Holy Spirit. That requires revelation that comes from Scripture and the church's tradition. Vatican Council I, a Roman Catholic Church council held in 1870, argued that God can be known with certainty, albeit incompletely, from that which has been created using the natural light of reason. The result is what we call "natural theology."[5] So special revelation and general revelation are on parallel tracks as it were, both headed in the same direction; it is just that special revelation takes us further into the kind of knowledge necessary for salvation. Even when special revelation iterates what we can know from general revelation, it might be the case that what Scripture and the church teach is doing a favor for those who do not have the time or intellectual ability themselves to arrive at truths such as God's existence.

3. The Protestant Reformed Model

This model was championed by John Calvin (the reason we use the word *Reformed*). It is the opposite of the Enlightenment model. In this model, special revelation measures, judges, and corrects what we think we know about God from reason and experience. God can only be known partially and distortedly in the "theater of God's glory." Because our understanding is finite and because our intellect is warped by sin, we cannot come to proper conclusions about God by ourselves. For instance, because of the evil we see in the world—both natural and moral evil—we might conclude that God does not care about us or, worse, that God is a sadistic killjoy. But God's self-disclosure in Jesus Christ, as he is known through Scripture and proclaimed and worshiped by the church, reveals that, despite how we process our experiences, God loves his creation and desires that none perish. Recall Calvin's simile that we read in

---

5. A caution is in order here: Roman Catholic thinkers would not typically say that natural theology is derivable from reason alone and would argue that it always requires prevenient ("coming before") or preparatory grace.

chapter 1: If you put a book before bleary-eyed old men, they might be able to discern that it is some sort of writing, but for them to read what is actually on the pages they need corrective lenses; in the same way, we need the lens of Scripture, said Calvin, to correct and clarify our distorted natural understanding of God and to reveal the heart of God.

We should mention an internecine debate with regard to this position that occurred between Karl Barth and Emil Brunner. It played out in a volume entitled *Natural Theology*,[6] in which Brunner argued that even after the fall humans still have a capacity for language, rationality, and responsibility that makes it possible for them to understand natural revelation. He granted that this understanding of who God is has been dulled by sin such that we fall into speculation and idolatry. But Brunner was saying that we have a "capacity" for receiving revelation, because the *formal* part of the image of God still functions even though the *material* part that has to do with original righteousness is lost; there is a "point of contact" between divine revelation and human thought, kept intact by a general, preserving grace that abolishes the worst effects of sin. Barth's response was entitled (in German) *Nein!* Barth argued that *with* God's revelation comes the divine gift of the necessary conditions for receiving it. A *human* "capacity" for receiving revelation can establish *no* "point of contact" on the *human* side. ("What has rationality and responsibility got to do with being able to hear God?!" Barth asked.) And even if we could "imperfectly" know the *true* God, what would be the sense of "imperfectly"? Because of the fall, the knowledge of God is in *principle*, but not in *fact*, possible. The *only human* possibility open to us is to know and worship the God of our *own heart*, and so we are without excuse. For Barth, the knowledge of God that comes in Christ *includes* a real knowledge of the true God in creation. It's as if Barth is saying that God is transmitting digitally, but we are still receiving in analog mode; the problem is not in the transmission, but in the reception, and until we are hooked up with a spiritual converter box, we cannot receive what God is transmitting.

4. The Anabaptist Model

Of all the labels, this one may be the most contrived, but its resonance comes from the fact that Anabaptists (e.g., Mennonites) have typically

6. See Emil Brunner and Karl Barth, *Natural Theology: Comprising "Nature and Grace" by Professor Dr. Emil Brunner and the Reply "No!" by Dr. Karl Barth* (London: Geoffrey Bles, Centenary Press, 1946; repr., Eugene, OR: Wipf and Stock, 2002).

distanced themselves from the prevailing culture. Not that an Anabaptist would necessarily hold the view to be described here, but there *are* those who espouse a *complete* separation of what people claim to know about God and human life from reason and experience and what God *tells* us about these subjects in Scripture (and primarily Scripture, not tradition, since most in this camp reject tradition). An example here comes in the works of Jay E. Adams, such as his early writing, *Competent to Counsel*. Adams disowns the science of psychology in favor of biblical explanations of what ails us, which can all be summed up in the word *sin* (not in words like *neurosis* or *psychosis*). So general revelation is largely rejected, and one puts all his eggs in the basket of special revelation.

Figure 2
The Relation of General and Special Revelation

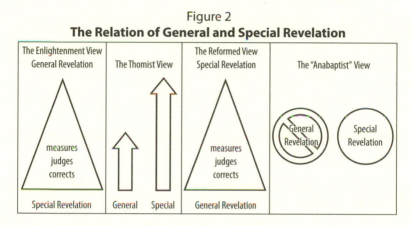

Making a decision as to where one should plant her flag among these models requires working through several issues. Among them are these questions: (1) How should we interpret Romans 1:18–3:20 (and 1 Cor. 2:14–16)? That is, how much weight does Paul want us to put on the knowledge of God through creation and moral conscience over against his claims about how sinful we are? (2) Relatedly, what are the effects of the fall—of our present sinful condition? How much weight should we give (if any) to the claim that there are significant noetic (intellect-related) effects of the fall? (3) How should we conceive the difference between God and humans? If God is such that even the word *being* or *existent* is not appropriate to apply to God, can we ever know God?

One's answers to such questions will determine the answers to other questions: Do humans have natural access to the revelation of God? Does the natural knowledge of God lead to anything but idolatry and despair? Does it even lead to that? Is a divine miracle of grace necessary to know the *true* God?

This *is* a significant issue, as Karl Barth, Dietrich Bonhoeffer, and a host of others understood as they lived out their Christian confession in the context of Nazi Germany. The German church had confused God's movement in history, "discernible" through history and rational thought, with the rise of German nationalism. The concern of the Confessing Church was that compromising its claim of God's definitive self-disclosure in Christ as *the* Truth (John 14:6; 18:37) would slowly devastate the church. George Hunsinger described it this way:

> The church prepared to offer binding loyalty to Hitler was a church which had died the death of a thousand smaller compromises. For more than two hundred years, it had been trying to divide its loyalty between Jesus Christ and other supposed sources of divine revelation. Whether reason, conscience, the emotions, history, nature, or culture, some second authority was continually proposed and ratified alongside the first. But no claim of exclusive loyalty can tolerate an external loyalty that is equally binding and obligatory. The attempt to turn an either/or into a both/and could only mean that the church's loyalty was compromised and divided. For whether the church realized it or not, no second authority, however apparently benign, could represent anything other than an exclusive and competing counter-claim to that of God's Word. By the time Hitler came along, the church was incapacitated by its history of compromises.[7]

Regardless of which of the above options one chooses, we do well to heed the German church's experience.

Scripture and Tradition

If the conjunction *and* can be dangerous, what should we say about Scripture *and* tradition? Though we encounter some different positions on this topic, it is helpful to begin with some comments about the early church's understanding of tradition.

Among other places in the Greek New Testament, the word *paradosis* ("tradition") is used by Paul in 1 Corinthians 11:2; 2 Thessalonians 2:15; and 3:6 to refer to teachings he handed down. First Corinthians 11, for instance, gives us the familiar words heard during communion that we refer to in the liturgy as the "words of institution." After Paul commends the Corinthian church for maintaining the traditions he handed on to them (1 Cor. 11:2), he writes,

7. George Hunsinger, "Where the Battle Rages: Confessing Churches in America Today," *Dialog* 26, no. 4 (Fall 1987): 264–74.

For I received from the Lord what I also handed on to you, that the Lord Jesus on the night when he was betrayed took a loaf of bread, and when he had given thanks, he broke it and said, "This is my body that is for you. Do this in remembrance of me." In the same way he took the cup also, after supper, saying, "This cup is the new covenant in my blood. Do this, as often as you drink it, in remembrance of me." For as often as you eat this bread and drink the cup, you proclaim the Lord's death until he comes. (vv. 23–26)

Essentially, Paul is saying that he is *traditioning* these words that have been *traditioned* to him, because the meaning of the word (similar to the word *traitor*) has to do with handing on to someone else what has been received. So *tradition* is not a bad word, especially when we realize that many churches continue to use in their celebration of communion these same words that Paul was handing on two thousand years ago.

Of course, traditions can become so routine that they are no longer effective in our lives. As John Leith has said, "Tradition is the living faith of dead people; traditionalism is the dead faith of living people."[8] But traditions, like habits, can still be good, even when we are taking them for granted. I have a "tradition" of brushing my teeth each morning and evening. I don't really think about it much, and I don't make a daily to-do list in order to remember to do it. But the routine is necessary for good physical health. In the same way, some of the church's traditions are necessary for good spiritual health, even when we are not giving them much thought. And some traditions, such as shaking hands, are appropriate whether or not we know why we do them or how we got them. Most Americans have no idea why we put our right hand over our left breast when the national anthem is played or when that tradition began, but we do it spontaneously because the action was handed on to us by a previous generation.

In the early church, before the canon of Scripture was fixed (something we will examine shortly), Scripture and tradition were neither separate nor contradictory.[9] But as time went on and for various reasons, some began to contest some of the traditions (both in practice and in thought) that had developed in the medieval church, so that even before we got to the Protestant Reformation in the sixteenth century, a significant degree of questioning occurred about that which had been received.

8. John Leith (borrowing from Jaroslav Pelikan), *An Introduction to the Reformed Tradition: A Way of Being the Christian Community*, rev. ed. (Louisville: Westminster John Knox, 1980), 31.
9. D. H. Williams, *Retrieving the Tradition and Renewing Evangelicalism: A Primer for Suspicious Protestants* (Grand Rapids: Eerdmans, 1999).

One of the marks of the Protestant Reformation is *sola Scriptura*—
Scripture alone. By this they meant that the Bible, as illumined by the Holy
Spirit, is sufficient to make known the will and word of God. At times this
is referred to as the *perspicuity* of Scripture. Did this mean that Protestants
such as Martin Luther and John Calvin had no use for tradition? Quite the
contrary, *sola Scriptura* did not mean *nuda Scriptura*. That is, tradition, while
not normative, was recognized as offering valuable insights for understanding
Scripture and thinking theologically. Both Luther and Calvin, for instance,
were heavily influenced and shaped by Augustine in their understanding of
the Christian Faith, and many times they resorted to the commentaries of
early church thinkers in their examination of certain doctrines. What is more,
they certainly affirmed the church's traditioned understanding of the Trinity
as expressed in the Nicene Creed. But they would not have opted for a parity
of Scripture and tradition.

Instead, that kind of parity was expressed in the Roman Catholic Church's
reaction to Lutheranism as it articulated its views during the Council of Trent.
During the fourth session of the council in 1546, the Church made this declaration: "The council is aware that this truth [the gospel] and this discipline
are *contained* in *written books* [Scripture] and in the *unwritten traditions*
which were received by the apostles from the lips of Christ himself or, by the
same Apostles, at the dictation of the Holy Spirit, and were handed on and
have come down to us."[10] The question is this: Was Trent teaching that there
is an "extra-biblical constitutive tradition"? In other words, was it saying that
there is a collection of revealed truths that the apostles received *in addition to*
inspired Scripture and that the church preserves by uninterrupted continuity
of the apostolic teaching office? Is there *one* or are there *two* sources of revelation? And are both sources needed for an adequate knowledge of the gospel?

The long-standing interpretation of Trent was that it *was* espousing two
sources of revelation of equal authority and that the Latin word *et* (and) implied "partly-partly"—the gospel is contained partly in the Bible and partly
in the church's traditions. Whether or not that is what Trent meant, that was
essentially the way Trent was understood until the late 1800s. And it would
have made sense, since the argument would be that the canon (i.e., what the
church decided should be in the Bible), the sacramental system, and the papacy
are truths not found in Scripture itself.

But modern scholarship has suggested that the primary and classical
Roman Catholic view on this is that *et* should be taken to mean totally-totally,

10. Henry Bettenson and Chris Maunder, eds., *Documents of the Christian Church*, 4th ed.
(New York: Oxford University Press, 2011), 264–65 (italics added).

not partly-partly.[11] In other words, there is one source (the gospel) with two currents or streams flowing from it. Scripture is "materially sufficient," which means that Scripture contains, at least implicitly, all revealed doctrines and provides a sufficient summary of the gospel. Nevertheless, while Scripture gives purity to tradition, tradition gives fullness to Scripture. Tradition interprets Scripture and fleshes it out. In this way doctrine must accord with Scripture but can develop what was only implied in it, just as an oak tree grows out of the acorn in which the tree was "contained."[12] So the Church moves forward toward the fullness of divine truth.

An analogy might be this: Paleontologists who dig up dinosaur bones and then reconstruct the dinosaur's skeletal structure for display in the museum sometimes put "flesh" on one side of the structure so that we can visualize what the beast originally looked like. The Bible is like the skeletal structure; the "skin" is supplied by tradition. Here is another way to think of it: If you walked into a room that was darkened to the point that all you could make out on the wall in front of you was that a framed painting was hanging on it, you might be curious about the painting and slowly turn up the rheostat on the light switch. As the light slowly grows brighter, you can see that this is a portrait, and as the light continues to increase, you can see that it is a portrait of George Washington. Washington's portrait was *materially* there all along, but in order to see it clearly and fully, you needed more illumination. In this analogy, the portrait is Scripture, and the illumination is supplied by the Spirit's guidance in the Church through the centuries.

Vatican Council II (the Roman Catholic Church council held in the early 1960s) provided a very dynamic and unified view of the relation of Church, Scripture, and tradition, with the gospel as the source of it all. It is instructive to hear the Church's own words:

> This tradition which comes from the apostles developed in the Church with the help of the Holy Spirit. For there is *a growth in the understanding of the realities and the words which have been handed down*. This happens through the contemplation and study of believers who treasure these things in their heart, through the intimate understanding of spiritual things they experience, and through the preaching by those who have received through episcopal succession the sure gift of truth. For as the centuries succeed one another, *the church*

11. On all of this see the classic study of George H. Tavard, *Holy Writ or Holy Church: The Crisis of the Protestant Reformation* (London: Burns and Oates, 1959).

12. This is one of the analogies used by John Henry Newman in *An Essay on the Development of Christian Doctrine* (Notre Dame, IN: University of Notre Dame Press, 1994).

constantly moves forward toward the fullness of divine truth until the words of God reach their complete fulfillment in her. (8)

Hence there exists a close connection and communication between sacred tradition and sacred Scripture. For both of these, *flowing from the same divine well-spring*, in a certain way merge into a *unity* and tend toward the same end. . . . The teaching office is not above the Word of God, but serves it, teaching only what has been passed on. . . . It is clear that sacred tradition, sacred Scripture, and teaching authority . . . are so linked and joined together *that one cannot stand without the others*, and that altogether and each in its own way *under action of the one Holy Spirit contribute to salvation.* (2.9–10)[13]

Like a three-legged stool that would be off-kilter if one leg were missing, this statement brings together tradition, Scripture, and the teaching authority of the Church.

In the end, Protestants and Roman Catholics will disagree on the relation of Scripture and tradition (and the Church's teaching authority), just as both will disagree with the Eastern Orthodox perspective that sees Scripture itself as part of a widely encompassing tradition. But at least we can agree when we are honest with ourselves that we *have* all been shaped by tradition as we come to Scripture, just as we discussed in chapter 1. Again, there is no view from nowhere. We all read Scripture from somewhere.

The Inspiration and Illumination of Scripture

All Christian traditions agree that Scripture is inspired. This is the claim made in 2 Timothy 3:16–17, which tells us, "All scripture is inspired by God and is useful for teaching, for reproof, for correction, and for training in righteousness, so that everyone who belongs to God may be proficient, equipped for every good work." In other words, the Holy Spirit was active in the origin of Scripture.

How exactly the Spirit was involved is not certain, because the text does not tell us. The word translated "inspired" here literally means "God-breathed." Those who study these texts call words like this a *hapax legomenon*—a word that only occurs once in the entire New Testament. Because we know what words mean when we understand them in context, a onetime occurrence makes it difficult to know what the author of 2 Timothy meant by

---

13. "Dogmatic Constitution on Divine Revelation," in *The Documents of Vatican II, with Notes and Comments by Catholic, Protestant, and Orthodox Authorities*, Walter M. Abbott, SJ, general ed., and Joseph Gallagher, translation ed. (New York: America Press, 1966, 2012), 115–18 (italics added).

this. At one end of the spectrum are those who insist that each word in the original writing was inspired, though not by divine dictation; this view is called "verbal plenary [literally, "all words"] inspiration." We will revisit this position when we discuss "inerrancy." At the other end are those who simply believe that the writers were inspired like a poet might be inspired to write her poetry.

Actually, since we do not know the details regarding the *process*, all that we can assert from this text is the *fact* of inspiration. In other words, in some way the Bible is *both* human *and* divine—and *fully* both in a way similar to the way in which the incarnate Son of God became *both* fully divine and fully human in the person of Jesus Christ. The *Catechism of the Catholic Church* makes this point eloquently: "To compose the sacred books, God chose certain men who, all the while he employed them in this task, made full use of their own faculties and powers so that, though he acted in them and by them, it was as true authors that they consigned to writing whatever he wanted written and no more."[14]

More important than trying to speculate about the process of inspiration are two points we need to remember with regard to the doctrine of inspiration.

First, it is clear from the 2 Timothy passage that the inspiration of Scripture should not be divorced from its purposes—to teach, reprove, correct, and train in righteousness so that everyone is well equipped to do God's work. Sometimes those who are adamant about the doctrine of inspiration are less concerned to live by the dictates of the text they are defending. I once had to remind a lawyer who sued church members whom he thought were compromising Scripture that he was acting contrary to the inspired Bible he so vigorously defended (see 1 Cor. 6:1–6).

Second, the doctrine of inspiration must be linked to the doctrine of illumination. That is, the same Spirit who inspired the writers of Scripture is still at work illumining the contemporary readers of Scripture. In fact, that is the point of the promise of Isaiah 55:10–11. Because God is actively involved with his Word *now*, what goes out does not return to God "empty"; it accomplishes God's purposes and succeeds in God's use of it. And that brings us back to the first point of keeping inspiration and God's purposes together.

In their worship services, many churches actually precede the reading of Scripture with a "prayer for Illumination," such as this: "Lord, open our hearts and minds by the power of your Holy Spirit, that as the Scriptures are read and your Word is proclaimed, we may hear with joy what you say to us

14. *Catechism of the Catholic Church* (Mahwah, NJ: Paulist Press, 1994), no. 106 (quoting Vatican Council II).

today. Amen."[15] The congregation is asking to receive and understand what God wants them to get out of Scripture as it is read and preached so that they can be better equipped to do what God wants them to do.

This idea that the reading of Scripture in worship is an event that involves not only the human readers and listeners, but also the life-changing activity of God whose Word it is, is beautifully articulated in Roman Catholic resources:

> When God shares his word with us, he awaits our response, that is, our listening and our adoring "in Spirit and in truth" (John 4:23). *The Holy Spirit makes our response effective, so that what we hear in the celebration of the liturgy we carry out in the way we live.* "Be doers of the word and not hearers only" (James 1.22).[16]

The apostle Paul seems to have something like the Spirit's illumination and empowerment in mind when he declares in 1 Corinthians 2:14–16 that "unspiritual" or naturally minded people cannot receive God's gifts (keeping in mind that God's self-disclosure is a gift), because they are spiritually discerned, but those who have the mind of Christ are able to understand what others consider to be foolishness.

John Calvin emphasized this Spirit-Scripture connection, insisting that it is the Holy Spirit who attests to the divine authority of the Bible. This is referred to as the self-authenticating character of Scripture.

In the end, we advocate maintaining a link between the internal Word (the Spirit's work in us) and the external Word (the Bible). Referring to the Bible as the "sword" (see Eph. 6:17), Donald Bloesch said it well: the sword cannot pierce by itself, but must be wielded and used by the Holy Spirit to be effective in our lives.[17] If we do not keep these linked together, we will end up with complete subjectivity with no basis to "test the spirits" that are supposedly speaking to us or with no rehabilitation of human reason by God's enabling grace.

15. *Book of Common Worship* (Louisville: Westminster John Knox, 1993), 90.

16. *General Introduction to the Lectionary for Mass*, 2nd ed. (Vatican City: Sacred Congregation for the Sacraments and Divine Worship, 1981), 3. Cited by Liam Tracey, OSM, "Word and Sacrament," in *The Study of Liturgy and Worship*, ed. Juliette Day and Benjamin Gordon-Taylor (Collegeville, MN: Liturgical Press, 2013), 57 (italics added). Tracey here makes clear why our appreciation for what is going on when Scripture is read in worship has become insipid: "This rich sense of the word as an event, an encounter with the risen Christ, was lost, largely when the Jewish sense of the word as an action and activity was forgotten, as the Jewish roots of Christianity faded away. When the word came to be seen as the communication or transmission of intellectual truths and polemics rather than a proclamation of what God has done in the past and continues to do in this worshipping community today, the importance of the word is soon obscured and seen as not even essential."

17. Donald Bloesch, *Essentials of Evangelical Theology*, vol. 1, *God, Authority, and Salvation* (San Francisco: HarperOne, 1982), 63–65.

Putting this all together and using an analogy that appreciates the resurgence of vinyl records, we could say that the vinyl record is Scripture, the phonograph on which it is played is the community of the Spirit (the church), the power that enables us to hear the vinyl being played on the phonograph is the Spirit, and the "voice" that is heard when the vinyl is played on the empowered phonograph is Christ. We need all of this in order to hear God's Word rightly and in order for it to make a difference in our lives as God intended.

How the Bible Came to Be

How Scripture came to play so prominent a role in the church's life has to do with what we call canonicity. While this topic is dealt with at length in books and courses having to do specifically with the text of Scripture, several comments are in order here as we begin to think about the *authority* of the Bible.

The word *canon* comes from the Greek cognate *kanōn*, referring to a ruler or yardstick. Some think that word derives from the Hebrew *qaneh*, which referred to straight reeds that grew in marshy areas in the ancient Near East. This lends itself to the concept of an instrument that can be used for measuring and for drawing a straight line. In that sense, "canonicity" refers to Scripture's authority as the standard or rule by which we measure the "straightness" of Christian faith and practice. For those familiar with some home-improvement projects, canonicity is like "snapping a chalk line."

The Greek word was first used to designate the "divinely inspired books of Scripture" in 373, referring to a list of the Bible's contents that Athanasius, bishop of Alexandria, mentioned in a letter in 367—a list that corresponds to the Bibles we have today. (Eusebius of Caesarea had made a similar list—with three divisions—over a century earlier.) Athanasius "measured" these books of the Hebrew Bible and our New Testament by the "rule of faith" (*regula fidei*)—something like what would become the Apostles' Creed, asserting his authority as a church leader (bishop) in harmony with what was the established practice in the churches at that time. He was making sure that his readers understood what was appropriate for liturgical reading. In other words, Athanasius was not defining what would be in an individual's Bible since there was no single "book" and most Christians would not even own parts of it. The issue was which books were to be used in the actual practices of the Christian community as they worshiped.[18]

18. See Andrew B. McGowan, *Ancient Christian Worship: Early Church Practices in Social, Historical, and Theological Perspective* (Grand Rapids: Baker Academic, 2014), 89–92.

Since the Bible did not invent itself, how did we get to the point in the late fourth century that Athanasius has described?

There is evidence that Christian letters[19] and "memoirs of the apostles" were being read in the church's assemblies as early as the late second century, though the memory of Jesus's words and actions and the proclamation of his death and resurrection were initially matters of oral rather than written discourse. (We have an account of publicly reading Gospel stories in literary form and a sermon in the context of a Christian assembly from Justin Martyr in his *First Apology*, ca. 160.) And it's fairly clear that the core of a canon— most of our present Christian Bible—was established from the time of the Apostolic Fathers (at least by mid-second century) as the most important books in the world, even though the edges of a canon were, as John Barton put it, still fuzzy.[20] What is called the *Muratorian Fragment*, which may be the oldest list of books of the Bible, dates from about the year 170. It is often cited to help make the case for an early core of books that were appropriate for liturgical reading.

In fact, we know that by about the year 200 Scripture was being read in the liturgical context, perhaps followed by a psalm, a homily (sermon), and prayers.[21] And as time went on, especially by the fourth and fifth centuries, appropriate texts were assigned for particular days and circumstances, such as Easter, Christmas, and celebrations of saints' days.[22] This was all accompanied by authoritative interpretations of these texts by church leaders.

Andrew McGowan sums up all of this so well that it is worth quoting at some length:

> Overall, there seems to have been an interdependent and complementary de-
> velopment of reading and preaching. The emergence of a more textualized
> and ultimately canonized approach to scriptural or revelatory discourse in the

19. We do know that Paul's letters were being circulated and read in the churches very early on: see Colossians 4:16; see also 2 Peter 3:15–16, where Paul's letters are referred to along with the "*other* scriptures." (Note some encouragement for us in this latter passage: *even 2 Peter* admits there are some things that are difficult to understand in Paul's letters!)

20. John Barton, *Holy Writings, Sacred Text: The Canon in Early Christianity* (Louisville: Westminster John Knox, 1997), 19, 25, 80–82. See McGowan, *Worship*, 110. Barton notes that the words of Jesus had intrinsic authority from the very beginning, much in the manner that some people prize "red letter" editions of the Bible today; the Gospel accounts became living guardians and literary guarantors of this sacred oral tradition. What was still "fuzzy" was universal acceptance of Hebrews, James, 2 Peter, 2 and 3 John, Jude, and Revelation; some books that would finally be rejected were accepted by a few, such as 1 Clement, the Shepherd of Hermas, and the Didache.

21. McGowan, *Worship*, 86.

22. McGowan, *Worship*, 99–101.

assemblies was accompanied by more authoritative, and indeed more clerical, exposition of those sacred texts. The interdependence of these two processes was liturgical, but more than that; for outside of communal events Scripture was generally not directly accessible to the individual, who was mostly neither reader nor interpreter but hearer, and so the development of an authoritative text implied the development of authoritative interpretation too.

Thus, the emergence of a liturgical ministry of the Word is not merely a feature of worship; it is the key to understanding how the earliest Christians in general knew and received Scripture itself, and how they encountered the God who spoke in Scripture: not for the most part on the page perused privately, but in hearing amidst the communal assembly of the people called by that God.[23]

What criteria did those who read and interpreted these texts use to determine authenticity? What should function as the *authoritative* texts for the Christian community? Certainly the identification of an author as fulfilling a *prophetic* role was one important mark, since a prophet was one whose life was devoted to revealing the messages and purposes of God for his people, who spoke by the prompting of the Holy Spirit (see 2 Pet. 1:20–21). For the New Testament letters and books, an *apostolic* connection was important, since an apostle was not just a spectator or reporter of Christ, but an active, contemporary participant with and witness to Christ in a way that was unique and unrepeatable. (One might wonder how that works with, say, Luke or Mark, since they were not apostles, but the argument is made that they had close ties with apostles.) *Internal consistency* and *integrity* also functioned as criteria, especially since those who ridiculed the Christian Faith, like second-century philosopher Celsus, pointed out contradictions and implausibilities in the texts. And as the preceding discussion should have made clear, *common use* and *universal acceptance* of the letters and books that became the Bible were significant factors in the development of the canon as the church read and preached these texts, especially in liturgical contexts.[24]

Two individuals who did not act as "criteria" did in fact provide further stimuli in the growth of Scripture and the canonization of its contents— Marcion for the growth and Montanus for the canonization. In Marcion's case, the question of the canon became explicit for the first time as the church considered what to *include*. In Montanus's case, the question of the purity

---

23. McGowan, *Worship*, 110. For our purposes, the second paragraph is very telling.
24. See Barton, *Holy Writings, Sacred Text*, 169n2, for a list of the criteria mentioned. Barton also mentions criteria such as "relevance to every reader" (by which he may be referring to something like universal acceptance), "nontriviality of text," and "excess of meaning" (134).

and reliability of the teaching forced church synods (councils) to consider what to *exclude*.[25]

Marcion (ca. 140) rejected the Old Testament as a *Jewish* book that was superseded by and incompatible with Christianity.[26] He insisted that the God Christians worship is distinct from and superior to the Creator portrayed in the Old Testament. He did regard the New Testament as a historically accurate record. The Old Testament he read literally and thus found it unable to support Christian beliefs.[27] But early apologists (defenders of the Faith) like Justin Martyr demonstrated that all Old Testament texts point to Christ (especially when they are interpreted allegorically and not literally), thereby reclaiming these books for the church and challenging the Marcionite heresy that denies that the Old Testament Creator is the God and Father of Jesus Christ. In a sense, Marcion "caused" the church to have an Old Testament and to be committed to the confession that identifies God the Creator as the same god as God the Redeemer.

Marcion's Bible included the Gospel according to Luke and ten of Paul's letters. These fit the Gentile (non-Jewish) context. So it has been argued that Marcion rejected the Old Testament because he was anti-Semitic. That may be, but it would not be a sufficient reason for his rejection, because the church itself did little to eliminate anti-Jewish sentiment and believed that Jews did not know how to read the Scriptures properly.

Montanus (latter half of the second century) is a person we will meet again when we discuss church authority (chapter 10). It is sufficient to say at this point that Montanus and the two prophetesses who accompanied him (Prisca and Maximilla) forced the church to reject certain writings and prophetic claims, especially when we keep in mind the point made earlier by McGowan that the development of the canon and its authoritative interpretation grew up together. Montanus declared that, while the Old Testament was the era of the Father and the New Testament was the era of the Son, the age of Montanus was the era of the Spirit, and what the Spirit was revealing to Montanus was that Jesus was returning soon so people should prepare by living extremely ascetic lifestyles. In a nutshell, the church rejected Montanism because of its concern regarding the *extent* of revelation (the limit being the apostolic era)

25. See Barton, *Holy Writings, Sacred Text*, 31, 36, 133–34, for this distinction between the two.

26. For this and what follows, see Barton, *Holy Writings, Sacred Text*, 42–45, 58, 65, 171n23, and 174n53.

27. Early Christians did not read the Old Testament as just prefiguring Christ but, if properly understood, as already an account of what Christ did and suffered; see Barton, *Holy Writings, Sacred Text*, 75–76. This is clear in the way that Paul begins 1 Corinthians 15. Also see 2 Clement 3:5; 13:2, which quote the Old Testament as if it is the words of Christ.

and the *manner* of revelation (since Montanus's revelations came in ecstatic utterances and the church was opting for guidance through the more sedate teachings of the duly ordained).

Biblical Authority

If this explains how the church's book evolved, how does the book function as the church's authority today? That must be answered with a splay of positions, since the spectrum of beliefs about the Bible's authority is wide. We will look at three representative positions that provide the ends and the middle of the spectrum, but there are many more options that we could also include.[28]

At one end of the spectrum is liberal theology. In theology, when we use the term *liberal* we are not using it pejoratively (as some conservatives might think), and it is not being used in the same way in which it is used in politics. It refers to a way of going about theology that emphasizes human experience and reason as starting points. As such, if a person were to read Scripture during the liturgy as a liberal, it would not be contradictory for her to preface the reading with the announcement, "Listen to the word of the human writer." In other words, in this view the Bible is merely a human text written by fallible people, open to criticism and correction, but bearing eloquent witness to profound truths. Besides its finer points, the Bible also includes internal contradictions, moral errors, legends, inaccuracies, and so on. In other words, it is not an infallible authority, but it is the medium through which we apprehend normative divine revelation. The practical result is that biblical authority is viewed selectively.

For this position, the Bible serves as a classical witness to the event of God's transforming reality in the lives of those in the past—a transforming reality that we experience now and that we associate with the paradigmatic figure of Jesus Christ. So God's truth is not located in a book from another era, but in the Spirit's work in the church, especially with the employment of Scripture as we rationally discern what resonates with the Spirit's voice. The Bible is a record of the spiritual and ethical narrative of human beings.

One proponent of this view is theologian Sallie McFague, and she nicely summarizes the liberal approach to Scripture:

---

28. See Donald K. McKim, *The Bible in Theology and Preaching* (Eugene, OR: Wipf and Stock, 1999), for a brief summary of twelve theological positions on the Bible's authority and sermons that accompany the positions to demonstrate how these theological points of view become reality in the church's worship.

What is the authority of scripture? . . . One such way is to see it as a "classic," analogous to other classics which have gained authority because of their intrinsic power to express certain truths about reality. A classic is given authority because it is judged to merit it. Likewise the writings which comprise the Bible are in this perspective given authority by people who experience the transforming love of God associated with the paradigmatic figure of Jesus of Nazareth, because these writings are judged to express dimensions of that experience more adequately than other rejected writings. The criterion is adequacy in expressing the event; as such, they become "classics," foundational but not exclusive texts, models which provide guidance but which are admittedly partial and biased.[29]

A question we need to ask those who hold this view is how this position keeps biblical authority from becoming captive to the cultural norms and the spirit of the age. This was certainly what dawned on Karl Barth as he began to question the liberal approach with which he had been equipped for his pastorate in Safenwil. And it came home to roost during the Nazi regime. It is something like what we discussed earlier about "Bible bits" getting recontextualized or, in this case, being rejected altogether because they do not resonate with our own theological and ethical ideas, which are often shaped by the culture or subculture we have imbibed. If the Bible's authority is viewed selectively, on what basis do we select? And does that "basis" thus become our ultimate norm in practice?

At the other end of the spectrum is the conservative view. In this case the reader in the liturgy might preface the reading with the phrase, "Listen to the Word of God," because the Bible is considered God's revelation in writing. This view is sometimes linked to "verbal plenary inspiration," which we discussed above. Its logic holds that God's Word can no more err than can an omniscient and truthful God lie. But not all who hold this view are on the same page.

Some conservatives say that Scripture is without error in what it *intends* to teach—in all that it *affirms* about God's redemptive acts in history and the way we are to live. In revelatory matters (theology and ethics) it is without error; in nonrevelatory matters (such as history, geography, geology, and astronomy) it can err. This view is often referred to as "infallibilist." This distinction appeals to the purposes of Scripture in 2 Timothy 3:16–17. The Bible is substantially accurate when it comes to history, but its human authors

29. Sallie McFague, "Epilogue: The Christian Paradigm," in *Christian Theology: An Introduction to Its Traditions and Tasks*, ed. Peter C. Hodgson and Robert H. King, rev. ed. (Minneapolis: Augsburg, 1999), 384.

reflect a premodern cosmology (e.g., Gen. 7:11; Ps. 104:5–7) and prescientific view of the world (e.g., cosmic monsters such as described in Job 41). And there are minor inconsistencies when reporting the exact words of Jesus (e.g., compare Matt. 10:9–10; Mark 6:8–9; Luke 9:3) or quoting Old Testament texts (such as Hab. 2:4, which is quoted differently in Rom. 1:17; Gal. 3:11; and Heb. 10:38–39). One contemporary proponent of this perspective is Fuller Theological Seminary.

Other conservatives take a stricter view labeled "inerrantist" (and here is where "verbal plenary inspiration" *does* fit). Given proper grammatical and linguistic analysis, as well as the historical and cultural context of the times in which the Bible was written, the words of Scripture affirm what is true and *never* what is false—whether it is talking about theology or geology. The "original autographs" (the original documents—none of which we have) are "inerrant." It is argued that Scripture teaches its own inerrancy (Matt. 5:18; Gal. 3:8; 2 Tim. 3:16; 2 Pet. 3:2, 15–16) and that Christ taught inerrant Scripture in generally reliable texts attesting to his views (Matt. 5:17–19; Mark 7:6–13; Luke 24:25; John 10:34–35). Historical precedent is thought to be found in Augustine, Luther, Calvin, and the like.

A classic exposition of this *more* conservative view was made by Harold Lindsell years ago in his book *The Battle for the Bible*. Because it is classic, it is worth quoting:

> The Word is free from all error in its original autographs. . . . It is wholly trust-worthy in matters of history and doctrine. However limited may have been their knowledge, and however much they may have erred when they were not writing sacred Scripture, the authors of Scripture, under the guidance of the Holy Spirit, were preserved from making factual, historical, scientific, or other errors. The Bible does not purport to be a textbook of history, science, or mathematics; yet when the writers of Scripture spoke of matters embraced in these disciplines, they did not indite error; they wrote what was true.[30]

A standard expression of this view is the "Chicago Statement" that was composed by the International Council on Biblical Inerrancy (ICBI) (and still stands behind, for instance, the doctrinal statement of the evangelical institution Wheaton College):

> We further deny that inerrancy is negated by biblical phenomena such as a lack of modern technical precision, irregularities of grammar or spelling, observa-tional descriptions of nature, the reporting of falsehoods, the use of hyperbole

---

30. Harold Lindsell, *The Battle for the Bible* (Grand Rapids: Zondervan, 1978), 30–31.

and round numbers, the topical arrangement of material, variant selection of materials in parallel accounts, or the use of free citations.[31]

As we did with the liberal view, we must pose some questions for this position, especially in its more strict form. Is the most rigid faith more vulnerable to complete destruction than that faith which lives with some doubt (analogous, perhaps, to earthquake-proof buildings in California that allow for some sway in order not to crumble)? Are the New Testament references to (Old Testament) Scriptures that we cited above talking about the autographs or the copies? Does inerrancy make sense if all we have are copies? Does inspiration of human authors entail inerrancy? Does "inerrant in the original autographs" die the death of a "thousand qualifications" in the ICBI quote, or is inerrancy just meant to be a methodological assumption that the Bible is *completely* reliable (in which case why is "inerrant" even needed)? What is the sense of saying that the Song of Songs is "inerrant"? If those who teach this view make factual errors in other claims they make, given the logic of this view, should we believe what they say about inerrancy?

A third position rests somewhere between the liberal and the conservative. It has been labeled neo-Reformed or neo-orthodox and is associated with Karl Barth. Persons who hold this view may precede the reading of Scripture in the liturgy by alerting hearers to "listen *for* the Word of God." In one sense this view is a reaction to the nineteenth- and twentieth-century liberal theologians we discussed above.

Theologians like Barth argue that the Word of God is mediated in and through the Bible—that the Bible is the *unique* "organ of the Spirit" through which God has chosen to confront the church in all ages. God speaks through the Bible in such a way that he *causes* the Bible to be his Word in a revelatory experience that ultimately witnesses to Jesus Christ. The Bible is the definitive human witness to divine revelation. We do not *give* it authority. It is God's chosen instrument—God's larynx or voice box, if you will. Here is the way Barth put it: "The Bible, then, becomes God's Word in this [revelatory] event, and in the statement that the Bible is God's Word the little word 'is' refers to its being in this becoming. It does not become God's Word because we accord it faith [cf. McFague above] but in the fact that it becomes revelation to us."[32]

This neo-orthodox view emphasizes the freedom and sovereignty of God, and revelation is understood as a personal existential encounter with God

---

31. Alliance of Confessing Evangelicals, "The Chicago Statement on Biblical Inerrancy," http://www.alliancenet.org/the-chicago-statement-on-biblical-inerrancy.

32. Karl Barth, *Church Dogmatics*, ed. G. W. Bromiley and T. F. Torrance (Edinburgh: T&T Clark, 1955–75), I.1:110.

(rather than propositional truths) that calls into question human control over God's Word. The Bible is a divinely inspired book, but it is also a human book (denial of which would be docetism—a heresy we will unpack in the chapter on Christology); as such, it contains legends, errors, and contradictions as any human book would. *But* Barth argued that we have no right to judge where Scripture errs. Again, that would be to compromise God's sovereignty to use the Bible as God's revelatory instrument. It has been said that Barth preached errancy but practiced inerrancy.

Once again, we must address this view with questions. Does this perspective turn out in the end to ground theology in the religious self-consciousness? In other words, can I be sure it is *God* speaking to me through his Word? And is the distinction between personal and propositional revelation a false dichotomy? If I write a note to my wife that includes the statement "I love you," years later she still reads that propositional statement as if I were saying it then and there, yet she is fully aware that it is also something that I have and will continue to say in person. And some have questioned whether Barth denies God's sovereign freedom by insisting that God does not and *cannot* communicate through propositional truths.

In the end, the crucial question for all of these views is this: Does it matter what view of biblical authority a Christian holds if he or she does not read the Bible and perform it?

The Interpretation of Scripture

It would be nice if all who accept the Bible's authority were in agreement on all matters of doctrine and morality, but everyone knows that Christians do *not* agree when it comes to faith and ethics. And they all use the Bible to make their case! That is because authority is one thing, but interpretation is another. This issue gets us into the area of hermeneutics (a word that derives from the Greek messenger god *Hermes*). We will not agree on many matters of biblical interpretation, in part because our personal experience and culture inform our hearing of the Word, but there are principles that all Christians should keep in mind as they discern what Scripture is saying. Here are several:

1. Keep Scripture at the top. As Stanley Grenz and John Franke put it, Scripture is the "norming norm."[33] Even for those who operate with what is called the Wesleyan Quadrilateral—working with Scripture, tradition,

---

33. Stanley Grenz and John Franke, *Beyond Foundationalism: Shaping Theology in a Postmodern Context* (Louisville: Westminster John Knox, 2001), 57.

reason, and experience as four sources of their theology—these sources line up in the formation of a diamond with Scripture at the top.

2. Remember our need for the Holy Spirit. We must not overlook the role of the Holy Spirit as the indispensable agent for correcting our understanding of the Word, keeping in mind the Spirit's role in the illumination of Scripture (1 Cor. 2:14–16).

3. Interpret Scripture christologically. While we do understand the Bible chronologically, we should recall the biblical narrative we outlined in chapter 1: Scripture's main purpose is, as John Calvin put it, to show forth Jesus Christ. We have already mentioned that the early church understood the Old Testament christologically; indeed, Jesus and Paul made this claim (see Luke 24:27; John 5:46; 1 Cor. 15:3–4).

4. Interpret Scripture intratextually or canonically. That is, allow Scripture to interpret Scripture. For instance, at many places in the New Testament, these Jewish Christian authors elucidate their understanding of Old Testament passages. So seek to understand the parts in light of the whole, keeping the "Bible bits" where they belong in the mosaic.

5. Interpret Scripture within the parameters of the "rule of faith"—the biblical framework that has been summarized by the early Christian church in statements such as the Apostles' Creed. For instance, since this creed is trinitarian, when Christians read the word *God* in the Bible, they should understand that as a reference to the God whose name is "Father, Son, Holy Spirit," unless the text makes it clear that it is referring specifically to one of the three.

6. Be guided by the doctrinal statements or confessions of your own faith community. Most churches position themselves with specific understandings of Scripture so that those who want to be part of that local community agree about certain doctrines. The apostle Paul admonishes us to understand all the dimensions of God's reality "with *all* the saints" (Eph. 3:17–18), reminding us that biblical interpretation is a communal endeavor.

7. Do not confuse our interpretations of Scripture with the Word of God itself. We must exercise humility while we hold to our interpretations with conviction, but we also must not confuse *conviction* with absolute *certainty*. (Keeping the communal context in mind will help us with this.)

8. Live the Scriptures. Ultimately, we understand Scripture as we *perform* it. Stanley Saunders and Charles Campbell have said this so well, and

it resonates with our earlier discussion of our place in the fifth act of the biblical narrative:

> According to [Nicholas] Lash, Christian Scripture is like the text of a drama or a musical score; its interpretation requires *performance*. That is, the Christian community's interpretation of Scripture is similar to the interpretation of a Shakespearean play by a company of actors or the interpretation of a Beethoven symphony by a group of musicians. The primary poles in biblical interpretation, Lash writes, are patterns of human action: on the one hand, "what was said and done and suffered, then, by Jesus and his disciples," and on the other, "what is said and done and suffered, now, by those who seek to share his obedience and hope." As Lash concludes, "the fundamental form of the Christian interpretation of Scripture is the life, activity, and organization of the believing community."[34]

The Response of Faith

If theology is a human response to God's prior revelation, then how should we characterize our response? Simply put, our response is one of *faith*. But there are two dimensions of faith that we must not separate.

There is the "faith *by which* we believe" (*fides qua creditur*). This is the *act* of faith—the subjective aspect of trust and confidence in God to be true to God's revealed Word and grounded in God's actions in the past. This is important lest Christianity become merely "academic." But the intensity of faith by itself is not sufficient. Belief does not make anything true or right in itself. In fact, faith in the wrong thing can be disastrous—even deadly. If I skate out onto a frozen pond in the winter, firmly believing that the ice is thick enough to support me, and if in reality the ice is not thick enough to support me, I will end up very wet and very cold. My firm belief did not make it true. Instead, I must tentatively creep out onto the ice, discovering its reliability little by little until I can be fully confident that it will not let me down. And that is much like our faith in a God who has demonstrated faithfulness in the past.

That brings us to the other aspect of faith—the "faith *which* we believe" (*fides quae creditur*). This is the *content* of faith—the objective facet of our doctrines and dogma, articulated in creeds and confessions and hymns and songs.

34. Stanley P. Saunders and Charles L. Campbell, *The Word on the Street: Performing the Scriptures in the Urban Context* (Eugene, OR: Wipf and Stock, 2006), 7 (quoting Nicholas Lash, "Performing the Scriptures," in *Theology on the Way to Emmaus* [London: SCM, 1986], 37–46).

John Calvin summarized both aspects of faith nicely in his definition of the term: "We shall have a complete definition of faith, if we say, that it is a steady and certain knowledge of the Divine benevolence toward us, which, being founded on the truth of the gratuitous promise in Christ, is both revealed in our minds, and confirmed in our hearts, by the Holy Spirit."[35]

As mentioned, doctrine is one way we express the content of faith. The word literally means "things that are taught" (just as the word *doctor* literally means "teacher"). This verbal content of faith can be taught and investigated. In one sense, it "translates" Scripture and tradition into instructive formulae that serve as summaries of topics (*loci*) in the Christian Faith. Some churches pass on their doctrine through catechesis, a term we mentioned in chapter 1. In that regard, Henri Nouwen remarked that doctrines "are not alien formulations which we must adhere to but the documentation of the most profound human experiences which, transcending time and place, are handed over from generation to generation as a light in the darkness."[36]

Some doctrine is given the label *dogma*. These are formulations of Christian doctrine that have obtained ecclesiastical (church) sanction and are embodied in the creeds, such as the Nicene Creed, which we will encounter in the next chapter. Dogma is normative and holds authority over members of a church community. That is, to be a member of a certain community one is obliged to accept such normative statements. For instance, when a Roman Catholic comes forward to receive the bread (the body of Christ), her correct liturgical response is to say "Amen," by which she is communicating that she believes the Roman Catholic dogma, especially as that pertains to that Church's understanding of the Eucharist. Of course, Protestant churches have a bit looser understanding of the binding force of their dogma. For Roman Catholics dogma is absolutely binding; it is infallible and adds to the "deposit of faith." But for Protestants dogma is relatively binding; it would not be seen as infallible or adding to the faith, but seen as a way of expressing the whole of the Christian Faith as it is found in Scripture.[37]

As we mentioned, doctrines and dogma are articulated in creeds and confessions—the church's historical expressions of its faith. These have functioned as instructional aids—fixed, precise, short, and unambiguous formulae

---

35. Calvin, *Institutes*, 2.3.7.

36. Henri J. M. Nouwen, *Reaching Out: The Three Movements of the Spiritual Life* (New York: Doubleday, 1986), 73.

37. Not all have seen dogma in a positive light. Adolf Harnack (1851–1930) viewed dogma as "a work of the Greek spirit on the soil of the Gospel"—a misunderstanding of Christianity and the "Hellenizing of Christianity." He argued that it was necessary in order to make the Faith relevant, but that it was also an unfortunate development.

that deal with heresies and determine orthodoxy. The Nicene Creed is one that functions this way for all Christian churches, but there are statements that are more elaborate and serve to more finely tune the faith for a specific Christian tradition. Examples of these include the Westminster Confession in the Reformed (Calvinist) tradition, the Augsburg Confession in the Lutheran tradition, and the Schleitheim Confession in the Anabaptist (think Mennonite) tradition. Not only do these serve as means to instruct the people who identify with these communities, but they also function as contemporary guides for understanding Scripture. They stand between Scripture and today's believers as hermeneutical tools that summarize the Christian Faith, often having arisen out of and in response to historical situations while meeting contemporary needs.

Doctrine, dogma, creeds, confessions—all are like maps that should not be confused with the reality they map. As someone has said, the doctrine of the atonement did not die for sinners. But, like maps, they do help us to stay on the right path to our journey's end. C. S. Lewis's analogy is instructive:

> Theology is like the map. Merely learning and thinking about the Christian doctrines, if you stop there, is less real and less exciting than the sort of thing my friend [who had an experience of God] got in the desert. Doctrines are not God: they are only a kind of map. But the map is based on the experience of hundreds of people who really were in touch with God—experiences compared with which any thrills or pious feelings you or I are likely to get on our way are very elementary and very confused. And secondly, if you want to get any further, you must use the map. You see, what happened to that man in the desert may have been real, and was certainly exciting, but nothing comes of it. It leads nowhere. There is nothing to do about it. In fact, that is just why a vague religion—all about feeling God in nature, and so on—is so attractive. It is all thrills and no work; like watching the waves from the beach. But you will not get to Newfoundland [from England] by studying the Atlantic that way, and you will not get eternal life by simply feeling the presence of God in flowers or music. Neither will you get anywhere by looking at maps without going to sea. Nor will you be very safe if you go to sea without a map.[38]

If the objective of this theological map is to keep us on course, then one of its functions is to keep us from veering off into heresy.[39] The word *heresy* derives from the Greek word *haireō*, which translates "I choose." In other words, heresy is my chosen interpretation of the Faith that runs contrary

38. C. S. Lewis, *The Joyful Christian* (New York: Touchstone, 1996), 33–34.
39. See C. FitzSimons Allison, *The Cruelty of Heresy: An Affirmation of Christian Orthodoxy* (Harrisburg, PA: Morehouse, 1994), for some of the thoughts about heresy that follow.

to what has been passed on, received, and taught by the faithful whose lives have been radically changed by Jesus Christ. Heresy ignores the maps that have taken travelers centuries to compile and instead decides to get to the destination "my way"—like traveling south from Los Angeles to get to Seattle. And heresy is usually the easy way out; it avoids the difficult terrain that we have to traverse to stay on the path of orthodoxy—a path that often involves seemingly irreconcilable dichotomies.

Over against heresy, there is *orthodoxy*, a word that literally means straight or correct (*ortho*) opinion or belief (*doxa*).[40] Just as orthodontics instructs us how to straighten teeth so that we might chew well and orthopedics instructs us how to straighten bones so that we might walk well, so orthodoxy straightens beliefs so that we might live well, because beliefs have consequences. Orthodoxy and orthopraxy go together: the purpose of good theology is obedience—a way of life mapped out by right belief.

An analogy from tennis helps. To play tennis we need to mark off the court, set up the net at the proper height, and establish rules (such as determining what is out of bounds) and a scoring system. But if after doing all of that we just sit down on the court, we cannot call that tennis. We need the markers and the net to play, but we also need to *play*.

Heresy hurts individuals, the church, and the world God created because it encourages either flight (such as a gnostic concept of salvation we will encounter later) or self-centeredness (such as legalism). (We will take note of these tendencies as we discuss heresies in the chapters to follow.) Heresy encourages some flaw in our fallen human nature; heretical ideas often appeal to ideas that will do damage to us in the end. And heresy actually narrows our understanding of God and reality with constricted and limited ways of understanding Christianity that are often one-sided. It's the easy way out. Orthodoxy, on the other hand, is the radical, risky way that requires balance between the both/and and the either/or.[41]

Ellen Charry has reminded us that classic theologians based their understanding of human nature as God meant it to be on knowing and loving God such that it resulted in human flourishing. In other words, orthodox theological reflection should be conducive to one's spiritual health, and this

40. The word *doxa* can also be translated "worship" or "glory," but Maxwell Johnson notes that in patristic Greek it is *ortho* (right, straight) and the verb *dokeō* (think, teach), not *ortho* and *doxa* (glory, worship), though that is certainly a proper sentiment. Maxwell E. Johnson, *Praying and Believing in Early Christianity: The Interplay between Christian Worship and Doctrine* (Collegeville, MN: Liturgical Press, 2013), xvi.

41. See the discussion of this in Ben Quash and Michael Ward, eds., *Heresies and How to Avoid Them: Why It Matters What Christians Believe* (Peabody, MA: Hendrickson, 2007; Grand Rapids: Baker Academic, 2007), x, 7, 133–34.

requires the kind of trust that a motorist places in signs along an unfamiliar highway because she knows that they were put there by those responsible for public safety. If the driver simply ignored the signs because she chose to take the next turn at eighty miles per hour rather than the recommended thirty miles per hour, she would not be acting in the best interests of maintaining her health. As Charry puts it, "It is surely rational that the driver on a mountainous road trust the traffic signs are reliable and authoritative whether or not he or she knows anything about the person who mapped the terrain."[42] Similarly, we listen to those who have come before us in the Christian tradition, trusting that they know terrain we have not yet traveled. We are certainly invited to make fine-tuning adjustments to the map so that it will be even more accurate for those who follow us, but it is good to know that dangers have been identified so that our lives might flourish as God intended.

So here we go, continuing the risky journey with the help of maps compiled by centuries of saints. As we head for various ports along the way, it is appropriate to pray with St. Augustine:

> Blessed are all thy Saints, O God and King, who have travelled over the tempestuous sea of this moral life, and have made the harbour of peace and happiness. Watch over us who are still in our dangerous voyage; and remember such as lie exposed to the rough storms of trouble and temptations. Frail is our vessel, and the ocean is wide; but as in thy mercy thou hast set our course, so steer the vessel of our life toward the everlasting shore of peace, and bring us at length to the quiet haven of our heart's desire, where thou, O our God, are blessed, and livest and reignest for ever and ever.[43]

42. Ellen Charry, *By the Renewing of Your Minds: The Pastoral Function of Christian Doctrine* (New York: Oxford University Press, 1997), 8.
43. George Appleton, ed., *The Oxford Book of Prayer* (New York: Oxford University Press, 1985), 123.

4

Who Is God? The Doctrine
of the Trinity

We Recite the "Creed" in Response to Hearing the Word

> *We believe in one God, the Father, the Almighty,*
>   *maker of heaven and earth. . . .*
>   *We believe in one Lord, Jesus Christ, the only-begotten*
>   *Son of God,*
>   *eternally begotten of the Father. . . .*
> *We believe in the Holy Spirit, the Lord, the giver of life. . . .*
> > *—The Nicene Creed (fourth century)*

As we have just seen, the response to God's prior revelation is faith that is often articulated in confessions and creeds. Indeed, in some liturgies, immediately after Scripture has been read and the sermon has been preached, the congregation stands to affirm its response of faith in the words of the Apostles' Creed or the Nicene Creed (from which the words above have been excerpted). And so we move in a similar fashion to consider theologically who this God is who is confessed in these creeds.

A Hymn Celebrating God's Attributes

Immortal, invisible, God only wise,
In light inaccessible hid from our eyes,
Most blessed, most glorious, the Ancient of Days,
Almighty, victorious, thy great name we praise.

Unresting, unhasting, and silent as light,
Nor wanting, nor wasting, thou rulest in might—
Thy justice like mountains high-soaring above
Thy clouds which are fountains of goodness and love.

To all life thou givest, to both great and small;
In all life thou livest, the true life of all;
We blossom and flourish as leaves on the tree,
And wither and perish; but naught changeth thee.

Great Father of Glory, pure Father of Light,
Thine angels adore thee, all veiling their sight;
All laud we would render: O help us to see
'Tis only the splendour of light hideth thee.

Words: Walter Chalmers Smith, 1876;
Revisions: W. Garrett Horder, 1884

The Attributes of God

How we should describe God involves the topic of God's attributes—God's properties or characteristics or "perfections." These four words all refer to the same thing, though theologians have organized the discussion of these attributes in different ways, typically categorizing them in pairs.

One way of discussing what characterizes God is to speak of relative and absolute attributes. The former include what are called the "omnis"—omnipotence (all-powerful), omnipresence (everywhere present), and omniscience (all-knowing). To make any sense of these requires that something besides God exists: God exercises power over whom? Is present where? Knows what? The latter include properties that do not require any existent but God, such as aseity or self-existence (God is the cause of God's own existence), eternity, and immutability (unchangeableness).

Another way of discussing God's attributes divides them into communicable and noncommunicable types. In other words, God communicates to human creatures God's goodness and righteousness and mercy. But it makes no sense to say that God confers on his creatures self-existence; in fact, that would be contradictory.

One more way that theologians sometimes divide divine characteristics is to speak of moral versus nonmoral aspects. When speaking of the former we might discuss God's love or God's holiness. When speaking of the latter we might be explaining omniscience, to mention one example, since knowing everything does not necessarily entail anything having to do with morality.

The more interesting question asks how we arrive at these attributes. How do we know what characterizes God?

One way of approaching this is *via negationis*—the way of negation. We think about our human existence with its limitations and imperfections, and then we think those away. Humans are finite, so God must be *in*finite. Humans are mutable (changeable), so God must be *im*mutable. But this leaves us with a rather static conception of God. In fact, it doesn't really tell us much about what God is, but only what God is not.[1]

Another approach is *via eminentiae*—literally, the way of eminence. This is the opposite of the tack taken by the previous method. Instead of discounting what is human, what is human is supersized, assuming that there is some analogy between the divine being and human beings (the *imago Dei* or image of God). If humans are powerful, then God must be *all*-powerful. If humans are knowledgeable, then God must be knowledgeable about *everything*. Care must be taken, though, because if we begin to think about God based on what we are, then we might end up just speaking about "human" in a loud voice—the "Man upstairs" or something like the reclining grandfatherly figure on the ceiling of the Sistine Chapel.

We might use the approach *via causalitatis*—the way of causality. This applies only to the relative attributes, but the idea is that an effect must have a cause; so if humans are capable of loving, then God must be the cause—God must be love. The problem here is that we cannot logically ascribe to the cause more than is required by the effect. Since humans are imperfect lovers, we cannot automatically assume that God is a perfect lover.

The problem with all of these approaches is that they begin with the human creature and speculate on that basis. We end up with a god made in our own image. Instead, given our definition of theology as a human *response* to divine revelation, we should *begin* with God's self-disclosure in history, especially as that occurred in Jesus Christ. What would that look like?

1. This is not quite the same thing as what Orthodox (Eastern) theology calls "apophatic" theology, though that approach does emphasize what we *cannot* say about God.

One example takes the attribute of "immutability." There has been a debate among theologians whether God's immutability means that God is inflexible in response to human activity. The disagreement comes to a head in the way that theologians understand the twenty-seven times that the Old Testament speaks of God changing his mind. (There are nine times that speak of God *not* changing his mind.) One case in point comes from the story in 1 Samuel 8 when Israel demanded a king. The prophet Samuel was told by God to tell Israel that they were not to have a king, but after the third plea God tells Samuel to inform Israel that God will allow them to have a king, as long as they remember that God is the true king, and that having a human king will lead to the same kinds of problems the other nations have. Then there is the story of Jonah: God shows mercy to Nineveh because they repented. At one point Jonah says to God, I fled to Tarshish the first time because "I knew that you are a gracious God and merciful, slow to anger and abounding in steadfast love, and relenting from disaster" (Jon. 4:2 ESV).

Are these examples of times when God actually *changed*? Though it is up for debate, it is at least clear in Scripture that God's immutability may have more to do with keeping his covenant promises. This is expressed in Psalm 89:34–35, where God says: "I will not violate my covenant, or alter the word that went forth from my lips. Once and for all I have sworn by my holiness; I will not lie to David." Paul expresses something of the same sort when he quotes, "If we are faithless, he remains faithful—for he cannot deny himself" (2 Tim. 2:13). It *is* curious that the LXX (the Septuagint or Greek translation of the Hebrew Scriptures) changed all verbs that referred to God "repenting" or "changing his mind" to static ones. And that is the danger—that by understanding immutability from what might be more of a human perspective than from the content of God's revelation, we end up with a static God. It *does* seem from the biblical narrative that the God who is faithful to his purposes and keeps his promises nevertheless is sovereignly free to change the way he accomplishes it all. Even Israel's stubborn demand for a king did not foil the plan God set in motion to redeem his fallen creation; God simply became incarnate through the royal line of King David.

Another example is the case of "omnipotence." For some this conjures up images of omnicausality. But the cross makes it crystal clear that God's conception of power is not the same as human conceptions of power. In 1 Corinthians 1:18–2:5 Paul argues that the cross, which makes no sense to the Greeks and is a stumbling block to the Jews, is God's power (*dynamis*, the Greek word from which we get *dynamite*) to save us. That is, God's omnipotence really refers to God's unconquerability. God is so powerful that God can work in and through his creatures without causing everything directly. Left to human ideas of power, we would end up with a distorted understanding of who God is and how God operates.

An attribute that may be more difficult to understand is divine "omniscience." Consider it in light of petitionary prayer: If God knows everything, why must we ask God to do certain things when apparently God already knows what the outcome is going to be? This attribute has generated extremely contentious debates; there have even been times when one side has accused the other of heresy. One aspect of the debate has to do with a very technical philosophical discussion about God's relation to time.[2] Another aspect has to do with what we have mentioned above: how theologians interpret biblical references to such statements as "God repented." Is that to be taken literally or in some sense figuratively (anthropomorphically)? At one end of the spectrum are those who insist that God's omniscience includes all things past, present, and future. At the other end are advocates of what is called "open" or "free-will" theism, arguing that God *does* know everything that is *possible* to know, but since future events are not possible to know because they have not yet happened, God only knows what might happen (though God has a very good idea what course of action will ensue). The first view might argue that we should continue to petition God because we are commanded to and God has already determined that those prayers are part of his plan. The second view might argue that our petitions are persuasive and that what God decides to do is affected by our prayers.

The Triune God

Now we turn our attention from God's characteristics to God's persons. That is, we begin an examination of one of the most essential and unique doctrines of the Christian Faith: the Trinity. No other religion confesses that the one God is three persons. But the church did not arrive at this conclusion overnight. In fact, it involved the first major doctrinal controversy that the church faced and took three centuries to find something of a "solution" in the words of the Nicene Creed. This "solution" was arrived at not only through ongoing theological arguments, but also by some nasty church politics and conflicts of personality. Not much about the life of the church has changed in that regard.

In addition, as we will see in the next chapter, the church's insistence that God the Son is the same divine being as God the Father made all the more

2. See Gregory E. Ganssle and Paul Helms, *God and Time: Four Views* (Downers Grove, IL: InterVarsity, 2001).

complicated a second major doctrinal controversy—namely, how God the
Son could become fully human and still be fully divine.

How and why did the church even feel compelled to think about God as
one being in three persons? What was it that called for the development of
the doctrine of the Trinity?

We must begin by remembering that the first Christians were Jews, and Jews
were adamant monotheists (believers in one god). Every day they would proclaim
the *Shema*: "Hear, O Israel, the Lord is our God, the Lord is one" (Deut. 6:4).[3]
The first Christians would not have compromised this conviction, yet they found
themselves worshiping Jesus, just as Jesus's disciple Thomas fell to his knees and
confessed before the resurrected Jesus, "My Lord and my God" (John 20:28).

In fact, it is the title "Lord" (*kyrios* in Greek) that provides one indication
that early Christians honored Jesus as God himself. Though it may not have
been in the earliest Jewish manuscripts, *kyrios* eventually replaced the Hebrew
proper name of God (*YHWH*) when the Hebrew Bible was translated into
Greek (which is called the Septuagint, abbreviated LXX). And this use of the
Greek *kyrios* for *YHWH* occurs in the New Testament when, for instance,
a psalm or a passage from Isaiah in the Hebrew Bible is quoted in the Greek
New Testament (e.g., Rom. 4:8 and Ps. 32:2; Rom. 9:27–29 and Isa. 10:22–23;
1:9). This lends force to the use of *kyrios* to refer to the risen Jesus in the New
Testament, as Paul writes in Romans 10:9, 1 Corinthians 12:3, and Philippians
2:11. Furthermore, passages such as 1 Timothy 6:15 that use the language of
Daniel 2:47 apply the same titles of honor to Jesus Christ—Lord of lords and
King of kings—that were applied to God in the Hebrew Bible.

The New Testament Christians also ascribed to Jesus what was ascribed
to God, particularly in the Gospel of John, placing Jesus in the "beginning"
with God (John 1:1–18), citing the time that Jesus upset the Jewish leaders
by calling God his own "Father" (John 5:18), and quoting Jesus when he said
"I and the Father are one" (John 10:30 ESV).

There are a few verses that might actually refer to Jesus as God, but we must
say *might* because they depend on how we punctuate the verses and which of
the ancient copies (manuscripts) we believe are the originals. (Punctuation
was not used in the original Greek of the New Testament; in addition, the
text was written without spaces between words.) Acts 20:28, Romans 9:5,
and 1 Timothy 3:16 are the verses that apply here.

Beyond the New Testament itself, Christians of the first three centuries of
the church—whether from a Jewish or a Gentile persuasion—were worshiping Jesus Christ in the liturgy.

3. There are different translations of the Hebrew, but this is its essence.

A late-first-century bishop, Ignatius of Antioch, wrote a letter to the Smyrnaeans asserting, "Our God Jesus Christ was carried in the womb of Mary." Later, to the Magnesians, he identified Jesus as one "who before time was with the Father" and "who has come from the one Father and who remained one in him and who has gone on to him"—a remark that is fitting with his reference to John 6:33 in his letter to the Romans, equating the "bread of God" with the "flesh of Jesus Christ."[4]

That makes us think of the church's celebration of the Lord's Supper. Indeed, in the church's early communion liturgy Jesus Christ is spoken of as God. For example, in the *Acts of John* (a second-century writing that did not become part of the canon), John is quoted in the act of breaking the bread:

> We give thanks to you, Lord Jesus Christ, because we believe that your grace is unchanging. We give thanks to you who had need of our nature that should be saved. We give thanks to you who has given us this sure faith, *for you alone are God,* both now and ever.[5]

And in a sermon that has a cadence comparable to one preached by today's black pastors, comparing the Christian Pasch (Easter) to the Jewish observance of Passover, Melito of Sardis (d. ca. 180) speaks of Jesus as incorruptible and "resurrected as God" in his "Homily on the Passion": "He is all things: the law in that he judges, the Logos in that he teaches, grace in that he saves, father in that he begets, Son in that he is begotten, sheep in that he suffers, man in that he is buried, *God in that he rises.*"[6] He concludes the sermon with a stem-winder:

> He is the alpha and omega; he is the beginning and the end,—the inexplicable beginning and the incomprehensible end—, he is the Christ; he is the King; he is Jesus; he is the Strategus [a Greek official with broad powers]; he is the Lord; he was raised from among the dead; he is seated at the right hand of the Father. He bears the Father and is borne by the Father; to him be glory and power forever. Amen.

In the next century, Cyprian of Carthage instructed Cecil, an African bishop, in procedures having to do with administering the Lord's Supper, referring to

4. Lawrence J. Johnson, *Worship in the Early Church: An Anthology of Historical Sources* (Collegeville, MN: Liturgical Press, 2009), 1:50.

5. L. Johnson, *Worship in the Early Church*, 1:87 (italics added).

6. L. Johnson, *Worship in the Early Church*, 1:91 (italics added).

the deeds and teachings of Jesus, "our Lord and *our God*, the founder and teacher of this sacrifice."[7]

So from its beginning the church was expressing its worship of Father, Son, and Holy Spirit on an equal basis. One of the most beautiful expressions of this worship is an ancient (perhaps second-century) hymn to Christ that accompanied the lighting of the lamps during the evening liturgy in the Eastern church—the "Phos Hilaron"—a hymn still used today in liturgical churches:

> Serene light of the Holy Glory
> Of the Father Everlasting Jesus Christ:
> Having come to the setting of the sun,
> And seeing the evening light
> We praise the Father and the Son
> and the Holy Spirit of God.
> It behooveth to praise Thee
> At all times with holy songs,
> Son of God, who has given life;
> Therefore the world does glorify Thee.[8]

In his discussion of the explicitly trinitarian liturgy of Justin Martyr (d. 165), patristics scholar Robert Louis Wilken makes the observation that "before there was a 'doctrine' of the Trinity, Christian prayers invoked the Holy Trinity."[9] Even more to the point of *lex orandi, lex credendi*, Wilken later reflects on Hilary of Poitiers's fourth-century book *The Trinity*, claiming that what Hilary is really getting at in this book is that "thinking about God begins with language that is given in the Scriptures and with *convictions formed by the church's practice, most notably in baptism in the name of the Father and of the Son and of the Holy Spirit.*"[10]

---

7. L. Johnson, *Worship in the Early Church*, 1:164 (italics added).

8. Quoted in L. Johnson, *Worship in the Early Church*, 1:222. This way of referencing the triune persons with the conjunction *and* is called the "coordinated form" and is very important for evidence of early church traditions in the liturgy that addressed God as a trinity (as opposed to the "uncoordinated forms," using *through* and *in*, that also appeared in the liturgy). See Maxwell E. Johnson, *Praying and Believing in Early Christianity: The Interplay between Christian Worship and Doctrine* (Collegeville, MN: Liturgical Press, 2013), 61.

9. Robert Louis Wilken, *The Spirit of Early Christian Thought* (New Haven: Yale University Press, 2003), 31.

10. Wilken, *Early Christian Thought*, 89 (italics added). In modern times, James B. Torrance has made a strong case that the church's worship practices *must* return to a robust trinitarian awareness of God (rather than the more unitarian conception that is implied even in much evangelical worship); see his *Worship, Community and the Triune God of Grace* (Downers Grove, IL: InterVarsity, 1996).

In baptisms, in communion liturgies, in sermons, in prayers, Jesus (let alone the Holy Spirit) was identified as God. This was all well and good, but a problem eventuated: "One could speak this way while kneeling to pray, but it was harder to do so when standing to teach or sitting to write."[11] Trinitarian dogma was firmly in the liturgy, but theology then needed to articulate and defend it. This was harder to do because the church had to figure out how to maintain two convictions: its commitment to monothesim without slipping into a pagan polytheism; and its rejection of any kind of unitarianism (belief in one person) because it insisted that the Father and the Son who were this one God were actually two different persons—a Son who came from the Father (Phil. 2:6–11), who made the Father known (John 1:18), and who prayed to the Father (John 17).[12]

Here's the problem in a nutshell: How could the church maintain the unity of God and the divinity and distinctiveness of Christ at the same time, without making Christ a separate or subordinate deity?

The Scriptures did not provide the solution. (The word *trinity* is not even in the Bible.) They simply expressed the relation of the persons in dyadic (Rom. 1:7; 1 Cor. 8:6) and triadic (Matt. 28:19; 2 Cor. 13:13) formulae. The church was forced to get off her knees and confess in some coherent manner who this one-in-three God is, especially when she had to explain her worship to polytheistic Greeks and monotheistic Jews alike.

There were well-meaning and early attempts at a solution, though all fell short of being fully orthodox. Still, they had value because they helped to chart the course that eventually led the church to articulate its faith in a trinitarian God. So, what were these well-meaning attempts that were crafted in the late first to early third centuries?

Early Attempts at a Solution

At one end of the spectrum was adoptionism (sometimes referred to as "dynamic monarchianism").[13] Simply put, proponents of this view taught that

11. Jaroslav Pelikan, *The Christian Tradition: A History of the Development of Doctrine*, vol. 1, *The Emergence of the Catholic Tradition (100–600)* (Chicago: University of Chicago Press, 1971), 178.

12. The church also identified the Father and the Son in passages such as Psalm 110:1 (the LORD said to my *Lord*), and the Father, Son, and Holy Spirit in passages such as Genesis 18:1–2 (the three visitors to Abraham, which became represented in one of the church's most significant icons).

13. The term *monarchianism* in these early views indicates an emphasis on the *unity* of God.

Jesus was the Son of God by adoption, not by nature. And some Scripture seems to warrant this conclusion. The oldest tradition had Jesus promoted to deity at his resurrection (see Acts 2:32–36 and Rom. 1:3–4). A popular view taught by Paul of Samosata (bishop of Antioch, 262–72) argued that Jesus was made Son of God at his baptism (appealing to Ps. 2:7; Mark 1:10–11; and Acts 10:37–38).[14] Finally, some pinpointed the timing of Jesus's adoption at his birth, using Luke 1:34–35 for support.

More fully, adoptionism was claiming that Jesus grew into or assumed divinity—something accomplished by the inspiration or empowering work of God's Spirit. The earthly figure of Jesus and the heavenly spirit of Christ come together to *make* Jesus Lord. He is *made* divine; his divinity is not intrinsic to his being.

The good thing about this view for trinitarian thinking is that the persons of the Father and the Son are distinct—but at the cost of a low Christology, for which it was definitively rejected by the year 269. It is divine sonship by inspiration, not by incarnation: God does not become human, but a human becomes God. In other words, it is divinity by promotion. Jesus's union with God is not natural or essential but ethical; Jesus gained such a victory over sin in his own life that he is able to gain victory over sin for us.

But it is precisely this last sentiment that alerts us to the danger of adoptionism: it can encourage self-centered legalism. (Legalism is *always* a form of self-centeredness.) If Jesus can get promoted to divine status by his efforts, perhaps we can do something of the same if we become like Jesus.

At the other end of the spectrum was modalism (sometimes referred to as "modalistic monarchianism"). Over against adoptionism, this view held to a high Christology. It accomplished this by teaching that God has disclosed himself in various *modes* or manifestations (referred to as *prosōpa* in Greek). Essentially, the person of Christ is the person of God the Father in another manifestation.

Because it was propounded by an early third-century priest named Sabellius, it is sometimes referred to as Sabellianism. Sabellius insisted that if we think of the one God (*Monas*), we must think in terms of a God who appears in different *energies* or three modes of actions or operations or revelations: the Father creating, the Son illuminating, and the Holy Spirit inspiring. These three are *names* for one and the same God who expands and contracts, each time getting nearer to humans. One God reveals himself successively in three modes or forms, much like masks, characters, or roles that a single actor might successively portray in a play performed on stage in ancient Greece.

---

14. This view is also found in the Shepherd of Hermas.

The late-second-century church leader Noetus stated his modalist position very clearly, as cited by another church leader, Hippolytus: "He [Noetus] alleged that Christ was the Father Himself, and that the Father Himself was born, and suffered, and died."[15]

Though this did affirm that the Son was divine by nature (unlike adoptionism), it lost sight of the distinct persons. In that regard it contradicted the church's Christ-oriented interpretations of Psalms 2:7 and 110:1. But it also called into question to whom Jesus was praying in John 17, to cite one example. Either he was delusional with multiple personalities or he was really speaking to another person—the Father. Modalism also drew the accusation of *patripassianism*, a term that literally means "father suffers." Tertullian made this accusation against another early advocate of modalism, Praxeas, arguing that essentially he crucified the Father, an accusation that makes sense if the Father and the Son are the same person wearing different masks at different times. Finally, some have countered that modalism has docetic tendencies. We will explore more fully what this means in the next chapter. It's enough at this point to mention that docetism (from the Greek word *dokein*, "to seem, appear") refers to the heretical view that God only *appeared* to be human in Jesus Christ, and if the Father became the Son before switching one more time to become the Spirit, then Jesus wasn't really human as we are.

The oft-used analogy that God is like three forms of water—ice, liquid, and gas—really ends up being modalistic (unless you are a physicist and know about "triple point"!), since the same substance takes on each of these forms successively instead of simultaneously.

A practical consequence of modalism is that it invites uncertainty over the completeness and definitiveness of God's self-disclosure. How could we know that God might not show up again as some other person, being revealed in four or more manifestations? There have been those who have claimed to be wearing the God-mask, and a modalist might have a difficult time making the case that such a claim is bogus. In addition, the modalist can never be sure that behind all the successive manifestations there isn't some being we will never know that wears the masks.

We begin to move closer to the church's confession of the Triune God it worships when we look at one figure from the Latin West and one from the Greek East (though both were from northern Africa, the home of many early church theologians).

15. Hippolytus, "Against the Heresy of One Noetus," in *The Ante-Nicene Fathers*, ed. Alexander Roberts and James Donaldson (Grand Rapids: Eerdmans, 1990), 5:223.

The Christian theologian from the West was Tertullian (ca. 160–225), sometimes called the "father of Western theology." As with most of the Latin theologians at this time, Tertullian emphasized and began with the unity or oneness of God, moving from that point to discuss how the one could be three. We especially owe Tertullian gratitude for giving us the vocabulary needed to talk about the Trinity—even the word *trinity* itself. Tertullian used *trinitas* to speak of a three-in-oneness, not three unconnected things. He referred to the oneness as *substantia*, while the three were *personae*. With a background in legal terminology (and often the Western theologians thought in legal categories), Tertullian explained that the persons possessed "legal rights" as joint holders of a common property (the divine substance). The problem came when the Latin got translated into Greek for Christian theologians in the eastern half of the empire. For instance, *trinitas* became simply *trias* (three).[16]

Tertullian is also associated with what we call the "economic" Trinity.[17] The Greek word *oikonomia*, meaning order or arrangement, was used to speak of God's ordered self-disclosure in the biblical story as God works out God's plan of salvation, beginning with creation and reaching its crescendo in the Son's coming in the flesh. So this involves theological discourse about God's orderly self-disclosure in human history. True, God is known in creation, as we saw in our discussion of general revelation (and in Ps. 19 and Rom. 1), but it is only through the economy—God's ordered self-disclosure in biblical history—that God can be known as Father, Son, and Holy Spirit.[18] For Tertullian (and especially for Eastern theologians), the Father is the sole source or ruler who manages and administers the other two persons of the Trinity. All of this is necessary for creation and revelation. The three are "consubstantial"; that is, their unity is organic, even though Tertullian emphasized that the three become one in terms of goal, function, task, and organization. Though all analogies for the Trinity are deficient, Tertullian likened the Father, Son, and Spirit to the sun, its rays, and the tips of the rays that we feel. He used some other analogies as well, all portraying three flowing out of one.

The Christian theologian from the East (Alexandria to be exact) came on the heels of Tertullian. He has been referred to as the first systematic

16. Discussion of this confusion goes beyond the agenda of this book, but if one is interested in pursuing this issue, a good classic study can be found in G. L. Prestige, *God in Patristic Thought* (London: SPCK, 1964; repr., Eugene, OR: Cascade, 2008). Prestige's discussion demonstrates how the translation of terminology ended up with the West viewing the East as Arian, while the East suspected the West of being Sabellian.

17. See the use of *oikonomia* in Eph. 1:10; 3:2, 9; Col. 1:25; and 1 Tim. 1:4.

18. See Wilken, *Early Christian Thought*, 89–90, for his discussion of this point with reference to Hilary of Poitiers.

theologian and, more for the purpose at hand, the "father of Arian heresy and Nicene orthodoxy."[19] This was Origen (ca. 185–254), who, with a typical Eastern orientation, began with and emphasized the "threeness" of God. One reason he complements Tertullian is not only because he was nearly a contemporary, but because, while Tertullian emphasized the economic Trinity, Origen is helpful for thinking about the "immanent" or "essential" Trinity—the internal workings and relationships among the three divine persons.

Origen taught that there are two types of being that are coeternal with the Father. There are angels who are coeternal with the Father, but they are created coeternal beings. That is, their existence is not necessary. Their existence is entirely dependent on the Creator. But their eternal existence makes sense of God's attribute of love, because love must have an object, and if God is eternally love, then God must have objects to love in eternity.

The other type of being that is coeternal with the Father is not created, but is generated, and that is the Son, because by definition a "son" is one who is generated or begotten. We will see this concept developed when we get to the church's confession in the Nicene Creed, which speaks of the Son as "eternally begotten." Though the phrase may seem contradictory, it is not to be thought of in the same temporal sense we have of the process of a child being born. The phrase is expressing a relationship that is eternal—the Father is always the one who begets, and the Son is always the one who is begotten. This is the essential relationship that exists eternally between these two persons.

With a Neoplatonic orientation, Origen saw reality in a graduated hierarchy of being. So on a sliding scale, as it were, you could slide down from Father to Son to Spirit to angels to humans, all the way down to rocks and such things. As one moves down the creaturely ladder, one is moving down to lesser levels of being. But this gliding scale might make it difficult to distinguish what is divine from what is merely creaturely. And this is why Origen could be aligned with those who end up in the Arian heresy or those of the Nicene orthodoxy, which we will be discussing. It all depends on where you draw the line. If you draw the line dividing the divine from the creature after the Father, then everything below the line, including the Son, is creature and you end up with Arius (to be discussed next). If you draw the line after the Spirit, then the three above the line are in some sense related as divine and not creaturely. And so we move ahead a century and enter the debate that gave us the Nicene Creed.

19. This is the label Prestige (*God in Patristic Thought*, 231) gives him for reasons that will become obvious.

Arius, Athanasius, and the Council of Nicea

Arius (ca. 260–336) was a priest in Alexandria, influenced by the thought of Paul of Samosata (bishop of Antioch) and of Origen—influences that had much to do with his own views about Christ. Arius taught that the Son was made—a creature. It is said that he set to music the refrain, "There was when he was not." He would have been careful not to say "a *time* when he was not," because even though the Son was a creature of the Father, he was "only begotten," which Arius took to mean that the Son was made only by the Father, unlike the rest of creation that was made by the Father through the Son. So, in that sense the Son existed before time; the Son was preexistent. In this regard Arius believed that he was taking the Bible at face value where Wisdom (aka the Son) was said to be with God at creation (Prov. 8:22–31) and where the apostle Paul called Christ the "firstborn of all creation" (Col. 1:15).[20]

According to Arius, Christ was the supreme angel—a finite creature who won the title "Son of God" because of his moral progress. He was passible (changeable), so he could have sinned, but God foresaw that he would not sin, so he was accorded the title Son of God and made the pioneer of our salvation.

Besides Arius's interpretation of Scripture, he was concerned to safeguard the oneness, transcendence, and impassibility of a God whose essence cannot be shared. Whatever else exists is created, so if the Bible and the church speak of the Son as "begotten," it must mean that he was created out of nothing. At least Arius was avoiding modalism, but in his own anti-Sabellian stance he made the Son subordinate to the Father.

Though Arius had his followers, there were those, like Athanasius (296–373; bishop of Alexandria three years after the Nicene Council), who pointed out the error of his theological thoughts. For one thing, he confused "beget" with "create"—derivation with creation. To beget or generate is to become the parent or source of the same thing. To create is to make something of a different essential sort. For example, I beget a child who shares my DNA, but I create her dollhouse that is made of balsa wood and glue. Like begets like; like creates unlike. So God begets God; God creates non-God. Christ is the begotten Son of God; Christians are the created sons and daughters of God.

Athanasius and others also pointed out to Arius that when as a priest he baptized in the name of the Father, Son, and Holy Spirit (as Jesus instructed in Matt. 28:19–20), he was baptizing in the name of both the Creator and

20. Arius also appealed to John 7:39; 17:3; Gal. 3:19–20; and Heb. 1:4. In the end, even Arius's mantra, "There was when he was not," was simply double-talk. If the Son came into existence, then there was a before and an after; there is simply no way that a creature could exist "before time."

a creature. Essentially he was calling the church to worship a creature. As Jaroslav Pelikan puts it, "Like the worship of the church, the offerings of the Magi [the "Wise Men" in the Christmas story] could be exonerated of the charge of idolatry only if the Christ child was king and God." Athanasius was arguing that the worship of Christ by people and angels indicated that he was essentially different from all creatures—even angels: "Only if he was not a creature, but true God by nature, could such worship be proper." The theological position of the Arians and their liturgical practice were irreconcilable.[21]

Long before Arius, Christians were offering prayer to Christ (1 Cor. 16:22; Rev. 22:20), and invocations to the Logos (the Word) appear in liturgies from the mid-second century.[22] Defenders of the Nicene Creed that condemned Arianism understood that true worship was the issue over against idolatry: "What's at stake here, liturgically, therefore, is the role of liturgical prayer not only in shaping but also in supporting and defending orthodox doctrine."[23] In fact, before the Nicene Creed and Apostles' Creed were composed—and in part what led to their composition—the Eastern church had been using the trinitarian formula in baptism (Matt. 28:19–20), and the Western church had been asking its baptismal candidates the three creedal questions, "Do you believe in God the Father . . . in Jesus Christ his Son our Lord . . . and in the Holy Spirit?" Once again, the church's liturgical language shaped the doctrinal formulations of the Christian Faith.

But the most significant argument against Arianism was penned by Athanasius in what has become a theological classic, *On the Incarnation of the Word*. Athanasius argued that the Son is *homoousios* with the Father. This word is not found in the Bible, but it succinctly expressed that the Son was *identical* in *substance* with the Father, though not in a Sabellian or modalistic sense. There was indeed debate about the meaning of the word—whether it *could* mean "identical" or simply "similar" or "equal" or "like." And there was debate about its appropriateness since it was a nonbiblical term. But there was not a single verse in Scripture that could refute Arianism with finality. What was needed beyond the use of this key word was a case to be made for the theological significance of the insistence that the Son must be identical in substance or being with the Father. And that was exactly what Athanasius did in his classic text.

In a nutshell, his concern was soteriological—that is, having to do with salvation. Only the one who created us in God's image is the one who has

21. Pelikan, *Emergence of the Catholic Tradition*, 207.
22. See M. Johnson, *Praying and Believing*, 34–49.
23. M. Johnson, *Praying and Believing*, 49.

the power and authority to redeem—or re-create—us and restore our God-likeness as God intended it. As Athanasius put it: "For he was incarnate that we might be made god."[24] But Arius's Christ could neither reveal God nor redeem humans. So the incarnation—God becoming human so that we might have a share in the divine nature—was the linchpin for Athanasius's argument.

Athanasius shared the Eastern (Greek) idea that our salvation is planned by God to bring out the glory of humankind by imaging God. In other words, the human destiny in God's economy is to be *deified*. But the image of God was damaged by the fall into sin. Now all of us reflect God no better than a cracked mirror. In order for God's original plan to go forward, God must do something to repair the human creatures who are to image God. But no creature can repair the damaged *imago Dei* in the creature. Not even a half-god could do this. Yet a half-god is all that Arius had. Arius's Christ was a being suspended between God and humans, identical with neither and yet related to both. So God had to become human so that, as Athanasius put it, the incarnate God could sit for the portrait, revealing what we were intended to be as God created us, and refashioning us into that image. Centuries later John Calvin would summarize the point nicely: "Since neither as God alone could he feel death, nor as man alone could he overcome it, he coupled human nature with divine that to atone for sin he might submit the weakness of the one to death; and that wrestling with death by the power of the other nature, he might win victory for us."[25]

Eventually Athanasius's ideas would win out and be expressed in the Nicene Creed, though after the Nicene council that originally composed the creed, he was exiled from his home five times, forcing him into the Egyptian desert, where he lived with monks, or sending him to Rome where he found sympathizers.[26] If the Arian doctrine had won, we might be encouraged to be self-focused in the kind of legalism we spoke of in connection with adoptionism, since, once again, the idea that the pioneer of our salvation won for himself the title of "Son of God" would lead us to strive for the same kind of moral perfection in order to merit status as a child of God.

The Council of Nicea was summoned in 325 by Emperor Constantine, who was more concerned with the unity of his empire than with doctrinal purity

---

24. Athanasius, *On the Incarnation*, trans. John Behr (Yonkers, NY: St. Vladimir's Seminary Press, 2011), 107.

25. John Calvin, *Institutes of the Christian Religion*, ed. John T. McNeill, trans. Ford Lewis Battles (Philadelphia: Westminster John Knox, 1960), 2.12.3.

26. The battle over Arianism went on for nearly five decades after the Nicene Council in 325. It even involved armies and monks. One positive outcome of Athanasius's exile into the Egyptian desert was his encounter with Antony, whose life Athanasius wrote about in a literary piece that became significant in the spread of Christian monasticism.

or theological clarity. Many gathered for what became the first ecumenical (all-church) council. The council issued four anathemas, condemning those who insist the Son of God is a creature, is not eternal, is not divine, is not immutable (unchangeable). Arius was wrong about the Son. When the church met again in 381 to reaffirm the creed at Constantinople, it added a statement about the Holy Spirit, who, by that time, was also affirmed as one God, "worshipped and glorified" with the Father.[27] But the key statement against Arius comes early in the creed when it confesses "the Son of God, begotten from the Father, only-begotten, that is, from the substance of the Father, God from God, light from light, true God from true God, begotten, not made, of one substance [*homoousios*] with the Father." (Note that twice the creed makes it clear that "begotten" does not mean the same thing as "created.") As Maxwell Johnson summarized, "In this Nicene and post-Nicene context, then, liturgical, Christological, and soteriological come together into a brilliant orthodox synthesis."[28] And of all the creeds and confessions that churches have written over the centuries, only this Nicene Creed is affirmed and used in liturgy by all three major branches of the Christian church—Eastern Orthodox, Roman Catholic, and Protestant—even though there is one variation in wording that separates the first from the second two.

Though we are not certain exactly when it was added to the creed, by the early fifth century the phrase "and the Son" appeared in the creed, asserting that the Holy Spirit proceeds from the Father *and the Son*. This has come to be known by its Latin terminology—*filioque*. The Western church used the phrase as standard practice in its liturgy by the seventh century. This was very upsetting to the East, in part because it was not in the original creed, but more importantly—and even today—because it runs counter to an important theological position that Eastern Christianity has insisted upon. Eastern Christian theology insists that the Father is the source and manager (if you will) of the other two persons; the Father begets the Son and breathes out the Spirit. Sometimes it is said that the Son and the Spirit are the Father's two hands.[29] The West would emphasize that the Father and the Son *together* send the Spirit, and the West has not emphasized the notion that the Father should be spoken of as source and manager of the Son and the Spirit. To this

27. We will review arguments for the deity of the Holy Spirit in a later chapter. The work of Basil the Great was especially instrumental in arguing for the full deity of the Spirit, and his argument in *On the Holy Spirit* dealt extensively with the language (especially prepositions!) that was used in the church's liturgy.

28. M. Johnson, *Praying and Believing*, 49.

29. See Kallistos Ware, *The Orthodox Way*, rev. ed. (Crestwood, NY: St. Vladimir's Seminary Press, 1979), 35, where he cites Irenaeus's words to this effect.

The Nicene-Constantinopolitan Creed
(as Revised/Amended in 381)

We believe in one God, the Father Almighty, Maker of heaven and earth, and of all things visible and invisible.

And in one Lord Jesus Christ, the only-begotten Son of God, begotten of the Father before all worlds, God of God, Light of Light, Very God of Very God, begotten, not made, being of one substance with the Father, by whom all things were made; who for us men, and for our salvation, came down from heaven, and was incarnate by the Holy Spirit of the Virgin Mary, and was made man, and was crucified also for us under Pontius Pilate. He suffered and was buried, and the third day he rose again according to the Scriptures, and ascended into heaven, and sits on the right hand of the Father. And he shall come again with glory to judge both the quick and the dead, whose kingdom shall have no end.

And we believe in the Holy Spirit, the Lord and Giver of Life, who proceeds from the Father [and the Son], who with the Father and the Son together is worshipped and glorified, who spoke by the prophets. And we believe one holy catholic and apostolic Church. We acknowledge one baptism for the remission of sins. And we look for the resurrection of the dead, and the life of the world to come. Amen.

day the *filioque* marks a significant point of disagreement between Christian West and East.

During the period when Athanasius was exiled five times—after Nicea in 325 and before Constantinople in 381—three Eastern theologians helped clarify the distinctions and relations of the persons, since Nicea was content to clarify only the unity of the persons. These three are called the Cappadocians because of their location in what is now modern-day Turkey. Basil of Caesarea, Gregory of Nyssa, and Gregory of Nazianzus separated the oneness and the threeness by restricting which words were used for what and then helping us to articulate something about the essential Trinity itself.

Those who had focused on differences that were economic spoke only of what distinguished the three manifestations of God as they appeared in the history of salvation. But the Cappadocians focused on *essential* differences among the three persons. There is one *ousia* (common substance) and three *hypostases*—the particular forms that the one substance assumes in each of the three individuals or the properties that are unique to the persons. All three have the same energy or divinity—the same substance or nature—but each expresses it in a different way—namely, in what the Cappadocians referred to as "modes of origin." The Father is ungenerate; the Son is generated; and the Holy Spirit is proceeding or spirated (breathed out). The mode of origin defines the particular way in which each one exists simultaneously in relation to the other two.

Another way of saying this points out that the Cappadocians were working with a social analogy of family-type relations. Because each finds its identity in relation to the other two, we can say that each "co-inheres" in the others. This conception of the relationship is referred to as *perichōrēsis*. Sometimes expositors of this idea speak of the Trinity as existing in an eternal dance, but Edith Humphrey has argued that this is really too trite (citing the popular novel *The Shack* as a case in point here). She maintains that *perichōrēsis* "refers to the deep indwelling and loving movement toward each other of Father, Son, and Holy Spirit, a mutual but ordered communion in which the Father retains headship, even while Father, Son, and Holy Spirit share each other's attributes, glory, and power. Their love is not the kind of undifferentiated love-fest that is pictured by some who are today co-opting the Holy Trinity as a kind of mascot for their own idea of what reality should be like."[30] In other words, in ordered relation, each contains the other two, dwells in the other two, makes generous room for the other two. Each person of the Trinity is present to the other two in a unique, eternal mode.

As Eastern theologians, the Cappadocians gave us insights into the very being of the Triune God—the one God who exists in three persons (not three existing in one)—yet in the end they confess that God's being is ineffable mystery.

There were theologians in the West who expressed trinitarian theology in slightly different but complementary ways. One of those was Augustine, who used what are referred to as psychological analogies that he spelled out in his treatise *De Trinitate*. We are made in God's image, so there should be traces of God's being in our human relations and self-experience, Augustine argued. For example, every time we think, we simultaneously employ memory, understanding, and will. Adequate self-knowledge also involves self-love and the mind at the same time. And any notion of love that makes sense must include three aspects: lover, beloved, and the love that relates them to each other. According to Augustine, all of these remind us that we are made in the image of Father, Son, and Holy Spirit.

Beyond the dangers associated with the heresies that we have noted, there are good reasons to have a robust understanding of God as "the ceaseless

30. Edith M. Humphrey, *Grand Entrance: Worship on Earth as in Heaven* (Grand Rapids: Brazos, 2011), 70.

exchange of vitality, the endless expense of spirit upon spirit in eternal trip-
licate life."[31]

First, if we are created in the image of a God who is eternally related *peri-
choretically* in three persons, then we are only fully human when we image
this God in our relations with each other, let alone in our relationship with
the Triune God. We are social beings to the core, and we are called to pour
out our lives into one another in the deepest, most intimate ways.[32]

Second, we will be rightly chastened when we are tempted to separate a
"God of love" from a "God of wrath" or baptism of the Holy Spirit from
receiving Christ. In other words, the three persons are a "package deal." We
get it all when we contemplate or enter into relationship with the God whose
name is Father-Son-Holy Spirit.

Third and most significantly for the agenda of this book, because Christian dogma and Christian doxology are intricately related, how we go about
the worship of God (and how we participate in the mission of God) is
determined by and flows from our understanding of who God is and what
God has done. As James Torrance has argued so forcefully, "Christian worship is our participation through the Spirit in the Son's communion with
the Father, in his vicarious life of worship and intercession. . . . The Christian doctrine of the Trinity is the grammar of this participatory trinitarian
worship."[33] Jesus Christ is the high priest (see the New Testament book of
Hebrews, especially Heb. 8:1–2), and when we worship—especially in the
Lord's Supper—we participate through the Spirit in this relationship that
the Son has with the Father. To compromise this is to end up with worship
that reflects a unitarian (one person) God and diverts the focus of worship
onto us and our religious experience. There is an eternal party going on into
which we are lifted up in the church's liturgy. (Think of the first words—the
sursum corda—of the communion liturgy: "Lift up your hearts!")[34] As Torrance puts it, "At the center of the New Testament stands not our religious
experience, not our faith or repentance or decision, however important these

---

31. Cornelius Plantinga, "Deep Wisdom," in *God the Holy Trinity*, ed. Timothy George
(Grand Rapids: Baker Academic, 2006), 155.

32. See Gary W. Deddo, "Persons in Racial Reconciliation: The Contributions of a Trinitarian Theological Anthropology," in *The Gospel in Black and White: Theological Resources for
Racial Reconciliation*, ed. Dennis Okholm (Downers Grove, IL: InterVarsity, 1997).

33. Torrance, *Worship*, 15, 22. Much of this paragraph relies upon Torrance's argument.

34. The *sursum corda*, which literally means "hearts lifted," is the first line of the *anaphora*
or the eucharistic prayer during which the bread and wine are consecrated or set apart as the
body and blood of Christ. It has been in use at least since the third century. The one who pre-
sides over communion begins the *anaphora* with this line, to which the people respond, "We
lift them up to the Lord."

are, but a unique relationship between Jesus and the Father"—a life of shared communion, mission, and service into which we are invited.[35] And our participation is made possible because the Son became incarnate in human flesh. It is to that extremely important confession of the Christian church that we turn next.

35. Torrance, *Worship*, 30.

5

Who Is Jesus Christ? Christology

We Ponder the Creed's Meaning
for Our Belief in Jesus Christ

*With one accord we teach all to acknowledge one and the same
Lord, our Lord Jesus Christ, at once complete in Godhead and
complete in manhood, truly God and truly man.*

— *The Definition of Chalcedon (451)*

I f, as the Nicene Creed insists, Jesus is to be thought of as fully divine, how
are we to understand his humanity? And how are the two related? If Jesus
preexisted as God the Son, how should we speak about the incarnation? Another way of asking this is, How are we to understand the meaning of John
1:14: "the Word *became* flesh"?

Early Attempts at a Solution

Just as the church attempted to explain the Trinity with early but insufficient
solutions, so the church attempted to explain the incarnate Christ with solutions that meant well but went amiss.

At one end of the spectrum is Ebionism. The word *ebion* means "poor ones" in Hebrew and reflects the fact that this view was associated with late first-century Jewish Christians in and around Jerusalem who were poor. (Recall Paul's allusion in Rom. 15:25–27 to his desire to hurry to Jerusalem with contributions from Gentile Christians during his third missionary journey [see Acts 21] to assist those who had suffered from famine and from ostracism from their fellow Jews.) Ebionites taught that Jesus was the natural-born son of Mary and Joseph who excelled in justice and wisdom. At his baptism "Christ" descended upon him, after which he revealed the Father and performed miracles. But just prior to the crucifixion, "Christ" flew away and left Jesus to suffer and die and rise again.

In keeping with its adoptionist leaning, Ebionism encourages a legalistic understanding of salvation, suggesting that if we are virtuous as Jesus was, perhaps we will experience something like he experienced at his baptism and be endowed with God's Spirit. In his treatise against heresy, Tertullian described Ebionites as those who maintained the customs of the Jewish law to the point that they accused Paul of falling away from it. The danger here, as in all cases of legalism, is that it tends to take the focus away from God and God's work and put it on ourselves and our performance.

At the other end of the spectrum is docetism. This word derives from the Greek word *dokein*, meaning "to seem" or "to appear." Often associated with gnosticism for reasons that will be clear when we discuss creation in the next chapter, those who held docetic views taught that Christ's human body was not real. That is, God only *appeared* to be human, suffer, and die, because the Absolute cannot unite with the finite, especially since the material world is evil. If anything, Christ was a heavenly being who was joined for a time to a human body, whose teaching helps us to overcome the material world. We can see that this view was around even at the time 1 John was written, since that letter argues that what has been seen and touched is what is being declared to the readers, and those who say that Jesus has not come in the flesh are not from God (1 John 1:1; 4:2–3).

Docetism still shows up in Christian circles today. A hint of it can be heard in our Christmas celebrations when we sing "Away in a Manger" and come to the line "no crying he makes." If God became truly human, then God experienced all that human babies experience, including hunger, defecation, and crying. In fact, what is wrong with docetism is that it encourages escape from the world God made: salvation is flight, perhaps typified by the bumper sticker that announces "Not of This World!"

Beyond these two alternatives, Logos Christology was also an option and a favorite among the early apologists (defenders of the faith in the early church around 120–220). The concept of *logos* was familiar to both Greek philosophy (as a cosmic principle governing and permeating the universe and giving unity to the universe) and Judaism (as the mediator of God's communication with humans, having creative power and a somewhat independent existence). In Christianity the Logos appears in the Johannine writings (John 1:1, 14; 1 John 1:1; Rev. 19:13) as identified with Christ.

Logos Christology taught that the preexistent *logos*—the divine reason in God—became externalized and personified to perform the will of God as the Son, who in turn, became incarnate in human flesh (John 1:14).

This approach was good as an apologetic device, since both Greeks and Jews were familiar with the concept. It might be something like telling Star Wars fans that the Son who became incarnate in the flesh is like the Force that could take on human nature. One problem with this apologetic approach: it was somewhat subservient to philosophical and religious concepts that already existed outside of the biblical narrative. Furthermore, proponents tended to emphasize the incarnate Logos as a teacher who would teach humankind the higher philosophy that embraces the one God—a task that could be accomplished by less than an incarnate deity. Finally, subordinationism was also an issue since the Logos comes from God (a tendency that can be seen in the *Dialogue with Trypho*, written by the apologist Justin Martyr).

Perhaps one of the most significant attempts at a solution was Apollinarianism. Apollinarius (ca. 310–390) was the bishop of Laodicea and later the archbishop of Caesarea. He was a forceful opponent of Arianism, and in the process of his attempt to avoid an Arian concept of an inspired man or two different sons, he stressed the unity of the two natures in Christ in such a way that he compromised the humanity of Jesus in his emphasis on Christ's divinity. The result was so devastating to orthodoxy that he was condemned four times and excommunicated twice! So what was so bad about his teaching?

In a nutshell, he taught that the divine Logos (Word) replaces the human mind, so that the divine Logos and human *sarx* ("flesh") make up one new nature. In other words, it has been said that he ended up with a "flesh-bearing God."

This was his reasoning: Christ must be both divine and human to be able to save the world through his suffering as our mediator. But how could he be both at once? For how can two complete entities (Logos and *sarx*) unite into one? It would seem there would have to be two sons. Furthermore, if Christ is *fully* human, he could change (because that is what humans do) and therefore sin; he could have a will different from the Father's. So one entity must be imperfect, and that could not be his divine nature because God is impassible (unchangeable). So it must be the human nature that is less than complete.

Apollinarius had a tripartite understanding of human nature—that we are body, soul, and spirit (see 1 Thess. 5:23). Spirit is the higher part of the soul, similar to what we often refer to as the mind. Since temptation begins in the mind, Christ's human nature must not have a human spirit or mind. Instead, the Logos functioned in the incarnate Christ as the soulful spirit does in us. The resulting blend is a mixture of Logos and *sarx*, such that Jesus's humanity was essentially only an animated body. The Son of God assumed the flesh of Mary's son and absorbed it into his divinity.

His attempt to work this out was well meaning, but his explanation of *how* Christ was both human and divine fell short. For one thing, it compromised salvation. As Gregory of Nazianzus famously put it, "That which he [Christ] has not assumed he has not healed; but that which is united to his Godhead is also saved." In other words, the Logos must take on a *complete* human nature with a *complete* human soul if we are to be saved. The mind has fallen just as surely as our flesh; it needs to be healed, so God must assume our human mind as well as our human flesh. (Gregory also insisted that any time the biblical authors refer to *parts* of our humanity—like flesh or mind—they are really connoting the *whole* person.)

Besides this soteriological issue, Apollinarius's Christology was essentially docetic. Jesus would have only appeared to be fully human, yet we are told that Jesus grew in wisdom (Luke 2:52) and that he even wrestled with the will of God the Father (Luke 22:42). The New Testament portrays Jesus as a complete human with a developing human mind that is at times in "conversation" with his divine mind.

Several years ago after my wife and I had moved to Illinois and were joining a new church, the well-meaning pastor was trying to impress upon the membership class the deep significance and sacrifice of God's incarnation in Jesus Christ. The analogy he used was of a human who wanted to communicate with a pack of dogs that were not getting along. It would be one thing to deal with them human to canine, he said, but wouldn't it be more effective if the human could enter into the pack by way of a brain transplant—the human brain taking the place of a dog's brain in order to inhabit the dog's body? That certainly emphasized the cost of the incarnation, but his analogy had slipped into a form of Apollinarianism. If the analogy was going to come anywhere close to orthodoxy, the pastor would have needed to teach that the human brain did not *replace* the canine brain, but that it was connected to the canine brain so that the human would not only become familiar with the limitations of the *bodily* life of a dog, but also experience the *mental* life of a dog.

We will see that a subsequent church council held at Chalcedon rejected Apollinarianism when it insisted that Christ is "true God and true man, of a *reasonable soul* and body." The insistence is important, because like docetism, Apollinarianism encourages an escapist view of salvation—an understanding of salvation that bypasses redemption of the mind and the struggles of disciplining the mind into alignment with God (Rom. 12:1–2).

Two Competing Schools

A century after Apollinarius, everything came to a head as two schools came to blows (literally) arguing about the best way to understand how Jesus could be both divine and human while not compromising the impassibility of the divine nature and yet appreciating the fact that in the incarnation it is our salvation that is at stake. The two sides consisted of an alignment of sees[1] or significant church centers.

On the one side were the Antiochenes, who held what is sometimes referred to as a Word-Human Christology. The most important representative of this school was Nestorius (d. 451), the patriarch[2] of Constantinople. He was condemned for emphasizing the separation of the two natures to such a degree that the person of Christ was split into two, but he repudiated the heresy of which he was accused. At the least, he was the victim of the power struggle between the two rival sees.

Whether Nestorius taught it or it simply represented a tendency, Nestorianism held that the immutable Logos dwells or resides in a mutable human person in such a way that the two natures remain distinct, each with its own properties. In other words, the divine nature cannot be born, suffer, or die; the human nature cannot be eternal, omnipresent, or omniscient. Jesus is a "God-bearing man."

Using the metaphor of the body as a temple (see John 2:19) or of dwelling in a body (Col. 2:9), the divine indwells the human in such a way that the two natures are conjoined (analogous to the description of marriage in Matt. 19:6). What is formed is an "ethical union" as the human nature morally develops in obedience to the divine nature (see Luke 2:52). The "temple" or "body" is sanctified more and more in this voluntary union, so that Jesus Christ *grew* into a complete God-human union. The human became the perfect receptacle

---

1. In this context the word *see* refers to a church that contains the "seat" (*sedes* in Latin) of a bishop—the one who oversees the liturgy in a geographical region of churches (a diocese). The bishop's church is called a cathedral (from the Greek *kathedra* and Latin *cathedra*, meaning "chair").

2. Essentially, the patriarch is the Eastern church's equivalent to the Western church's bishop. Nestorius was joined by others, including Theodore of Mopsuestia (d. 428) and Theodoret (d. 466).

> ### "Sub tuum praesidium"
>
> An early third-century Greek liturgical hymn:
>
> To your protection we flee,
> holy Mother of God (*Theotokos*);
> Do not despise our prayers in [our] needs,
> but deliver us from all dangers,
> glorious and blessed Virgin.
>
> Cited in Maxwell E. Johnson, "The Apostolic
> Tradition," in *The Oxford History of Christian Worship*,
> ed. Geoffrey Wainwright and Karen B. Westerfield
> Tucker (New York: Oxford University Press, 2006), 66.

of the divine, allowing a fellowship of the two natures that grew closer and closer until it reached its peak at the resurrection.

Using a contemporary analogy, one way to think of this is to picture each nature as a 2x4 Lego piece. As we bring them together they end up interlocking perfectly. From a distance (assuming they are the same color), they look as if they are one piece, just as to look at Jesus Christ was to see one person. But upon closer examination we see that one has fit perfectly into the other—two separate pieces that are conjoined because the pegs of one conform to the holes of the other.

This way of speaking about Christ provided a pattern for the way we could speak about our redemption: as we become increasingly obedient to the will of God, our salvation becomes more complete.

Those following the rival Alexandrian view were easily discovered by the way they referred to Mary, the mother of Jesus. In the Alexandrian liturgy, Mary had for some time already been referred to as *theotokos*—"bearer of God" or "Mother of God." But the Antiochenes crusaded against this term, insisting that a human cannot give birth to God, and God cannot be born. Mary's son was the God-man, Christ, so Mary is to be called *Christotokos*— bearer or Mother of Christ. Nestorius objected to the idea of transferring the characteristics (*idiomata* in Latin) of Christ's human nature to the divine Logos: "You can't say God is two or three months old." So it made sense to the Antiochenes that Mary could not be the bearer of God.

The Antiochenes fought hard to avoid the impression that their view ended up splitting Christ into two persons and that, essentially, Mary was the mother of only one part of Christ, thereby denying the incarnation. They insisted that if you looked at the two natures in their harmonious relationship, you would see only one person in appearance. But what was missing was a full appreciation of the significance of John 1:14—that "the Word *became* flesh and dwelt among us" (ESV). In fact, when the church customarily read the entire first chapter of John's Gospel at the end of every communion service, all the worshipers would kneel when they came to that mysterious acclamation: "the Word became flesh."[3] Furthermore, one might be tempted to find her salvation by emulating Jesus, conforming her will to God's until salvation is achieved.

And so, Nestorianism was condemned at the third ecumenical Council of Ephesus in 431, and Nestorius was deposed from his position as patriarch.

The Alexandrians represented the other side of the conflict, led especially by the patriarch of Alexandria, Cyril (d. 444). They contended that the divine Logos takes on or absorbs the human nature (the flesh) in such a way that it is not necessary to speak of a human soul. (Recall that Apollinarius was from Alexandria.) Christ, then, is a "man-bearing God."

With the metaphor of a garment, Cyril understood the word *became* in John 1:14 to mean that the Logos deifies the human nature by making it its own. This results in something more than a conjunction of the human and divine natures. It results in what is called a "hypostatic union"—a union of the two natures such that, while each nature preserves its own attributes, there is a mysterious exchange or communication of one with the other (or, in Latin, *communicatio idiomatum*, meaning a "communication of properties"). At the incarnation the two natures come together so closely that the two seem to disappear, or at least the human seems transformed by the divine. The union is such that the divine had a share even in the sufferings of Christ, though *in itself* the divine nature did not suffer.

One of the analogies Cyril used was that of an iron poker in a fire. When you leave an iron poker in the fire and then take it out, the poker has taken on the properties of the fire; it is hot and red, yet it is still solid iron. On the other hand, the fire has taken on the properties of the poker; what was formerly amorphous has taken on the shape of the poker, yet it is still fire.

A contemporary analogy might be a tattoo, such as a ring of forget-me-nots on an ankle. The ankle has taken on the characteristics of the ink, becoming blue, green, and black, even though the ankle is still the color of flesh. Meanwhile the ink takes on the shape and actions of the ankle, so that what was once a fluid now stays in place while it twists and turns.

3. See A. N. Williams, "Nestorianism: Is Jesus Christ One Person or Does He Have a Split Identity, with His Divine Nature Separate and Divided from His Human Nature?," in *Heresies and How to Avoid Them: Why It Matters What Christians Believe*, ed. Ben Quash and Michael Ward (Peabody, MA: Hendrickson, 2007; Grand Rapids: Baker Academic, 2007), 38.

This way of speaking about Christ dovetailed well with a soteriology (a doctrine of salvation) based on the deification (*theōsis*) of the human, which we spoke of when we unpacked the ideas of Athanasius (another Alexandrian) in the previous chapter.

The liturgical designation of Mary as *theotokos* made sense, given the Alexandrian position, and it would become a significant element in securing the church's orthodox Christology. While it is true that God cannot be born, just as the iron poker experiences the characteristics of the fire while remaining an iron poker, and just as the ankle experiences the characteristics of the ink while remaining an ankle, so God can experience the birth, suffering, and death of a human named Jesus while remaining God. The Logos cannot suffer but suffers *in* the human nature that became its own in the incarnation.

The only problem with the Alexandrian position, for which Cyril was put on the spot, was that it tended toward monophysitism (one nature). After the incarnation there is a *new* union on God's side—something completely new and *singular* (not two sons as seemed to be in the Antiochene view). There is one new divine-human nature of the Word incarnate. Christ was *from* two natures. Before the union and in abstraction we speak of two natures; after the union and in concrete we can only speak of one divine-human nature. To be clear, this is neither a mix nor alteration nor confusion of the two natures; those options would be heresies that were already or would be condemned. No, Christ is *homoousios* with the Father on the Logos side and *homoousios* with Mary on the human side. The two natures *can* be seen, but they are so fused that the union is in the *hypostasis* (i.e., the essential thing). While this sounds sensible, we will see that it was easy to slip into full-blown monophysitism. This position also made it somewhat difficult to explain passages of Scripture that refer to the growth and development of Christ (such as Luke 2:52), since the Alexandrians insisted that all Scripture terms referring to Christ apply to *both* natures *united*.

So the fight between the two schools raged on. Emperor Theodosius deposed both Cyril and Nestorius at the 431 council. A compromise confession formed the basis of a truce between the Alexandrians and the Antiochenes in 433, after which Cyril regained his position. (Nestorius returned to a monastery to which he formerly belonged.) But the truce was too tenuous. It did not solve the doctrinal issue. So when Cyril died in 444, he was succeeded by Dioscorus, who tried to make Alexandria the dominant see in the East and persecuted Antiochenes. He tried to do away with the doctrine of the two natures and favored doctrinal statements with an Apollinarian bent.

Then came Eutyches (d. 454) espousing full-blown monophysitism. He was the abbot of a monastery near Constantinople who sided with the Alexandrian school. But he carried the Alexandrian view to an extreme with his assertion: "Before the incarnation, two natures; after the incarnation, one nature." In other words, the incarnate Son was some sort of tertiary thing—something like the strange creature that resulted when a fly got into the experimental chamber with the scientist in the movie *The Fly*, resulting in a hybrid that was neither human nor fly.

The problem with Eutychianism (as the heresy came to be named) is that God cannot take on our sin, since Christ was not truly human. C. FitzSimons Allison has provided an analogy that helps us understand this point.[4] Those who drive in cold climates know that at times water condenses in the gas tank so that the spark plugs cannot fire. Gas and water do not mix, just as God and sin do not mix. So, to get rid of the water an alcohol-based liquid is poured into the gas tank. The alcohol is able to take on the water in a tight molecular bond, just as Christ who knew no sin was able to become our sin by virtue of his human nature. Alcohol will fire in the spark plugs, at which point the water is burned away, just as at the crucifixion Christ was able to "burn away" our sin, again by virtue of his human nature.

These problems did not go unnoticed in the church fight. Eutyches had appealed to the bishop of Rome, Pope Leo, hoping to get the Western church's support against the Antiochenes. But when Leo was apprised of Eutyches's views, he wrote his *Tome* to Flavian, the archbishop of Constantinople, repudiating Eutychianism and asserting the doctrine of one person and *two* natures. Eutyches was at first condemned in 448, but a year later acquitted in an unfair council called by Emperor Theodosius (who wanted to rid the church of the Antiochene leaven), which Leo would label the "Robber Synod." Theodosius would not allow Leo's *Tome* to be read, condemned the two-natures doctrine, restored Eutyches, deposed Flavian, and put Dioscorus in his place.

Leo demanded a new council to be led by Rome, so when Theodosius died in 450, the emperor's sister and her husband, who favored Leo and detested Dioscorus, rose to power, and a new ecumenical council was held at Chalcedon.

Besides deposing Dioscorus, declaring Cyril orthodox, and ratifying Nicea, this fourth ecumenical council, held in 451, resolved the issue, not so much by articulating what we *must* say about the two natures, but what we *cannot* say about the two natures, using four phrases that begin with the word "without." The formula insisted that we must not confuse the natures (as Apollinarius and Eutyches had done) or compound the person (as Nestorianism had done). Christ is one person in two natures "without confusion

4. C. FitzSimons Allison, *The Cruelty of Heresy: An Affirmation of Christian Orthodoxy* (Harrisburg, PA: Morehouse, 1994), 149–50.

The Definition of Chalcedon

Following, then, the holy fathers, we unite in teaching all men to confess the one and only Son, our Lord Jesus Christ. This selfsame one is perfect both in deity and also in humanness; this selfsame one is also actually God and actually man, with a rational soul and a body. He is of the same reality as God as far as his deity is concerned and of the same reality as we are ourselves as far as his humanness is concerned; thus like us in all respects, sin only excepted. Before time began he was begotten of the Father, in respect of his deity, and now in these "last days," for us and on behalf of our salvation, this selfsame one was born of Mary the virgin, who is God-bearer [theotokos] in respect of his humanness. [We also teach] that we apprehend this one and only Christ—Son, Lord, only-begotten—in two natures; without confusing the two natures, without changing one nature into the other, without dividing them into two separate categories, without contrasting them according to area or function. The distinctiveness of each nature is not nullified by the union. Instead, the properties [idiotetos] of each nature are conserved and both natures concur in one person and in one hypostasis. They are not divided or cut into two prosopa, but are together the one and only and only-begotten Logos of God, the Lord Jesus Christ. Thus have the prophets of old testified; thus the Lord Jesus Christ himself taught us; thus the Symbol of the Fathers [Nicea] has handed down to us.

From *Creeds of the Churches*, ed. John H. Leith, 3rd ed. (Atlanta: Westminster John Knox, 1982), 35–36.

(contra Eutychianism), without change (contra Apollinarianism), yet without division and without separation (contra Nestorianism)." There was a slight correction of Cyril by using "*in* two natures" rather than "*of* two natures," thereby stressing the unity of Christ's person (reflecting Alexandria) and the duality of the natures (reflecting Antioch). But essentially it was a "solution by negation." Each "without" acted as a signpost indicating how far we could go before crossing into heretical territory, but not telling us exactly *how* the natures are related or exactly *who* suffered and died.

The fighting did not end with Chalcedon. A fifth ecumenical council was held in 553 at Constantinople to rein into conformity those who continued to espouse monophysitism, but it did not succeed with Coptic, Jacobite, Ethiopian, and Armenian churches that still confess a monophysite Christology.

Another question that arose was whether Jesus had one will or two wills. Put differently, does a will go with the person or with the natures? The sixth ecumenical council at Constantinople (681) insisted that Christ had two wills,

---

"O Monogenes (Only Begotten)"

This is a sixth-century hymn sung in the liturgy at Constantinople that sum- marizes the councils from Nicea to Chalcedon:

Only-Begotten Son and Word of God, immortal as you are,
You condescend for our salvation to be incarnate
from the Holy Theotokos and ever-virgin Mary,
and without undergoing change, You became Man;
You were crucified O Christ God, and you trampled death by your death;
You are One of the Holy Trinity;
equal in glory with the Father and the Holy Spirit:
save us!

Cited in Maxwell E. Johnson, *Praying and Believing in Early Christianity: The Interplay between Christian Worship and Doctrine* (Collegeville, MN: Liturgical Press, 2013), 92.

---

the human being subject to the divine, though the East and West were not in complete agreement on this.

Kenotic Christology

A more recent view has been critical of the classical view that we have discussed. Kenotic Christology (referring to the Greek word *kenōsis*, meaning "emptying") teaches that in the incarnation the Son relinquished his divine prerogatives without ceasing to be God. In fact, the argument is that Jesus *expressed* his divinity by *emptying* himself (Greek *ekenōsen* in Phil. 2:5–8, esp. v. 7; cf. 2 Cor. 8:9; John 17:5).

Some theorize that the Son temporarily left behind his divine attributes, such as omnipotence, omniscience, and omnipresence (but not eternality), to become human. Others suggest that the incarnate Son restrained the use of divine attributes to make possible a truly human experience, even though it was his prerogative to exercise them. Those who hold this position insist that it is better at explaining why Jesus did not know some things (Mark 13:32) and had to be made perfect (Heb. 5:8–9). Furthermore, the humanity of Jesus as our example, especially as one who did not usurp power, is taken quite seriously with this option.[5]

---

5. See Sarah Coakley, *Powers and Submissions: Spirituality, Philosophy and Gender* (Oxford: Blackwell, 2002).

Those who hold this position argue that it avoids what they consider to be tendencies toward some heretical positions in the two-natures model—heresies such as docetism, in that the kenotic theory emphasizes that God really *became human*. Advocates also suggest that this view is more coherent—that it simply makes more sense.

6

How Did the World Come into Existence, and What Keeps It Going? Creation and Providence

We Join in the "Prayers of the People": Thanksgiving and Intercession for the World and the Church

Lord, in your mercy, hear our prayer.

Whether it is the Nicene Creed or the Apostles' Creed that is used, the first dogma that the church confesses when it recites the creed is its belief that God is the maker of all that exists:

> We believe in God the Father, maker of all that is, seen and unseen.

> We believe in God the Father, maker of heaven and earth.

It is important that we really hear what we are saying. We are not confessing our faith in the creation. We are confessing our faith in God the Creator. This means that the doctrine of creation is first and foremost part of our understanding of who God is, and only secondarily part of our understanding of what the world and human existence are.

This distinction will be important when we get to the problem of evil, when we will be reminded that we must understand the creation in light of who God is rather than vice versa.

In the creeds we also express our faith in Christ, through whom all things were made (see Col. 1:15–17). This is appropriate because, as we saw in our discussion of the Trinity, God's redeeming work is related to God's creating work. The doctrine of creation must not be separated from the doctrine of redemption, especially because we can only truly know God the Creator through God's self-disclosure as Redeemer.

This seems to be the biblical pattern. The Hebrews had become a people after God brought them out of Egypt and redeemed them from slavery. It was only after that experience that they wrote about creation in Genesis. They got to know the God of the exodus first.

We see the same pattern in the New Testament. John's Gospel is written from a post-resurrection perspective, so it is significant that his Gospel echoes Genesis 1: "In the beginning was the Word." The redeemed author had come to know the risen Christ as the God of creation.

It is commonly thought that even the Apostles' Creed began with the second "article"—that is, with the confession about Jesus Christ, before the first article was added about God the Father who made all things. The Bible and the creed begin where the action is *now*—our redemption—before moving backward to the beginning and forward to the ending.

Another way to say this is that the creation provides the *ontological* basis for redemption, while redemption provides the *epistemological* basis for creation. In other words, creation establishes the *fundamental relation* of God to the world and the validity of God's claim on the humans he has made as the only one who has the power and authority to redeem or re-create us. But because Jesus Christ has revealed the Father to us (John 1:18), we can *know* the meaning and purpose of creation and the Creator's love for us. We cannot know the heart of God simply by looking at the stars or taking a walk in the forest, but it is the God who made the stars and the forests who has come to us in Jesus Christ. Karl Barth put it this way: creation is the external basis of the covenant, while the covenant is the internal basis of creation. What Barth meant was that creation sets the stage on which God's choice to be with humanity is played out. The identity of God the Creator and God the Redeemer is the theological axis of the good news.

So the doctrine of creation is not as interested in an explanation of the beginning—in a theory of origins—as it is interested in establishing who God is and who we are in relation to that God.

The Biblical Narratives

The biblical narratives that speak of creation complement each other. The first (Gen. 1:1–2:4a) is cosmological, focusing on the creation of the entire cosmos; the second (Gen. 2:4b–25) is anthropological, centered on the creation of Adam and Eve. (Of course, there are other creation narratives in the Old Testament, such as Pss. 8 and 104.)

Some consider Genesis 1 to be matter-of-fact—that is, to be telling us precisely the way in which God created the world. Those who hold such a position explain the six days of creation as either twenty-four-hour days, six ages (since the Hebrew word *yom* can mean day or age), days with gaps between them, or the week that follows an original creation (the "formless void" in Gen. 1:2) after a long interval.

Others point out how much poetry we find in Genesis 1–11; perhaps lyrically, even the first Hebrew sentence in Genesis contains seven words. They might refer to this material as religious drama or myth or "saga" (Barth). They do not mean this is some fairy tale, but it is truth being communicated in something like the perennial stories of Washington admitting that he had chopped down the cherry tree and of Lincoln walking miles to return pennies that he had overcharged someone. While these events may not have happened as told, their purpose is to illustrate the integrity of these iconic American presidents. The argument asserts that Genesis 1–11 deals with what we might call "prehistory"—like the orchestra that performs the musical themes before the play actually begins. And since our knowledge is dependent on our experience as creatures within an *already* existing world, the Genesis account of creation does the best it can to communicate something that transcends human experience.

Walter Brueggemann has even noticed a pattern in the telling of stories in Genesis 1–11. A crisis occurs in God's creation that is followed by divine intervention in the way of judgment and a promise. Adam and Eve sin; God sends them from the garden, but promises Eve's seed will crush the serpent's head and then clothes them with animal skins. Cain kills Abel; God punishes Cain, but marks him with protection. Humanity becomes wicked; God sends a flood, but provides the human race with another beginning by preserving Noah and his family. The tower of Babel is built, rebelling against God's command to fill the earth (Gen. 1:28); God confuses their language, but the confusion forces them to scatter in obedience to God's mandate, leading to the story of Abraham and God's command to "Go!" (Gen. 12:1)—the beginning of a nation through which all the nations of the earth will be blessed.[1]

---

1. Walter Brueggemann, *Genesis*, Interpretation: A Bible Commentary for Teaching and Preaching (Louisville: Westminster John Knox, 2010), 11–22.

Ultimately, we have to accept the creation narratives in Genesis 1 and 2 on their own terms, understood within the context of the ancient Near East several millennia ago. We should not force the texts to answer the questions of twenty-first-century Western minds. These opening chapters of the Bible are at least a prologue to the drama of human redemption that will be played out in the life of Israel. So the creation accounts are making religious or theological claims, not telling us new "facts" about the stuff of the world. The biblical narratives are neither scientific nor unscientific; they are simply *nonscientific*. As a result, no scientific facts can disprove these theological truths. For some who have a difficult time reconciling evolutionary theory with creation, this is good news.

Not only is Genesis 1 not providing a scientific account of the origin of the universe, but contemporary scholars of the Hebrew Bible and of ancient Near Eastern culture have argued that Genesis 1 is a description of how God's cosmic temple was set up.[2] In the ancient Near East, temple building was described in cosmic terms, and temples were described as having cosmic functions. The temple was considered the control center of the cosmos, so when we read that God "rested" on the seventh day, we should not think that God is now disengaged, but that God is now commanding the universe. The previous six "days" describe how God sets up the cosmic temple so that God can mount his throne, take his place, and assume his role. So Genesis 1 is not about creating "stuff"; it is about installing functionaries. Temples were built in the ancient Near East to be miniature models of the cosmos, as it were—places in which the deity dwelt as in a control room. And seven-day temple inaugurations are mentioned in temple-building records, so scholars surmise that Genesis 1 is similar to such temple-inauguration accounts. In other words, Genesis 1 itself is a kind of ancient liturgy.

If the cosmos is God's temple, then an ancient element in the church's liturgy celebrates what Genesis 1 is depicting in that part of the eucharistic prayer called the *Sanctus*, a conflation of Isaiah 6:3 and Matthew 21:9 (cf. Ps. 118:25–26). One current rendering that is usually sung is this:

> Holy, holy, holy, Lord, God of power and might.
> Heaven and earth are full of your glory.
> Hosanna in the highest.
> Blessed is he who comes in the name of the Lord.
> Hosanna in the highest.

2. For what follows, see John Walton, *The Lost World of Genesis One: Ancient Cosmology and the Origins Debate* (Downers Grove, IL: InterVarsity, 2009); see also, Greg K. Beale and Mitchell Kim, *God Dwells among Us: Expanding Eden to the Ends of the Earth* (Downers Grove, IL: InterVarsity, 2014).

Indeed, the creation that is filled with God's glory is a sanctuary—God's temple—and we are his priests.

Theological Claims about Creation

If the biblical narrative and the Christian tradition are making theological claims, then what are they?[3]

First, God's primary and essential relation to his creatures is expressed in the phrase *creatio ex nihilo* (creation out of nothing). The cosmos is the result of a divine act of purposive will. Ten times in Genesis 1 we hear the refrain "And God said, let there be." This is echoed by Psalm 33:6, 9 ("By the word of the LORD the heavens were made, / and all their host by the breath of his mouth. . . . For he spoke, and it came to be; / he commanded, and it stood firm"), and Hebrews 11:3 ("By faith we understand that the worlds were prepared by the word of God, so that what is seen was made from things that are not visible").

This implies that there was no preexistent matter. God is the ultimate source of *all* that is. There is no eternal dualism of God and some reality apart from or alongside God. If there were, then God would have to answer to the creation. If a carpenter could create *de novo* the lumber with which she builds, she would not have to put up with the knots and warped boards that she *does* have to work with; she has to answer to the wood from time to time because it is a given. But God ultimately answers to nothing in God's creation, which gives us hope, because nothing in creation is to be ultimately feared (Col. 1:16) or worshiped (Rom. 1:24–25).

This also implies that creation is not an emanation of God. It is not *creatio ex deo*. This distinguishes Christian theism from pantheism, the idea that all is God. The world is *not* God, and God is not the world. Again, we have hope, because if all that exists is God, then we have nowhere to turn outside of our own reality to make things right. "God" would be severely limited. A salesperson who came to our house once on a lovely spring evening warmed us up for her pitch by telling us that on the way to our house she rolled down the car windows and let god in. I concluded that her god could not permeate glass.

Second, because God is omnipotent and all-wise, God created in freedom and with purpose. God was under no obligation to create. But there is an orderliness in the creation account that moves from chaos (Gen. 1:2) to cosmos (Gen. 1:31). This is evident especially in the progression from day

---

3. See Langdon Gilkey's classic, *Maker of Heaven and Earth: The Christian Doctrine of Creation in the Light of Modern Knowledge* (New York: Anchor Books, 1965).

two to day three. Day two is the only one of the seven days on which the text does not repeat the phrase "and God saw that it was good." The reason is that on that day the waters were created, but they were not given boundaries until the next day. Unbounded waters or "seas" represented chaos in Meso-potamia and Egypt, where events such as floods could be devastating. We see the same sort of thing in the life of Jesus's disciples. Caught in a storm on the lake, the frightened disciples were amazed when Jesus calmed the storm. They wondered, "What sort of man is this, that even the winds and the *sea* obey him?" (Matt. 8:27). In other words, who is this who can change chaos into cosmos? And when John envisions the new heaven and new earth, it is because "the first heaven and the first earth had passed away, and the *sea* was no more" (Rev. 21:1). In God's redeemed creation there will be no more chaos. (One has only to think of cancer as chaos in the human body to know that this is good news.)

The orderliness of what God has created makes possible science, tech-nology, art, math, and so on. Our lives depend on God's purposiveness in creation.

Third, creation is good as God made it. It has divinely derived value or worth. Over and over in Genesis 1 God sees that what is established is good; in fact, it is "very good" when all is set in place (Gen. 1:31). And God still finds the creation valuable: God became flesh in it, suffered and died for it, remains Lord over it, and will re-create it. (The word *new* in Rev. 21:1 refers to a qualitative distinction, not a quantitative difference; we will take this up again in the final chapter.) Romans 8:18–25 assures us that the creation groans with birth pangs for its redemption. God will not waste what God has made good.

And this includes all of creation—the physical as well as the spiritual, matter as well as spirit. In other words, the Christian Faith is not dualistic. Gnostic dualism pits "evil" matter over against "good" spirit, but we have seen in our discussion of Christology that even the New Testament contests this heresy in the guise of docetism. The incarnation itself is a testimony that the stuff of created matter is not untouchable even by God. Moreover, the two most significant liturgical acts of the church—her use of water in baptism and bread made from wheat and wine made from grapes—remind us that God and God's relation to us are communicated through the stuff of the earth.

This understanding of creation makes Christians world affirming, not world denying or world escaping. True, we are warned in 1 John 2:15 not to love the "world," but this is a case in which we must contextualize the meaning of the word, since John 3:16 tells us that God loves the world. In the former case the word refers to a worldview that is confined only to the material. In the

> A seventeenth-century hymn from Roman Catholic Jesuits in Germany celebrating creation and Jesus, its Creator:
>
> Fairest Lord Jesus; Ruler of all nature,
> O Thou of God and man the Son.
> Thee will I cherish; Thee will I honor,
> Thou my soul's glory, joy, and crown.
>
> Fair are the meadows; fairer still the woodlands,
> Robed in the blooming garb of spring.
> Jesus is fairer; Jesus is purer,
> Who makes the woeful heart to sing.
>
> Fair is the sunshine; fairer still the moonlight
> And all the twinkling starry host.
> Jesus shines brighter; Jesus shines purer
> Than all the angels heav'n can boast.
>
> Beautiful Savior! Lord of the nations!
> Son of God and Son of man!
> Glory and honor, praise, adoration,
> Now and forevermore be Thine!

latter case the word refers to that which God has made. And if God loves the world God has made, then those who worship God must also love it. In fact, because we love the divine Artist, we work to protect the artwork. Christians are ecologically minded not because they are devotees of any political ideology, but because they are devotees of the Creator. Furthermore, as worshipers we also find the creation worthy of scientific study.

Finally, humans are created in the image of God—the *imago Dei* (Gen. 1:27; 2:18–24). And this includes male and female. The Triune God made *us* (plural) in the image of the three persons who are in perichoretic unity. If we think of the word *image* not just as a noun but also as a verb, then we image God when we are in right relation with each other. In fact, we were made to be social animals; we can only be human in relation to another. The second greatest commandment (Matt. 22:37–39) is not meant to be an imposition; to love one another is simply to express what it means to be human. Though Christians celebrate individuality and particularity, they are not to embrace individual*ism*.

The social constitution of our human existence is expressed throughout the church's liturgy. As we will discuss in chapter 11, when infants or new believers are baptized (depending on the church tradition), they are immersed into a new relationship with other baptized believers. And in many churches, after confessing sin and hearing that they have been forgiven and reconciled to God, worshipers pass the peace of Christ to one another as a sign that they have also been reconciled to each other. Participation in the Lord's Supper that often follows is the paramount sign of our connectedness—of our unity in Christ. The apostle Paul warned Corinthian believers who were eating and drinking communion in an "unworthy manner" that they were not "discerning the body"—presumably the body of Christ, the church—and were therefore bringing judgment on themselves (1 Cor. 11:27, 29). As he reminded them, "Because there is one bread, we who are many are one body, for we all partake of the one bread" (1 Cor. 10:17). In these ways and others, the church's worship images the Triune God.

Insofar as humans are made in God's image, they are distinct from the rest of creation, but in another sense humans share continuity with the rest of creation. The creation narrative implies such continuity: Adam (Man) was created from the ground (Gen. 2:6–7, 15); the ground is cursed because of human sin (Gen. 3:17–19); the blood of Abel, Cain's slain brother, cries out from the ground (Gen. 4:11–12). God's first command was for humans to have "dominion" over creation (Gen. 1:28–30; 2:15, 19–20; cf. Ps. 8:5–8). We are inextricably related to the rest of creation such that what we do affects the creation, and the creation can affect us. To be obedient to the first commandment God gave to his human creatures (Gen. 1:28)—a command God has never rescinded—we must participate in God's care for his creation, whether that is being eco-friendly or campaigning for social justice.

The Doctrine of Providence

The inseparable flip side of the doctrine of creation is the doctrine of providence. One implies the other. Providence has to do with the Creator's involvement with the creation—the wisdom, omnipotence, and goodness with which God maintains and governs in time this distinct reality according to the counsel of his own will. In other words, this is God's knowing, willing, acting upon, and providing for his creation. God is not an idle spectator of his creation, unlike the song sung by celebrities during the First Gulf War ("Operation Desert Shield/Storm," 1991), assuring us that "God is watching from a distance." Ultimately, that is not terribly reassuring, especially when human beings are lobbing weapons at one another. John Calvin put it this way: providence refers to God's *acts*—God's "hands," not just God's "eyes."[4]

Traditionally, theologians have discussed this doctrine under several headings. For instance, they have spoken of general, special, and extraordinary providence: in other words, God's involvement in the universe, individual lives, and the miraculous. At times it is helpful to understand the aspects of God's providence by referring to conservation, governance, and concurrence.

God *conserves* or preserves the creation through what is sometimes called "common" or "general" grace. God causes the rain to fall on the just and the unjust (Matt. 5:45). God institutes what have been called "orders of creation"—such gifts as marriage and government, which are enjoyed by all. This "grace of preservation" is contrasted with the "grace of redemption," which has to do with God's gift of salvation through Jesus Christ. That raises an interesting and debated issue: How is common grace related to special (redeeming) grace? More specifically, for instance, how is civil government related to the church? Is one supposed to serve the other? Or are the two relatively distinct? Calvinism has sometimes been seen to prefer the former option, ending up with a theocracy in which the secular government is to provide space for and to support the church. (Rousas Rushdoony and the Reconstruction movement is a good example.) Lutheranism has often been linked with the latter, referred to as a "two kingdoms" approach whereby the state and the church operate in separate spheres, each with its own ethic. We will examine these positions when we discuss the doctrine of the church.

God also *governs* or guides his creation toward the purpose or end that God has chosen. God works out his purposes in time and space. This means that Christians do not endorse fatalism. There is meaning to history. But how far God's guidance extends is debated. At one end of the spectrum is Calvin's statement that "not one drop of rain falls without God's sure command."[5] At the other end is open or free-will theism; this position holds that God does not even know for certain what is going to happen in the future, for while God is omniscient, the all-knowing God cannot know what cannot be known—namely, future events that are freely chosen by human agents.

Finally, God remains involved with creation *concurrently* with human creatures. A relationship exists between divine and human agency—between divine rule and human responsibility. Sometimes this is described as a division of labor. Other theologians speak in terms of divine "permission" for human

4. John Calvin, *Institutes of the Christian Religion*, ed. John T. McNeill, trans. Ford Lewis Battles (Philadelphia: Westminster John Knox, 1960), 1.16.4.

5. Calvin, *Institutes*, 1.16.4. A contemporary Reformed (Calvinist) theologian even insists that every stroke I am making on my computer is ordained by God.

actions. Still others use categories such as primary cause (God) and secondary cause (humans). The difficulty is this: the God-universe relation is sui generis. That is, it is one of a kind. There is no other like it. There is only one God and one universe. So all analogies that come from our experiences of agency within the universe fall short. Somehow God works in and through all things without compromising their freedom. In fact, God's continual preservation of the human creature is necessary for the creature to be free to act. One way to think about this issue is to ask yourself, What specifically am I asking God to do when I pray for someone to become a Christian?

In the end, the Christian doctrine of providence must avoid dualism and pantheism. The former is represented by deism—the notion that God created the universe and then let it run on its own according to natural laws. This position emphasizes divine transcendence at the cost of divine immanence. The latter is the notion that all things *are* God; it emphasizes divine immanence at the cost of divine transcendence.

Two Problems: Miracles and Evil

Typically two problems have been associated with the doctrine of providence: miracles and evil.

Our belief in miracles is problematic on two counts. The first has to do with metaphysics (the branch of philosophy having to do with the underlying nature of reality). If we are convinced that the universe is governed in an orderly fashion (as we have claimed above) by natural laws, then how can we take seriously narratives that claim Jesus walked on water or produced bread and fish for thousands of people when all he had to work with was a child's sack lunch? This assumes that the definition of *miracle* is "exception to natural laws." That definition is debatable. But even if we accept such a definition of *miracle*, we must realize that what we call "natural laws" are generalizations of recurring events made from our finite human perspective. Why should that matter?

Consider this analogy.[6] Let's assume I have been invited to the Hollywood Bowl to hear an orchestra play Tchaikovsky's *1812 Overture* for a Fourth of July celebration. And let's assume I am not familiar with this piece. Unbeknownst to me, there are cannons poised behind the audience, ready to be discharged at just the right times as the music reaches its final crescendos. As they blast away, I am startled because I did not expect them. For one thing, they are not typical orchestral instruments. But I would not have been startled and

6. This analogy was prompted by a reading of C. S. Lewis's book *Miracles* (New York: HarperCollins, 1996 [1947; rev. 1960]).

I would have expected them if I had known what the composer of the piece intended. Perhaps in a similar fashion, because I do not have God's perspective on the ways in which God has ordered the universe, and because my perspective on its orderliness is finite and limited, miracles are not exceptions from a divine point of view. This is not the only way to deal with the metaphysical problem of miracles, but it *is* one way to rethink the issue.

The second problem with miracles is epistemological (the branch of philosophy having to do with knowledge). In his treatise *An Inquiry Concerning Human Understanding*, eighteenth-century philosopher David Hume asked how it is we expect regular events to happen, such as the rising of the sun in the east and its setting in the west. The answer is that we have been used to this regularity day after day, so there is a psychological necessity involved in our expectation that this regularity will continue. As a result, we would be incredulous if someone reported that *this* morning the sun arose in the west. No matter how much evidence they produced, we would not be convinced.

Now propose a different scenario: the resurrection of Jesus Christ, on which the Christian Faith is grounded. All of our experiences with and reports about death have been consistent: when people are dead for three days, they stay dead. Hume asked why Christians believe that Jesus was an exception. The answer states that it was reported by contemporaries. So Hume pressed further, asking who it was that reported this event, and the answer is the disciples of Jesus. In other words, we are being asked to weigh the comparative evidence. On the one side of the scale is our experience. On the other side of the scale is the report of biased witnesses to something that goes against everything we know about living and dying. To be clear, Hume was not denying that miracles such as Jesus's resurrection do occur. He was just arguing that we have a very significant epistemological problem when we make such claims.

Perhaps in the end it is wise to remember that the biblical report of miracles is unconcerned with these modern problems (not that there weren't detractors in the first century). The biblical view of miracles places the emphasis on events that are new and surprising acts of God that lead to the exclamation, "Oh my God!" Ultimately, miracles in the biblical narrative are witnesses to and aimed at bringing about salvation and establishing the kingdom of God. As Emil Brunner said, they are not to be thought of so much as "against nature" in a closed universe as "against sin" in an open universe and through which God's plan of salvation is realized.[7] In the end, they can only be "seen" from the standpoint of faith.

7. Emil Brunner, *The Christian Doctrine of God*, vol. 1 of *Dogmatics*, trans. Olive Wyon (Philadelphia: Westminster, 1950), 253.

The other major issue that comes up when discussing the doctrine of providence is the problem of evil. And the answers to the problem are called theodicies—justifications of God's providential rule of creation in the presence of evil.

The problem has been redefined in recent years, but its classical statement is helpful for understanding what the issues are. Traditionally, it has been argued that if God is all-powerful, he is *able* to prevent evil from happening, and if God is all loving, he *wants* to prevent evil from happening. But evil exists. Therefore, either God is not all-powerful or God is not all-loving.

Before suggesting some ways of dealing with this problem, we need to make it clear that evil is a problem for Christianity *because* of the doctrines of creation and providence, especially since the One who created is revealed in Jesus Christ (Col. 1:15–16), who went about healing people and witnessing against injustice. Because of the Gospel witness to Jesus Christ, Christians know that the world should be better than it is presently. For the atheist, evil is not or should not be a "problem" but simply a dynamic of the cosmos in which we reside—and which one can hope to overcome in order for life to run more smoothly for everyone.

Any Christian "solution" cannot accept a dualism that pits evil against good in an eternal contest, or a monism that does not distinguish between good and evil (as if they were only illusions), or a naturalism that must simply accept things as they are. The Christian answer must not begin with evil, but must begin with a confession that God is righteous, loving, wise, and omnipotent. We are to try to understand the presence of evil in light of our confession of who God is, not try to understand who God is in light of evil's presence. But that doesn't resolve all the issues.

Two traditions of theodicy run like threads throughout the history of Christian thought.[8] One follows the path laid out by Irenaeus (second century), who believed that the fall recorded in Genesis 3 was not so much a fall downward as a fall forward—an event necessary if humans were to mature, learning through failure what it means to live in the likeness of God. Friedrich Schleiermacher (nineteenth century) was a modern proponent of an Irenaean theodicy. The other follows Augustine (fifth century), who taught that, since everything God created was good, evil is a privation of God's good creation—the nothingness that, like rust or tree rot, takes away from God's creation. (If you've seen the movie *The Neverending Story*, then you have been introduced to this Augustinian tradition.) Karl Barth (twentieth century) was a more recent advocate for an Augustinian theodicy,

---

8. See John Hick, *Evil and the God of Love* (New York: Palgrave Macmillan, 2010).

calling evil *das Nichtige*—the nothingness that cannot exist, even though it does.

Much ink has been spilled dealing with and arguing about the problem of evil, and this book is not the proper context for an exhaustive treatment of it, but a few comments might be helpful for those just entering into the fray.

A few cautions are in order. First, it is usually assumed that evil exists because God took a chance with free will. The argument is that if humans are going to be free to love God or reject God, then God must allow for the possibility of evil choices and actions. Yet there is nothing illogical about claiming that God could have created a material human world in which evil was neither chosen nor done. God could have created a world in which we were free and never sinned; in fact, in the next chapter we will see that Augustine argued that in the afterlife we will finally be perfectly *free* and *unable* to sin.

Second, it is often stated that evil must exist for there to be good. But that cannot be true, since before the world was created all that existed was God, and God is good; evil did not exist. In fact, evil is a parasite on the good, not the other way around. In other words, good must exist for there to be evil, but evil does not have to exist for there to be good.

Third, we want to know how evil got started, but in a world created good (Gen. 1), the Bible provides no ultimate explanation for the origin of evil.[9] If we attribute it to the free will of Adam and Eve, then there would have to be an evil choice to choose among the options in the good world God created. If we attribute it to the fall of some angel (as some interpret Ezek. 28:12–17; Isa. 14:12–15; John 8:44; and 1 John 3:8 as recording), we have only traced the explanation one step back from Genesis 3, but would need an explanation for the fall of that angel.

It helps to distinguish natural evil from moral evil (though sometimes evil involves a combination of the two, such as when people dwell irresponsibly in fire-prone areas).[10] Natural evil may simply be the result of God's all-wise decision to create a world that is material—a world in which rusted parts fall off of jets, resulting in crashes, and lions devour lambs simply because that is what lions do and lambs suffer. In that sense, God is the *indirect* cause of the evil that is suffered by people and animals.

9. On this point, see Austin Farrer, *Love Almighty and Ills Unlimited: An Essay on Providence and Evil* (Garden City, NY: Doubleday, 1961). Karl Barth called sin the "ontological impossibility": it is a denial of human freedom and our being as those who exist only insofar as we choose God's determination of our existence and correspond to the Creator. See Karl Barth, "The Gift of Freedom: Foundation of Evangelical Ethics," in *The Humanity of God*, trans. Thomas Wieser (Louisville: Westminster John Knox, 1996).

10. Some of the ideas about evil in the next few paragraphs are explained well by Herbert McCabe in *God Matters*, rev. ed. (New York: Continuum, 2005), chap. 3.

As we have already said, moral evil is not a *necessity* in a human material world. But it is the case that human beings commit morally wrong acts. And what is morally evil about such acts is not what it does to the one harmed, but what it does to the one who inflicts the harm. Sometimes a morally evil act can have a good effect. The morally evil rape of a woman resulted in the existence of Ethel Waters, an amazing jazz and blues singer and actress who memorably sang "His Eye Is on the Sparrow" at Billy Graham crusades. But the rape was morally wrong not because of the harm it caused Waters's mother—harm that is not to be minimized—but because the rapist's unjust act diminished the rapist's humanity.

Now God could prevent such evil acts, even without interfering with the perpetrator's freedom, but God is under no obligation to prevent morally evil acts, lest there be something greater than God that put constraints on God. God was not obligated to create the world, and God is not obligated to keep us from sinning. Still, why God permits such moral evil to occur is something we cannot answer. Somehow God is infinitely good *and* God allows sin. Sin does not demonstrate God's goodness, but neither does it demonstrate that God is not good. As Herbert McCabe says, all we know of God's purposes is that God loves us and wishes us to share his life of love.[11] Other than that, in the end, evil is a mystery.

Ends of the Spectrum

The ideas just presented display something of a compatibilist approach. That is, we have suggested that God allows or permits evil and sin to exist in God's providential oversight of the creation. But others have gone to one extreme or the other in their approach—extremes we have mentioned above in passing—so we conclude this investigation of the doctrine of providence with a brief description of these two options that come home to roost when it comes to the presence of evil.

On one end of the spectrum is Reformed theology. We mentioned Calvin's comment about each drop of rain being ordained by God. Some Calvinists say the same regarding evil events. Just as Calvin rejected language suggesting that God "permits" evil to happen, he would also not go along with the sentiment that, in referring to something like 9/11, "God did not cause the incident, but God will bring good out of it." A contemporary Calvinist might insist that God "ordained" 9/11 or even caused it, in the sense that God decided that it would occur and then brought it to pass. But he would also insist that this

11. McCabe, *God Matters*, 38.

neither destroys human responsibility nor implies that God takes delight in catastrophes, since God is compassionate and ordains evil for a greater good (appealing to Prov. 21:1; Rom. 11:33–36; and Eph. 1:11). The prime example is the crucifixion of Christ, in which those who crucified Christ carried out what God had planned for them to do (see Acts 2:23; 4:28). John Calvin even argued that the fall (Gen. 3) was ordained by God, but that Adam and Eve were still at fault for exercising their will to sin.[12] So, God is the direct cause of good and is worthy of all the glory for it, but God is the indirect cause of evil and deserves none of the blame. In other words, divine control does not compromise human accountability.[13]

At the other end of the spectrum is open (or free-will) theism.[14] Those who take this position argue that when Scripture speaks of God changing his mind (e.g., Jer. 18:8, 10), regretting decisions he has made (e.g., 1 Sam. 15:11), or experiencing disappointment when events don't turn out as expected (e.g., Jer. 3:7), these are to be taken literally. (Reformed theologians would say these are figurative expressions: God does not actually experience changes of mind, regret, or disappointments.) The reason open theism sees God as actually changing a decision is that some events in the future are settled, while others remain open. God is omniscient in that God knows those future events that are already settled either by God's foreordaining will or natural causes, but with regard to future events that are not yet settled, God knows all the *possibilities* of future events that are still open. The latter are the result of the future free actions of humans who create the future by their actions, some of which are the result of evil choices. God gave humans free will, which includes the potential for evil, such as the events of 9/11. God is not responsible for those freely decided choices and actions, so God cannot be blamed for evil.

12. Calvin, *Institutes*, 1.15.8; 3.23.7–8.

13. Some of the comments in this paragraph are based on an email correspondence with Matt Perman of Desiring God Ministries, October 4, 2001.

14. A good introduction to this view is provided by Gregory A. Boyd, *God of the Possible: A Biblical Introduction to the Open View of God* (Grand Rapids: Baker Books, 2000).

7

What Is a Human Being?
Theological Anthropology

We Kneel in the "Confession" of Our Sins

In many Christian liturgies, after the congregation has been welcomed into the presence of God and confronted by the reality of Jesus Christ through the Word of God that has been read and proclaimed, a realization of our present human condition sets in, leading the people to get on their knees and pray:

> Most merciful God, we confess that we have sinned against you in thought, word, and deed, by what we have done and by what we left undone. We have not loved you with our whole heart. We have not loved our neighbors as ourselves. We are truly sorry and we humbly repent. For the sake of your Son Jesus Christ, have mercy on us and forgive us, that we may delight in your will and walk in your ways, to the glory of your name. Amen.[1]

How did we get into this mess? We saw that the major emphasis in the trinitarian and christological controversies was soteriology. The issue of salvation raises questions about our origin, our present condition, how we got the way we are (that leads us to pray confessions like the one above), and where it is we are headed. This immerses us in theological anthropology: Whence

---

1. *The Book of Common Prayer* (New York: Oxford University Press, 2007), 360.

have we come? What are we now? Where are we headed? and How do we get from what we are now to what we shall be?

This is an important area of theology. For one thing, the way we answer these questions forms the presuppositions for understanding and dealing with humans in society, economics, politics, psychology, medicine, and religion. And knowing what it means to be human essentially becomes the basis for making decisions about many ethical questions, including women's issues, the protection and preservation of life, biogenetic engineering, cloning, racism, proper sexual behavior, equality of persons, human rights, and so on.

As we approach this topic, we do well to remember that the Christian understanding of human existence insists that the knowledge of human nature and of the human self can never be isolated from the knowledge of God. An adequate view of human existence proceeds from an understanding of God—not vice versa. The biblical view of human nature *begins* with God (Ps. 51:6). To this end, Calvin wisely said: "Man never attains to a true self-knowledge until he has previously contemplated the face of God and come down from such contemplation to look into himself."[2]

Of course, as we mentioned, we are currently a mess, and so even our understanding of who God created us to be is complicated by the fact that we are, in the Bible's way of putting it, sinners. There is something wrong with us. Yet, at the same time, as G. C. Berkouwer has observed, we are convinced that there is a "*real* human" who is better and nobler than the "actual" human with its empirical dark side.[3] Thankfully, the knowledge of self and human nature through the knowledge of God occurs primarily through an encounter with Jesus Christ, who is the definitive paradigm of humanity—the "second Adam" (but really the original Adam) as Paul calls him in Romans 5:12–18. By entering into our history, God reveals not only who God is, but also who we humans are—and can become.

2. John Calvin, *Institutes of the Christian Religion*, ed. John T. McNeill, trans. Ford Lewis Battles (Philadelphia: Westminster John Knox, 1960), 1.1.2. Calvin began all eight editions of the *Institutes* with this sentence: "Nearly all the wisdom we possess, that is to say, true and solid wisdom, consists of two parts: the knowledge of God and of ourselves" (*Institutes* 1.1.1). Pascal put it this way: "The Christian religion, then, teaches men these two truths; that there is a God whom men can know, and that there is a corruption in their nature which renders them unworthy of Him. It is equally important to men to know both these points; and it is equally dangerous for man to know God without knowing his own wretchedness, and to know his own wretchedness without knowing the Redeemer who can free him from it. The knowledge of only one of these points gives rise either to the pride of philosophers, who have known God, and not their own wretchedness, or to the despair of atheists, who know their own wretchedness, but not the Redeemer." *Pensées*, no. 556, in *Pensées*, trans. W. F. Trotter (n.p.: CreateSpace, 2013).
3. G. C. Berkouwer, *Man: The Image of God* (Grand Rapids: Eerdmans, 1962), 18.

The Two Dimensions of Human Existence

In the Christian perspective, human existence has two aspects that form a unity.

First, there is our *creatureliness*. We are to be understood within the context of the creative and re-creative work and purposes of God. As such we are *dependent* on God. We are not gods; but we are not junk either. So we neither applaud the self-worship of much pop psychology nor engage in the self-denigration of some distorted representations of Christianity.

Our creatureliness implies limitations and partial determination by environmental factors. We share similarities with other animals and their relationship to the rest of the created order (Gen. 2:7; 3:19). Thus, humans are objects of scientific study, as well as creatures who must exercise humility in scientific study.[4] Humans are similar to and connected with the rest of creation. In other words, we are biodegradable. We are made from the dust of the ground (Gen. 2:7; 3:19; cf. Rom. 8:19–23).

Creatureliness implies *dependence*, which is the fundamental orientation of humans toward God, an orientation that led Karl Barth to speak of humans as "beings-in-gratitude," for thankfulness must characterize beings whose very existence depends at all points on the Creator of all things. Further, we should understand human existence as rooted in the overarching creative and redemptive purposes of God.

Second, there is our *personhood*. We are free, self-conscious, decision-making, and valuing agents who act on our own decisions and who can purposefully enter into relationships. It follows that humans are not merely at the mercy of heredity and environment (nor are we therefore merely "sick" or "victims").

Our agency implies a responsibility to God to transcend environmental determinants at times and to make self-determining choices as persons, particularly in light of the fact that God has invited us to be coworkers with him. For this reason the Christian must reject reductionism, determinism, and materialism.

Made in the Image of God

Humans were created as a special part of creation—namely, the only creatures to be made in the image and likeness of God. As we briefly discussed in the preceding chapter, it is perhaps the most important thing we can affirm

---

4. We should make it clear at this point that sin does not reside in our creatureliness or finitude, but has much to do with the *denial* of our creatureliness and finitude, along with a corresponding misuse of self-transcendence. See Reinhold Niebuhr, *The Nature and Destiny of Man: A Christian Interpretation*, vol. 1, *Human Nature* (New York: Scribner's Sons, 1941), 16, 137–38, 140, 145.

about human existence in terms of the essence of human nature. The biblical data include Genesis 1:26–27; 5:1–3; 9:6–7 (and Ps. 8:4–7, which some have interpreted as a commentary on the Genesis 1 verses); 1 Corinthians 11:7; Ephesians 4:24; Colossians 3:10; and James 3:9. And it is affirmed in a striking manner—like the announcement at the end of a drum roll—in the contrast between the repeated conjunction "and" in Genesis 1:3, 6, 9, 14, 20, 24, and finally the "then" in 1:26.

But what does it mean to be made in God's image? What does this biblical data tell us about the *imago Dei*? In one sense, not much! For being such an important word, the biblical passages are brief, scarce, and not very detailed. (As a result, as we shall see, there are many different views as to how to understand what "image" means.) But the importance of the concept is out of proportion to its mention in Scripture and the lack of precision with which it is defined in Scripture.[5]

Before explaining what it might mean, a caution is in order. We must avoid eisegesis—reading our own ideas *into* Scripture. For example, we must avoid identifying the *imago* with the spirit over against the body—something the biblical text itself does not do. This identification might be made because God is spirit or because of some eagerness to distinguish human existence from the rest of the material world. But Scripture affirms that the *whole* human was created in God's image. Furthermore, though God breathes the spirit or "breath of life" into Adam in Genesis 2:7, we were already told in Genesis 1:30 that the animals also have the "breath of life."

Many suggestions have been given regarding the meaning of the *imago*. These are not mutually exclusive options necessarily. Among serious contenders is Augustine's suggestion that there are vestiges of the Trinity within human nature, such as memory, understanding, and will—all aspects of the mind—that image the divine Trinity.

Other theologians have selected various features of human life to pinpoint what *imago* is. For instance, Thomas Aquinas suggested rationality. That does distinguish us from the rest of creation. It is especially evident in our use of language, perhaps a reflection of *the* Word. Humans are the only animals who can recite poetry, write novels, and compose hymns of praise to the Creator. But the text does not indicate that rationality is what *imago Dei* connotes, and to make that connection might exclude from full membership in the "image of God" club those with severe mental disabilities.

---

5. The word for "image" is the Hebrew *tselem* (in the Greek LXX *eikōn*), while the word for "likeness" is *demuth* (*homoiousios* in Greek). Medieval exegetes tended to separate these two terms, but most today see them as synonymous words in a Hebrew parallelism—as Hebrew poetry.

Some argue that the *imago* refers to human dominion over the rest of creation (see Gen. 1:28; 9:6–7; Ps. 8:6–7; Heb. 2:5–9), though here the text is not clear: Does the *imago* consist of dominion, or was dominion a result of having been made in the image of God? This "dominion" or oversight of creation seems to have been exercised initially when God gave Adam the task of *naming* the animals—an act of power (Gen. 2:20).

"Personality," which C. Stephen Evans says encompasses purposing, self-shaping, rational, moral, responsible agency, has been identified as the *imago*.[6] This, too, excludes those who do not have this ability because of a physical or mental disability or limitation. Of course, in this case or in the case of rationality, it may be that bearing God's *imago* does not require the actual operation of these characteristics, but refers to the potential to function in these ways (for certainly an infant would not otherwise qualify).

Finally, relationality has been stressed by Karl Barth—the capacity to live in communion with God and fellow humans, after the fashion of the triune Creator who said, "Let *us* make humankind in our image . . . *male and female* he made *them*" (Gen. 1:26–27).

This last suggestion seems to be supported by the Genesis text. In the previous chapter we suggested that imaging the Triune God appears to have something to do with our relationality. Humans were not meant to live alone (Gen. 2:18), because we were made male and female by a God who is Father, Son, and Holy Spirit: "Let *us* make *them*." We can only be human in relation to an "other"; no human can find fulfillment in and by one's self. As we have mentioned, that is why the second greatest commandment (e.g., Matt. 22:37–39) is not onerous, but simply an acknowledgment that the only way we can live as the humans God created us to be is by living in relationship. Love—being-for-another—is essential to human creatureliness. We see this more clearly if once again we think of the word *image* as a verb as well as a noun. We *image* God when we live together in just or righteous relationships—in right-relatedness. But this implies that while we are *made* in God's image, we are not always *living* in God's image. This contrast requires some explanation.

The biblical data seems to indicate two different conditions of the image. On the one hand, Scripture implies in Ephesians 4:24 and Colossians 3:10 that the *imago* has been lost and needs to be restored. Theologians have referred to this with various terms: "material image," "narrower image," "actual image," "essence," and "analogy of relation." At the very least, from these two Pauline texts, it seems that something of the true knowledge of God and righteousness

6. See his development of this in *Preserving the Person* (Vancouver, BC: Regent College Publishing, 1994).

and holiness constituted aspects of the *imago* that have been lost. This corresponds to Calvin's notion that "integrity" or "rectitude" is the supernatural aspect of the image that has been lost and is in need of restoration. On the other hand, Scripture implies in Genesis 9:6–7 and James 3:9 that even after the fall something of the *imago* still remains. Theologians have referred to this with terms such as "formal image," "wider image," "ontic image," "nature," and "analogy of being." Though it is not clear what this includes, it is something like what Calvin had in mind when he referred to a *spark* of the image that remains in those who are fallen such that we recognize their humanity and our obligation to serve them.[7] It bears mentioning that, though many scholars surmise *image* and *likeness* were synonyms in the Hebrew parallelism of Genesis 1:26, the Eastern Orthodox tradition has argued for a distinction that corresponds to these two conditions of the image: we remain in God's *image*, but we must be restored into God's *likeness*.

Methodologically, we do not figure out what the *imago* is from a description of humanity's fallen state; instead, we must understand what it is from a description of humanity's redeemed state. We have two clues at this point. First, we have references that describe the goal of our regeneration or redemption: 1 Corinthians 15:49; 2 Corinthians 3:18; Ephesians 4:24; and Colossians 3:10. Second, we have references that point us to Christ, who, as *the* "Adam," is also the very image (*eikōn* in Greek) of God: 2 Corinthians 4:4; Colossians 1:15; and Hebrews 1:3. From this New Testament perspective, we then read back into the Old Testament text, particularly Genesis 1. In other words, the New Testament leads us to understand the *imago* in the contexts of Christology, soteriology, and eschatology (our final state).

We are growing into our humanity, which involves glorifying God by expressing God's character. The *imago* is being restored in those who are being regenerated—who have become "new creatures," the "new Adam"—a renewal that involves becoming like Christ, who is himself the very image of the invisible God (Col. 1:15). And this regeneration involves the restoration of three dimensions of relationships that have been perverted by the fall: our relation to God is being redeemed from idolatry; our relation to others is being redeemed from treating people as means to self-centered ends; our relation to creation is being redeemed from a posture of domination to one of stewardly dominion. In other words, we are being renewed in righteousness, which is nothing less than "right-relatedness." The image is expressed in and through the human insofar as the human individual expresses a proper relation to God, fellow human beings, and nature.

7. See Calvin, *Institutes*, 1.1.15.

All this demonstrates that humans are always "humans-in-relation-to-God," even in their fallenness, since we are always to be seen in the context of God's original aim for creation, either as those who live according to that aim or as those who are alienated from that purpose. But the being-redeemed human is *imaging* God as she is reoriented toward God to become like Jesus Christ and restored into the right-relatedness that God originally intended for his human creatures to occupy.[8]

More specifically, what does this restoration of the image involve?

First, the restoration of the *imago* that involves *becoming like Christ* (Rom. 8:29; 1 Cor. 15:49; Col. 1:15) is not an option for the Christian; it is an imperative. It involves putting off the "old Adam" and putting on Christ (Eph. 4:21–24; Col. 3:5–10), or, as Paul says elsewhere, imitating Christ (Eph. 5:1; Phil. 2:5–11). We mentioned earlier that the *imago* involves the whole person, not simply one's soul or spirit life. These imperatives involve one's whole existence in very concrete, observable, ethical behavior, and they involve the *analogia relationis*—being related to God and other humans as Christ is to the Father (as Son) and to us (as brother). So, the more we correspond to God or become like Christ, the more perfect the *imago* is in us—that is, the more perfectly we reflect God as a mirror that is being renewed from its cracked and twisted condition.

Second, the restoration of the *imago* is a *continual process* (2 Cor. 3:18). We "grow into" the image, so that this is a dynamic concept of the image, not simply some qualities that are conferred on us at the initial stage of our salvation. And the growth continues until "we shall be like him"—Christ, who, again, is the perfect *imago Dei*.

Third, the restoration of the image *takes places in community*. More accurately, it takes place *as community* (Eph. 3:17b–19; 4:12–13, 15–16; Col. 3:10–11). Relationships are restored as we grow up together into Christ. The restoration of the image is not an isolated project of the individual. In fact, according to Paul in Ephesians 4, we either grow up *together* into a maturity measured by Christ, or we do not grow up.

A Biblical Theological Anthropology

One debated issue asks whether the biblical understanding of humans is dichotomist (body and soul) or trichotomist (body, soul, and spirit).[9] Most

8. It is significant that in the Colossians 3 passage, in which Paul talks about the restoration of the image, he relates it to the baptism that newly defines us no longer by gender, race, or socioeconomic class, but by our new identity as people in Christ.

9. There are those who insist on a monist option. Among them, Nancey Murphy articulates a physicalist option that is not reductive. For an introduction to this position, see her *Bodies and Souls, or Spirited Bodies?* (Cambridge: Cambridge University Press, 2006).

likely the latter can be ruled out. For one thing, Jesus easily moves from talking about three aspects of human existence to four; compare Matthew 22:37 with Mark 12:30. The Bible is not interested in an abstract analysis of the constitutive parts of human existence, nor does it use terminology with great precision and exclusivity (as a study of the biblical use of "soul" and "spirit" will attest). As we have mentioned, it is interested in the human's total existence in relation to God.

One can summarize Scripture's view in this way: a human being is constituted as a *fundamental unity* of body and soul organized around a *center*, which can be referred to from *different perspectives*. John Cooper classifies such a perspective as "functional holism."[10] But the holism presupposes a dualism of body and soul. This is not to be thought of as some sort of gnostic dualism whereby good spirit is to be saved apart from the body, nor is it some Platonic preexistent immortal soul trapped in the prison house of a body. In fact, from a Christian perspective it is unnatural and incomplete for a human being to live in a disembodied state—even in the resurrection (see 1 Cor. 15:35–57). That is why Christians who confess the Apostles' Creed in the liturgy affirm that they believe in "the resurrection of the *body*." This dualism and what amounts to a temporary separation of body and soul (whatever "soul" is) is demonstrated persuasively in the New Testament's teaching on the "intermediate state" (our existence between physical death and resurrection). Jesus's parable of Lazarus and the rich man (Luke 16:19–31) is illustrative of what Jesus thought of the intermediate state. Though the precise description of such a state is debated, it is undeniable that we somehow exist apart from the body *and* that the body is an *essential* part of the human such that the redeemed are not perfected (completed) until the resurrection of the *body*.

The body (*sōma*, not *sarx*, which is translated "flesh" and which is usually used by Paul to refer to the principle of sin) is *not* intrinsically evil in the Christian view. In fact, God made it as part of his good creation. God intended for humans to exist bodily and to relate to him and to the rest of creation in an embodied way. Still, the body (like the mind) can be used as an instrument of sin or as an instrument of righteousness (Rom. 6:13). Yet it is as embodied beings that God wants us to offer our worship to him and wants to indwell us as his temple (Rom. 12:1; 1 Cor. 6:18–20).

At this point it is important to understand that when Paul says a "physical body" is sown at death while a "spiritual body" is raised, he is not speaking of a nonphysical resurrection. As N. T. Wright puts it, he is referring to a new

10. See John Cooper, *Body, Soul, and Life Everlasting: Biblical Anthropology and the Monism-Dualism Debate* (Grand Rapids: Eerdmans, 2000), 206.

A Theological Anthropology Word Study

The word *soul* can refer to life on earth in its external and physical aspects (Rom. 11:3) or to the seat and center of a person's inner life and its varied aspects (Mark 8:37; 14:34 [ESV]; Luke 12:19; James 1:21). It is sometimes difficult to distinguish it from the word *spirit*, though the emphasis of the latter is sometimes on the life-principle that God instills in humans, or *spirit* can refer to a spiritual state, state of mind, or disposition that is often set against that which characterizes the present age or the finite world (see 1 Cor. 2:12; 4:21; Gal. 5:16, 22). In other words, humans could be said to *be* a soul and *possess* a spirit-animating principle. "Spirit" is often set over against "flesh" when the latter is used to refer to the "willing instrument of sin," as in Romans 7:18. But *flesh* (*sarx*) can refer simply to the physical life (as in John 1:14 and 1 Cor. 15:39), though that is often reserved for *body* (*sōma*), physical existence created by God (Rom. 12:1; 1 Cor. 6:20).

mode of physicality that is "much more real, more firmed up, more *bodily* present than our present body." The Greek word that is translated "physical" here—*psychikos*—does not refer to the material out of which the body is made, but the *power* or *energy* that animates the body. It's like the difference between a steamship and a sailing ship. The present body is animated by the human *psychē*, but the future resurrected body will be animated by God's *pneuma*. This is why "flesh and blood" cannot inherit the kingdom of God—because the body must be *transformed*, not merely replaced.[11]

So we should keep in mind that a Christian theological anthropology must always refer to the whole person. Scripture uses body (*sōma*[12]), soul (Hebrew *nephesh*, Greek *psychē*), and spirit (Hebrew *ruach*, Greek *pneuma*) to refer to the whole person from different perspectives of our human existence. These are not things *in* a person. They *are* the person expressed or considered from a specific focus—from the dimensions of living that involve our thinking (cognitive), our feeling (affective), and our moving (physical) (see figure 3). And the Bible usually refers to the center around which this functional unity of a person is organized as the "heart" (*leb, kardia*). This stands for the center of a person's life—that which integrates and expresses

11. See N. T. Wright, *Surprised by Hope* (San Francisco: HarperCollins, 2008), 154–56. Wright argues that words with the *-ikos* ending in Greek are referring to the power or energy that animates, not the composite material.

12. There is no one word in biblical Hebrew that refers to the whole body, as *sōma* does in New Testament Greek.

itself through the different aspects or foci (see Matt. 15:18; Luke 16:15; Acts 14:17; 2 Cor. 5:12; also Prov. 4:23; 23:26). The heart works through one aspect or more of a person's life (Ps. 119:2, 10). We pattern and develop our intellectual, emotional, and behavioral life according to our "heart." In turn, these three dimensions of life influence the orientation and development of the "heart." (This is why Jesus says where your treasure is there your heart is, rather than vice versa!)

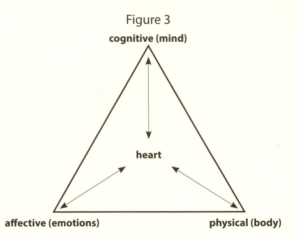

Figure 3

A couple of illustrations might help to understand what all of this means. If "heart" stands for the center of a person's life, then, given what Jesus says in Matthew 6:21 about the heart locating itself where one's treasure is, what a person "invests" in with respect to her thoughts, emotions, or behaviors will shape the orientation of her life. This should call to mind what we discussed in chapter 1 about the formative role that liturgies play in our lives, and it should reinforce the notion that worship should involve not just the cognitive (such as listening to sermons) and the affective (such as emotions that accompany singing), but also the physical (such as kneeling, raising hands, crossing one's self, and passing the peace—what Nadia Bolz-Weber once referred to as "liturgical aerobics").[13]

Also, given the integrative nature of the biblical understanding of human existence that we have developed, it makes sense that a person's orientation in life (the "heart") could be moved in the direction of a commitment to Christ's lordship either by apologetic reasoning (the cognitive), a traumatic experience (the affective), or coming forward at an evangelistic meeting (the physical).

13. Nadia Bolz-Weber, speech, ELCA (Evangelical Lutheran Church in America) Youth Gathering, New Orleans, LA, 2012.

Why Do Some Christians Cross Themselves?

Some Protestants think that the gesture of signing one's self with the sign of the cross is a "Catholic thing," but it has been practiced from the earliest times of the Christian church. Tertullian (second century) wrote, "In all our travels and movements, in all our coming in and going out, in putting on our shoes, at the bath, at the table, in lighting our candles, in lying down, in sitting down, whatever task occupies us, we mark our forehead with the sign of the cross."

Early Christians traced the cross on their foreheads with their thumbs, as well as on objects like food. Over the years this gesture has taken on various forms. In the West, typically the fingertips of the right hand touch the fore- head, breastbone, left shoulder, and right shoulder. Often when the Gospel is read, parishioners will sign the cross on their forehead, lips, and heart, as if to signal "Christ in my mind, my mouth, and my heart." Eastern Christians typi- cally cross themselves using the first two fingers and thumb to symbolize the Trin- ity, while the last two fingers touch the palm to represent the human and divine natures of Christ.

The Trinity, the incarnation, and Christ's redeeming work are captured in this gesture, just as many aspects of American patriotism are symbolized when citizens cover their left breast with their right hand as they face the flag.

From Scott Hahn, *Signs of Life: 40 Catholic Customs and Their Biblical Roots* (New York: Doubleday, 2009), 25–29.

And if the commitment is genuine and deep, no matter which dimension of human life was involved in the conversion, the other aspects of the person's life will follow suit.

The Beginnings of a Human Life

If it is the case that "functional holism" permits a soft kind of dualism, what accounts for the origin of the "soul"? (We obviously know what accounts for the origin of the person's body.) There have been three ways of answering this question in the history of Christian thought.

The most popular theory is called *traducianism*. This view teaches that the soul is generated by the union of the parents and comes into existence with the body. It was thought that this accounts for the transmission of Adam's sin to the rest of the human race. Tertullian taught that there is nothing spiritual without corporeality, so sinful parents pass on their sinfulness to their children, who are therefore born with the inclination to choose evil.

The least popular theory has been *preexistence*. Those who hold this position believe that souls exist before they enter into bodies. Often this has taints of Platonism; Plato taught that souls were immortal but fell into materiality, and the goal of salvation is the soul's release from the "prison house" of the body. Origen provides a good example with his doctrine that God's first creation was of spirits—an intellectual universe from which some fell even before Genesis 3, which is described as the separation of light and darkness in Genesis 1. So the creation of a material world recounted in Genesis took place for the punishment and purification of fallen spirits. (Latter Day Saints also teach the preexistence of the soul.)

Somewhere between most and least popular is *creationism*. In this case each soul is created by God with each propagation of a body by the human parents. God creates the soul *ex nihilo* (out of nothing) and implants it in the body at birth or conception (or at some time in between). Athanasius seemed to hold this view.

Although these theories are somewhat arcane, they do or could have implications for some theological and ethical issues. For instance, that Mary must have been "immaculately conceived" (in other words, born without sin), as the Roman Catholic Church teaches, seems necessary with a traducianist theory (if sin might otherwise have been passed on to Jesus by the propagation of a sinful soul) but not for the other two theories. Or, again, such theories might come into play for someone wrestling with his position on abortion; in other words, he might be more tolerant of abortion if he believed that the body was not soul-ful until birth (a creationist option) rather than believing that the body was soul-ful from the moment of conception (a traducianist option). It might be unusual to hear such doctrines voiced in discussions of such ethical issues, but it has come up in my conversations with pastors.

The Mess We Are In: Sin

Speaking of the possible transmission of sin brings us back to where we began this chapter—the mess we are in. This beginning point involves one of the most significant teachings of the Christian Faith that has much to do with how our human lives begin—the doctrine of original sin. But before we get to that doctrine and the argument that swirled around it when Pelagius and Augustine were at odds with each other, we need to define "sin." While there

An Excerpt from the Catholic Catechism on the "Reality of Sin"

"Only the light of divine Revelation clarifies the reality of sin and particularly of the sin committed at mankind's origins. Without the knowledge Revelation gives of God we cannot recognize sin clearly and are tempted to explain it as merely a developmental flaw, a psychological weakness, a mistake, or the necessary consequence of an inadequate social structure, etc. Only in the knowledge of God's plan for man can we grasp that sin is an abuse of the freedom that God gives to created persons so that they are capable of loving him and loving one another.

"With the progress of Revelation, the reality of sin is also illuminated. Although to some extent the people of God in the Old Testament had tried to understand the pathos of the human condition in the light of the history of the fall narrated in Genesis, they could not grasp the story's ultimate meaning, which is revealed only in the light of the death and Resurrection of Jesus Christ. We must know Christ as the source of grace in order to know Adam as the source of sin. The Spirit-Paraclete, sent by the risen Christ, came to 'convict the world concerning sin,' by revealing him who is its Redeemer."

From *Catechism of the Catholic Church* (Mahwah, NJ: Paulist Press, 1994), nos. 387–88.

is no one way of talking about sin in the Bible, there is a unity in the biblical witness about the sinful condition of humans and the consequences.

As we said in the previous chapter, ultimately sin and evil are mysteries (2 Thess. 2:7). One who gives too facile an explanation of these realities has not understood the gravity of our problem—of our human predicament. In fact, we cannot comprehend the mystery of sin apart from the equally mysterious reality of grace!

What we must *not* say about sin is that it is due to our finitude or creaturely existence. That would make sin intrinsic to being a creature of God. We in the modern era have done that, for example, by seeing "sin" as the expression of our incomplete evolutionary development or the result of ignorance or the manifestation of the pressures and structures of society. As a result, many have sought salvation in science, technology, or education.

On the other hand, sin can be a *denial* of our finitude. This leads to one of two extremes. On the one hand, we can assume that we are not confined to our creaturely status but can transcend it, leading us to self-exaltation. Or we can resign ourselves to our finitude in a begrudging manner that leads to self-denigration.

The Bible begins its description of sin with the narrative in Genesis 3:1–6. In this narrative the serpent exaggerates ("Did God say, 'You shall not eat from *any* tree in the garden'?"), lies ("Surely you will not die" [NET]), tells half-truths ("You will be like God"), and questions or twists God's statements. Eve corrects the serpent's hyperbole, but ends up exaggerating too ("God said, 'You shall not eat of the fruit of the tree that is in the middle of the garden, *nor shall you touch it*'"). In the process, God's word is misrepresented by both parties, and the human is invited to pit her opinion over against God's word. God's character is misrepresented as being miserly and withholding something good from his human creatures. (And notice the focus on the only thing that is prohibited rather than on a garden-full that is permitted.)

Getting at the root of this first sin might help us understand the essence of sin. We will describe three ways of thinking about the essence of sin, each of which is true and compatible with the others.

First, sin is concupiscence—love that is misdirected or inordinate. Eve looks and lusts or desires (v. 6; compare with 1 John 2:16 and with Jesus's temptations in the wilderness).[14]

Second, sin is disobedience or rebellion against God's will: Eve and her companion, Adam, eat what God forbids.

Third, and perhaps most penetratingly, sin is essentially pride, which amounts to a self-centeredness that takes the place of God. The idea behind the command not to eat from one tree in the garden was really all about this question: Who will be at the center of the human creature's world? Who is in charge?[15] When Eve eats of the tree of the knowledge of good and evil, she decides that the human creature will be at the center—will be in charge. And in that sense the serpent had told a half-truth: she *did* become like God, knowing good and evil as God knows it, insofar as the creature has assumed the right to apprehend and legislate morality as a god. In that sense, Genesis 3:4–5 is not far from Romans 1:21–25, where Paul tells us that our problem is that we end up worshiping the creature rather than the Creator. This is the autonomy that manifests itself so clearly in a desire to be one's own god. It is a misuse of human freedom that frustrates rather than furthers God's plan.

In becoming his own god, the human creature wants to become more than he is. The human person is a finite creature, but in becoming a god he denies his creaturehood and ends up serving and worshiping the creation. This is

14. Here is where some have suggested that the first sin was sexual in nature (as Augustine understood Gen. 3:7 and Ps. 51:5). But we sin *in* our sex lives, not because sex is inherently sinful.

15. Walter Brueggemann makes this observation: "The destiny of the human creation is to live in God's world with God's other creatures on God's terms." *Genesis*, Interpretation: A Bible Commentary for Teaching and Preaching (Louisville: Westminster John Knox, 2010), 40. Brueggemann goes on to comment: "The human creature, in or out of the Garden, still finally must live on God's terms" (50).

idolatry—an infraction of the first commandment. And it is not confined to the human individual. It manifests itself on many levels—human systems, governments, products, -isms. The irony is this: in wanting to be what they were not, human beings lost what they could become.

This sinful orientation expresses itself in our desire to be *in control*—to center the world around *self*. But since our true center is outside of us (Christians are supposed to be a bit "eccentric"), to center our lives on self throws everything else off-center—*everything*. Like a wheel with a misplaced hub, all that revolves around the autonomous human creature—marriages, governments, businesses—is in for a bumpy ride.[16]

Another way to characterize this sinful orientation is *covetousness*—the desire to have what is not rightfully mine as a creature. It is interesting that the Decalogue (Ten Commandments) ends where it begins: to idolatrously be my own god is to covet what is not mine to have. This is a point not lost on the apostle Paul, who equates greed with idolatry (e.g., Col. 3:5—note the location; it is the same passage in which Paul teaches the renewal of the *imago*).

Idolatry now brings us to what some argue is the real human problem. It has to do with worship. N. T. Wright says it well: "The primary human problem . . . is not 'sin,' but 'ungodliness.' [Rom. 1:18] It is a failure not primarily of behavior (though that follows), but of worship."[17] Maxwell Johnson concurs in a statement that brings us back to chapter 1 of this book. Noting that the worship of God at mid-eighth-century BCE Bethel and Dan was not authenticated by the people's ethical behavior (Amos 5:21–24), he writes, "Christians act morally or ethically because of what they believe, and what they believe is continually shaped by worship, by how they are formed by the words and acts of worship."[18]

Recalling the two dimensions of human existence, then, sin is a denial of the creaturely and an overreaching of the transcending personhood. Sin is therefore not simply to be thought of in moralistic, atomistic, external terms. It is a *direction* or *orientation* of the *heart*; Paul calls it the *flesh* (see Rom. 5–8; Gal. 5–6). This is a point that Augustine makes as well.

So, the present sinful condition of humans is not the way God originally willed for us to be. We have already seen that the *basic* truth about us is that

16. In a context such as this, Cornelius Plantinga's characterization of sin as "culpable shalom-breaking" or the "vandalizing of shalom" is apropos. See *Not the Way It's Supposed to Be: A Breviary of Sin* (Grand Rapids: Eerdmans, 1996), 7, 10, 14.

17. N. T. Wright, *The Day the Revolution Began: Reconsidering the Meaning of Jesus's Crucifixion* (San Francisco: HarperOne, 2016), 268.

18. Maxwell E. Johnson, *Praying and Believing in Early Christianity: The Interplay between Christian Worship and Doctrine* (Collegeville, MN: Liturgical Press, 2013), 98–99.

God made us in his image and he made us good. So the Christian sees the present world as not what it is meant to be or what it will be.[19] Our sinful condition is such that we keep trying to be what we were not meant to be. In the end, sin is a *lie* about who we really are and what we were originally meant to be.

The "Mess" Is All-Encompassing

At this point theologians sometimes introduce the concept of "total depravity." This does not mean that humans are as bad as they can be. Nor does it mean that everything human is completely bad. Nor does it mean that an individual indulges in every sin. It does mean that sin has penetrated the whole of our existence—like a virus or a cancer that has metastasized—and that we are beyond mere human repair. As Paul puts it repeatedly, we are dead in our sin—slaves to it (see John 8:31–36; Rom. 7:7–25; 8:7–8; 2 Pet. 2:18–19).

Genesis 3–4 makes clear the infectious spread of sin to the whole creation, something that should not surprise us if we are indeed integrated whole beings.

Obviously there were *spiritual* effects of the fall: the God-human relation is no longer what it was. The human creatures stand ashamed in their nakedness before God (Gen. 3:8–11); they want to hide from God now that their sin has been uncovered (cf. Ezra 16).

In *psychological* terms the fall took its toll as well. Though guilt and fear can be healthy dynamics in a person's life, in this case they become destructive. As Walter Brueggemann put it: "Perfect love casts out fear. But [Adam and Eve] learned another thing. Perfect fear casts out love and leaves only desire (cf. Gen. 3:10)."[20]

Family relationships are distorted. The husband-wife relationship is altered: subordination and domination become characteristic of the cursed relation (Gen. 3:16b, 20). In fact, male and female become subservient to the sources of their own created existence—Adam to the ground, Eve to the man. The first case of fratricide is recorded (4:8) as the human creature takes out his rebellion against God by attacking the image bearer (cf. Ps. 83:1–3). Our neighbor stands in the way of achieving our own will; we therefore assume the divine role and decide their destiny.

As we move further into the "prologue" of the Old Testament, *sociological* effects of sin become apparent. Genesis 3:15 points toward two humanities:

19. Plantinga, *Not the Way It's Supposed to Be*, 7.
20. Brueggemann, *Genesis*, 53.

a people of God (the offspring of the woman) and a people against God (the offspring of the serpent). Lamech appears to belong in the latter camp (Gen. 4:19–24). Babel becomes the attempt of the human creature to disobey God's first command to scatter and fill the earth (1:28); God in untiring grace forces them to fulfill the command, but it will not be the last time that group rebellion against God is recorded in Scripture.

There are *physical* effects of the fall, typified in Eve's increased pain in childbirth (Gen. 3:16a). (Having watched my wife deliver our two children—something that far exceeded my pain threshold—I cannot imagine that there would not have been pain in this process without the fall; the word *increase* should be taken quite seriously!) The physical effects of the fall have implications for the way that Christians think about scientific research that finds genetics are involved in some diseases, in sexual orientation, and the like; we need not shy away from such conclusions of empirical research since sin has affected even our gene pool.

Ecological disaster results from the fall, characterized by weeds that make work (which was commanded by God in the garden and which was good for the human—Gen. 2:15) to degenerate into a toilsome task (3:17b–19).[21] Work becomes a burden, as the earth is no longer hospitable to humans. What the human creature does affects the environment, and the environment retaliates.

Death is the last enemy. As we know it post-fall, death has a "sting." Death *as we know it* was not intended by God, but intruded into God's good creation. It is not to be welcomed as a Platonist would welcome the release from the prison house of the body (see John 11:32–35; Rom. 5:12; 1 Cor. 15:54–56). Though theologians debate whether there would have been death without the fall, it is undeniable that *how* we die has been a penalty of the fall.

Even without the Genesis text, it is crucial to note that a Christocentric theology would lead us to the same conclusion: the consequences of the fall were of cosmic proportions (see Eph. 2:1–3), since the effects of Christ's reconciling work are of cosmic proportions (Rom. 8:18–25), leading to the restoration of the whole creation (Col. 3:10; 2 Pet. 3:10; Rev. 21:1).

The Universality and Inevitability of Sin

After the fall sin is not only universal and pervasive but also inevitable. The problem is that the lie about who we really are as God intended is perpetuated generation after generation. In other words, we are born in sin. Like a compass

21. Note again that the Genesis author links the ground and the human creature repeatedly: 2:7; 3:17b–19; 4:10.

needle that always points north, our lives are inclined toward sin from the very beginning. We are sinners from the moment of conception (Ps. 51:5). At the very least, we would say that we have all been shaped by the consciousness of post-fall civilization.[22] We don't have to teach the preschooler to *take* the other child's toy; we have to teach him to *share* his toy.

This inborn inclination is what theologians call "original sin." Reinhold Niebuhr once observed that the doctrine of original sin is the only empirically verifiable doctrine in Christian theology.[23] Yet, still, it's painful to admit. We usually try to mask our problem or shift the blame for it (e.g., "It's natural" or "Boys will be boys" or "He made me do it"). It even manifests itself in that we blame others or our circumstances for the evil we do, while we are quick to take credit for the good we do. Yet we still have an uneasy conscience because we are aware that we are not just hapless victims of forces beyond our control; we are aware of endorsing behavior that goes against God (Rom. 1:32; 2:1, etc.). Despite the fact that we seem helpless to do anything but sin, we have a sense of responsibility for who we are and what we have done.[24]

The doctrine of original sin is the way theologians have dealt with the inevitability yet responsibility for sin—with the juxtaposition of our inborn proclivity toward sin to which we, nonetheless, freely give assent. The fall in Genesis is represented as a momentous decision on the part of our first parents that sets about a chain reaction—an event that shapes subsequent history. Though the Old Testament (interestingly) has no *explicit* statement about the effect of Adam's sin on his posterity (beyond Gen. 11) or about how the rebellion was passed on, moral evil is spoken of as characteristic of all humans (Gen. 8:21; Ps. 51:1; Jer. 17:9). Theologians have turned to Romans 5 for a passage that tries to explain original sin. And a debate between Augustine and Pelagius in the early fifth century helps us to understand the issues.

Augustine and Pelagius were in contention over the relationship between God's grace and human free will. At issue was the extent to which Adam's sin affected us and, consequently, what is now needed for us to choose what is good.

Pelagius was a British monk who was a moral reformer. He had been appalled by the low level of Roman morality when he had visited Rome around 400, so he preached to a worldly church an ethic much like the Sermon on the Mount.

---

22. See Jacques Ellul, *The Ethics of Freedom* (Grand Rapids: Eerdmans, 1976), 194–96.
23. Niebuhr, *Nature and Destiny of Man*, 121.
24. Reinhold Niebuhr put it this way: we sin inevitably but not necessarily; see *Nature and Destiny of Man*, 242–43, 255, 260, 263. We sin because we fully choose to sin *and* because the human condition into which we are born after Adam moves us in that direction.

Purportedly, he went to North Africa around 410 to visit a major church leader whom he respected—Augustine. Among other things, he had been disturbed by an Augustinian prayer: "You command continence [i.e., controlling urges, especially with regard to sex]; give what You command, and command what You will" (see Augustine's *Confessions*, 10.40). Pelagius thought that such a prayer undermined morality because it implied that we are not able to do what God commands. And it belittles the grace of a God who would command us to do what God knows we cannot do and then damn us for our inability. What kind of God is this? What kind of God would issue commands that we cannot follow? And why even try to obey as a result?

Pelagius published a commentary on Romans that emphasized the idea that if God commanded something for which he holds us accountable, then we should be able to do it. Surely we have the power to fulfill God's law. In other words, the degree of ability determines the degree of responsibility. This is a stance that our legal system endorses, since we assign lesser penalties to those who commit crimes with mitigating circumstances, such as in the case of those who plead insanity in the course of committing an illegal act.

To make his case, the key for Pelagius was the assumption that humans have a totally unconditioned and undetermined free will to do what God commands, for if a person is coerced in either direction, it lessens her responsibility and culpability. In fact, theoretically Pelagius believed that it was possible for a person to go through life without ever sinning, though practically speaking he believed that would not happen. We have the power of contrary choice or "formal freedom"—the inalienable power of human nature to do what is right. As evidence, consider the fact that there are pagans who cultivate virtue and perform righteous acts. Nothing in us compels us to sin.

In fact, Pelagius insisted that we are not born with sin: "Everything good and everything evil, in respect of which we are either worthy of praise or blame, is *done by us*, not *born with us*. We are not born in our full development, but with a capacity for good and evil; we are begotten without virtue as without vice, and before the activity of our own personal will there is nothing in man but what God has stored in him."[25]

So Pelagius challenged the idea of original sin that is passed down from generation to generation. We are not inclined to sin from birth, since no sinful tendency or condition is transmitted from parent to child.[26] When faced with temptation, our choice today is as real as it was for Adam. But we are

25. Henry Bettenson and Chris Maunder, eds., *Documents of the Christian Church*, 4th ed. (New York: Oxford University Press, 2011), 56 (italics original).
26. Pelagius seems to have been a creationist when it came to the origin of the soul; only the body, not the soul, is traceable to Adam.

not held accountable for Adam's sin. The fall (Gen. 3) set a bad example for humanity—an example that has been influential and started a "long custom of sinning." We come into a world that is sinful and *learn* to sin.

Lying behind Pelagius's view is an atomistic conception of sin. Sins are wrong acts of disobedience of God's law, and we cannot inherit wrong "acts" from our parents. Still, all of these individual acts cluster over time into such a weight that sin is universal. The attraction of all these bad examples tempers our otherwise ethically indifferent sensual nature so that Pelagius admitted that sin ends up being a necessary condition of humans.

But there is hope, because God's grace is available to *everyone* to change and obey God's law. This comes in the form of enlightenment and enforcement— namely, the publication of God's law and the sanctions (carrots and sticks) that encourage us to obey and discourage us from disobeying. Along with these come good examples to offset the bad, especially in Jesus Christ. In these ways God facilitates or assists our reason and will so that we can do what God wants us to do. And when we fail, Christ has provided for our forgiveness.

When Pelagius had gone to Carthage to visit Augustine, he didn't find him there, so he left Celestius in charge to represent his views. Apparently, Celestius represented Pelagius's ideas "too well," such that he was excommunicated and Pelagius's ideas were considered heresy in 412 at Carthage. But the ideas spread, so that Augustine, along with some others, began to publish tracts against Augustine's critics. Pelagius had not wanted any controversy and convinced some people that Celestius's condemned opinions were not his own—especially the misrepresentation that God's grace was not necessary. So it may well be that Pelagius was not a Pelagian. Nevertheless, after decisions went back and forth, Rome finally condemned Pelagius, Celestius, and the Pelagians in 418, and further denounced them at the third ecumenical Council of Ephesus (431).

Augustine's position is inseparable from his life story (which he writes about in his *Confessions*). For some years he had lived with a mistress with whom he had had a son. He had embraced several philosophies, affirming the determinism of Manichaeism at one point and free will at another. But he finally rejected an optimistic view of free will, reflecting on his own conversion that led him to conclude that humans in their natural condition are incapable of any positive cooperation with grace and that faith is a gift of God (Rom. 9:16; 1 Cor. 4:7; Eph. 2:8; Phil. 2:13).

Augustine explained that in the garden, before the fall, Adam and Eve existed in "original righteousness" that included an intimate knowledge of God, perfectibility, the harmony of soul over body, and free will. They were enabled by a helping grace that made it possible to persevere in their righteousness.

In other words, they were in a state of *posse non peccare*, "able not to sin." But the human weakness was creaturely changeableness, and change they did.

Giving up constant dependence on grace, the first humans fell. The root of their sin was pride, and from then on self became the goal. This fall was not a single wrong act (as Pelagius taught), but an act that implicated all of humanity. The entire human race existed seminally (in seed form) in Adam. Now fallen humanity is caught in a wrong *orientation* from which it cannot free itself. This is the grip of concupiscence in which the will is dominated by sensuality over against the spirit, finding satisfaction in what is material and changeable. It is the state of *non posse non peccare*, "the inability not to sin."

All of us are in this predicament, according to Augustine. It is a "damned mass," since the collective will of the human race was operative in Adam's sin. Augustine argued this position on three counts: (1) a mistranslation of Romans 5:12 (reading "death came to all *in whom* [i.e., in Adam] all have sinned"); (2) childhood experience; and (3) the practice of infant baptism, which had become a widespread practice by this time and which Augustine argued was for the forgiveness of sin before the doctrine had been developed (another case in which the church's liturgical practices would shape doctrine).[27]

The only way out of the "damned mass" is through prevenient (coming before) justifying grace—the free, undeserved gift that awakens and heals the will that cannot help itself and that turns the will toward God. Grace received by faith (which is itself a gift of grace) does what the law with its demands could not do—namely, overcome concupiscence. As a result, the divine "Do what I command" of Pelagius is wrongheaded; the prayer "Grant what You command" is the right approach. Grace changes the inclination of the heart, which the will follows. And then God gives the grace to persevere in the healed life—to grow in faith, knowledge, and love. This is the subsequent sanctifying grace from which individual good acts naturally arise.

At death, the soul of the new creature in Christ enjoys the vision of God and enters into a state of *non posse peccare*, "not able to sin." This is true freedom: the inability to sin. (As Augustine argued: Can God sin? No. Is God free? Yes.) Until this beatific vision becomes a reality, the soul is restless until it finds its rest in God.

Augustine's view has two significant implications. First, grace is irresistible. If God chooses to change a person's life, he is going to be changed. Second, what follows is predestination: justice demands that all go to hell, but God, in God's inscrutable grace, has chosen some for salvation by a decree of

27. Maxwell Johnson (*Praying and Believing*, 4) points out that in the ninth century infant baptism came to be based on a *developed doctrine* of original sin.

predestination that precedes any merit and any asking. Grace is offered to all and willed for all, but we cannot tell to whom it has been actually *given*.

As time went on Augustine's views regarding the irresistibility of grace and predestination were considered extreme and novel, even by those who did not accept Pelagius's views. Eventually, the Council of Orange (529) established that grace was not irresistible, though it was necessary if one was to respond to God in faith. The council insisted that humans are completely depraved, that they lost their spiritual freedom when the fall took place, and that there is no merit in salvation. After a few centuries, the council's decisions were forgotten, Pelagian ideas made something of a comeback, and the equivalent of semi-Pelagianism was affirmed in the late Middle Ages leading up to the Protestant Reformation. We will pick up the story at that point when we discuss Luther and the doctrine of justification in the next chapter.

Table 3
Pelagius vs. Augustine

	Pelagius	Augustine
Sin	Wrong choices	Wrong orientation
The effect of the fall on humanity	A "long custom of vice"	A "damned mass"
Grace	Carrots and sticks: the law and sanctions, good examples, forgiveness of sins	The awakening and reorientation of the heart, which the will follows
True freedom	The ability to choose	The inability to sin

For the time being, some reflections on the interpretation of the key passage, Romans 5:12–21, are in order for further considerations about the notion of original sin.

Christ is central in Romans 5. Adam is introduced for the sake of making the point about Christ, not vice versa. It is a typology of two men—one righteous, one unrighteous. It summarizes the effect of the one act on the many (while Rom. 1–3 focuses on the sins of the many). In this passage, verse 12 is crucial, particularly the phrase "death spread to all *because all have sinned*." (Note the correct translation uses "because" rather than Augustine's "in whom.")

What does the phrase mean? What *is* the relationship between Adam's sin and ours? There have been many explanations of the meaning of this phrase.

For Pelagius, "have sinned" simply refers to our actual sins rather than our having sinned in Adam. We reenact Adam's transgression in our own lives. "Pelagianism" makes sense in that God's judgment would fall on each one of us because of what each one of us does; it stresses the moral responsibility for our own actions. But it does not do justice to verse 18 in this passage, which implies that what Adam did has brought condemnation on all of us.

For Augustine, as we have seen, it depicts the whole human race seminally in Adam—a view we refer to as "realism." We participated in Adam's sin, but not in such a way that we actually sinned in our own person. But Romans 5 does not attribute guilt to the *act* of *all* people. And why wouldn't we be guilty for *all* the sins that Adam and Eve committed? We are still left with what seems to be an injustice.

"Representationalism" or "federalism" argues that Adam is our "federal head," our representative, whose decisions implicate all of those "under" him, such as happens when a nation's president or prime minister declares war, implicating all the citizens of that nation. In this case, the whole race represented by Adam is guilty. This has some merit with what is said in Romans 5, yet detractors have argued that this introduces a massively new concept in biblical theology that is found nowhere else. And the parallel doesn't quite work: it appears that Christ's righteousness is applied only to those who accept it, but, given what is claimed about our involuntary connection with Adam, in a parallel fashion it would seem that salvation must come to all regardless of faith.

John Calvin taught that Adam's sin corrupted our human nature and transmitted the habit of sin (like pollution flowing down a stream), so humans sin in their own persons, but as a result of the corrupt nature inherited from Adam. So Romans 5 would be teaching that at least the *guilt* of Adam's sin is immediately applied (or imputed) to the entire race of human creatures, while the *corruption* of our human nature has been inherited from Adam. Some question whether this is really what is taught in the text.

What might be the best explanation harkens back to the corporate solidarity of Old Testament conceptions of the relation between the individual and the tribe (e.g., consider Achan, Edom, Ishmael). With this understanding, Adam is our ancestor and we are "his kind" (Gen. 5:3)—like a tree with root and branches. One person embodies the group, which is joined in a racial solidarity. This resonates with some cultural and religious worldviews of societies that see themselves "not as separate, autonomous individuals, but as intimately interconnected nodes in large webs of kinship. The same blood, the same life, which they received from their first ancestor, runs through the veins of all. . . . Central to this corporate view of life is the concept of 'linkage' or connectedness."[28]

---

28. Paul G. Hiebert, R. Daniel Shaw, and Tite Tiénou, *Understanding Folk Religion: A Christian Response to Popular Beliefs and Practices* (Grand Rapids: Baker Academic, 2000), 104–5. The authors point out that this is exemplified by the Yoruba of Nigeria.

Scripture and empirical evidence *do* seem to teach the solidarity and univer-
sality of sin and its effects, and humans *are* caught up in a sinful predicament
that they did not create. Further, there does seem to be a social heritage of
sin—something wrong with the world that goes beyond the individual and
involves even Christians.

Meanwhile, on the "Eastern Front"

Eastern Christianity was developing its own approach at this time. We can
see it most clearly in the views of John Cassian, a contemporary of Augustine
and Pelagius, whose position has been labeled "semi-Augustinianism" (since
he had no dealings with Pelagius). It has been described as a *successive* view
of free will and grace.[29]

Over against the Western brand, teaching about grace was not always logical
in Eastern Christian theology. It showed little interest in theories and doctrines
of grace and free will. Eastern theology tended to be more concerned with the
practical and moral consequences of what was taught. So, there was a simultane-
ous stress on absolute dependence on God *and* full responsibility of free will to
choose between good and evil. Cassian put it this way: What is necessary for the
farmer to have good crops—good weather or human toil? The answer is both!

Through ascetic practices (such as fasting), one is to cut away the passions—
the earthly barriers that hinder the entry of grace, and then grace will be
able to flow. God's mercy is bestowed only on those who labor and exert
themselves—given to those who ask, opened to those who knock, and found by
those who seek.[30] It wasn't Augustine's concern with pride that most troubled
theologians like Cassian; it was the laziness of those who had received the
grace that was absolutely necessary for salvation from start to finish (which
is why Cassian was not Pelagian). In addition, Cassian would not agree with
Augustine's treatment of original sin—that we all fell in Adam, a disagreement that was partially fueled by Cassian's *creationist* account of the soul's
origin over against Augustine's tendency toward *traducianism*; still, Cassian
did argue that the human will is affected by heredity, society, and environment.

Another way to see the differences is to compare the state of the precon-
verted will in Augustine, Pelagius, and Cassian. For Augustine the will to good

29. See Owen Chadwick, *John Cassian: A Study in Primitive Monasticism* (Cambridge:
Cambridge University Press, 1950); Columba Stewart, *Cassian the Monk* (New York: Oxford
University Press, 1998).
30. See John Cassian, *The Conferences*, trans. Boniface Ramsey (Mahwah, NJ: Paulist Press,
1997), 12.14.

is basically dead, needing to be awakened by God's prevenient grace. For Pelagius the will is born healthy and perfectly capable of doing good without the assistance of internally reorienting grace. For Cassian the will is sick, needing constant attention from healing grace, but, like a sick person, still capable of healthy acts at times if revived by medicine. For Augustine grace re-creates the whole person; for Cassian, grace is a necessary medicine. So, for Cassian there are those who cannot even make the first little turn toward God without divine intervention igniting the spark, while there are others who do make a little turn of the free will toward God, to which God responds with grace.

8

What Did Christ Do for Humans?
Soteriology

We Hear That We Are Forgiven in the "Absolution"

Once we have confessed our sins to God, the pastor or priest declares that we are forgiven. In churches with a more formal liturgy, you might hear this: "Almighty God have mercy on you, forgive you all your sins through our Lord Jesus Christ, strengthen you in all goodness, and by the power of the Holy Spirit keep you in eternal life. Amen." This "absolution," as it is called, is often followed by what are labeled "The Comfortable Words" (Scripture, such as 1 John 1:9). In other churches the absolution is simply referred to as something like "Words of Assurance"—that is, assurance of God's forgiveness, quoting Scripture such as Psalm 103:8–13 or 1 John 1:9.

But salvation is not simply about forgiveness. In fact, salvation involves three "moments" or tenses of the verb "to save": "I have been saved" (justification); "I am being saved" (sanctification); and "I will be saved" (glorification). Unfortunately, the evangelical church has often reduced salvation to the first one of these three, forgetting that salvation is an ongoing process until it is completed in what N. T. Wright calls "life after life after death."[1]

Soteriology (the study of salvation) is often divided into two aspects: the objective (what Christ has done for us) and the subjective (what happens to

1. See N. T. Wright, *Surprised by Hope* (San Francisco: HarperCollins, 2008).

us). And so we begin this chapter with objective soteriology and end it with the first "moment" of subjective soteriology.

What Christ has done for us is often referred to as the doctrine of the atonement. The first thing that must be said about this doctrine is that it is just that—a doctrine. In fact, the four Gospel accounts (Matthew, Mark, Luke, and John) and the book of Acts give us no formal doctrine about how the death and resurrection of Jesus saves us. And there is no single uniform teaching about the atonement in the rest of the New Testament (such as in Paul's letters), though there is an essential unity of witness regarding the cross, summarized succinctly in 1 Corinthians 15:3: "Christ died for our sins according to the Scriptures."[2] This last phrase is a reminder that any consideration of what was accomplished on the cross has to be understood in the context of the whole biblical story (recall the six acts in chapter 1); however, as we shall see, many understandings of the atonement ignore the biblical narrative in their explanation of how we are saved by what Christ has done.

Perhaps because the church has recognized the diversity of understandings in the New Testament and that no single historical understanding is sufficient to capture all that needs to be said, there is no creedal insistence on any one view of the atonement as there is with the Trinity and Christology. The New Testament uses various metaphors when it speaks of salvation. These include images that have to do with finance, the military, law courts, slavery, and sacrifice. Historically, the church's understandings have often been expressed in a particular cultural context, as we will see when we describe Anselm's satisfaction theory of the atonement. Because of cultural context, models of the atonement can also fall out of favor. For instance, because of today's cultural sensitivities, there are objections to portraying the cross-event as an act of violence, yet we will see that the violence of evil forces *did* and *does* have a role to play in Christ's atoning work. In any case, we must be careful not to hold theories of the atonement in cultural captivity, while recognizing the

2. See John Stott, *The Cross of Christ* (Downers Grove, IL: InterVarsity, 2006). Stott outlines six biblical themes or emphases that are central to the New Testament witness regarding the cross: it was necessary (Mark 8:31; Acts 2:23; Gal. 1:3–4); it was sacrificial (Mark 14:22–25; John 1:29; Rom. 3:24–25; 1 Cor. 5:7; 11:23–26; Eph. 5:2; 1 Pet. 1:2, 18–19; 2:24; Heb. 9:22–28; 1 John 2:2; 4:10); it was vicarious (Mark 14:24; John 10:15; Rom. 5:6; 8:32; 1 Cor. 15:3; Gal. 2:20; 1 Thess. 5:9–10; Heb. 2:9; 1 John 3:16) and representative (Rom. 5:19; 2 Cor. 5:14; Heb. 7:26–27); the servant of the Lord's humiliation and death has sin-atoning power for the many (language of Isa. 53; John 1:29; Acts 3:13; 4:27, 30; Rom. 4:24; Phil. 2:6–11; Heb. 9:28; 1 Pet. 2:21–35); its goal is reconciliation of God-human fellowship and of human-human fellowship (Rom. 5:10–11; 2 Cor. 5:18–19; Heb. 10:19–25); and it is understood as penal substitution (Gal. 3:13; 2 Cor. 5:21). As we will see, there is some disagreement about the last on the list.

biblical truth that is expressed when it appears in these historical conceptions. It is good to have access to all of these views since together they overcome deficiencies in each one and help us to understand the multifaceted aspects of Christ's saving work.

One more point needs to be made before we unpack these views: though the focus of Christ's atoning work is the cross and resurrection, that, too, must be placed in the context of the *life* of Jesus of Nazareth. It has been said that cradle and cross are made of the same wood. In other words, the incarnation was as costly for God as was the crucifixion. A reminder of that would be a weekly occurrence in churches that recite the Apostles' Creed in their liturgy if they simply moved a comma. Instead of confessing that we believe in Jesus Christ who "was born of the Virgin Mary, suffered under Pontius Pilate, was crucified and buried," we might rephrase it "was born of the Virgin Mary, suffered, under Pontius Pilate was crucified, and buried."[3] Jesus did not suffer only at the time of the Passion, but, as the Gospel accounts make clear, God the Son suffered throughout his incarnate life.

Historical Understandings of the Atonement

One of the earliest theories of the atonement—recapitulation—is found especially in the thought of Irenaeus (late second century). The Latin word *recapitulatio* literally means "summing up," echoing the apostle Paul, who wrote that God "sums up" or "gathers up" all things in Christ (Eph. 1:10). Christ is the Second Adam (Rom. 5:12–21), who restores the fallen creation by reversing, as it were, all the sin done in Adam. Adam was tempted through the woman; Jesus was brought into the world through a woman. Adam's fall involved a tree; Jesus's victory took place on a tree—the cross. He reigns from the cross as king on his throne. In other words, Jesus recapitulates the story of Adam, undoing Adam's disobedience that led to damnation with Jesus's perfect obedience that has led to our salvation. And as Jesus sums up all that God originally had in mind for humanity, he becomes the head of a new race, just as Adam was the head of the old humanity.

Philip Pfatteicher discusses this theory in the context of liturgy, especially a line in the ancient "Gregorian Preface of the Cross" as it is rendered in the Lutheran Book of Worship: "through Christ our Lord, who on the tree of the cross gave salvation to all, that, where death began, there life might be restored, and that he [Satan], who by a tree once overcame, might by a tree

---

3. I believe it was from Marva Dawn that I first heard or read the suggestion of this subtle change.

be overcome."[4] Pfatteicher goes on to recount the medieval legend that traced the journey of the wood of the forbidden tree that was centuries later used to fashion the cross of the second Adam. Another legend had Adam's bones buried under Golgotha, "the place of the skull," where Christ was crucified; that accounts for Adam's skull at the base of medieval crucifixes and in Byzantine icons. "The fall and the restoration, paradise lost and paradise regained, are to be understood together."[5]

Much of Eastern thought (Greek especially) speaks of salvation as *theōsis*—deification (see Ps. 82:6; 2 Pet. 1:4; 1 Cor. 15:49). Deification does not mean that humans become divine by nature. The Creator-creature distinction is not erased. Instead, deification has to do with the renewal of the image of God. In chapter 3 we read how Athanasius understood the work of the incarnate Son as revealing who God is and restoring the image of God in humans after it was damaged in the fall. As we progressively bear the image of God that has been distorted and defaced by sin, we become more like God and fulfill our human destiny in Christ. As Athanasius said, "God became man so that man might become God." The goal is union with God, achieved by means of a ladder of ascent that begins with repentance (conversion of the will) and progresses to purification or purgation of the passions (such as lust or anger) that interfere with the life of unceasing prayer. That makes possible a deep knowledge of the things of God and a perfect love that is the fullness of grace, until the soul is fully united with God, either in this life or the life to come.[6] While this is characteristic of Eastern thought, iterations of it are not entirely absent in Western Christian thought, such as in Bonaventure's *The Mind's Road to God* (thirteenth century).

In fact, this notion that God became humanized so that we might be deified is echoed in the collect for Christmas Day that comes from the Leonine Sacramentary (seventh century)—the earliest collection of prayers (especially from the fifth and sixth centuries) in the worship that follows the Western tradition (known as the Roman rite). So the "wonderful exchange" gets expressed even in the Western church:

> O God, who wonderfully created, and yet more wonderfully restored, the dignity of human nature: Grant that we may share the divine life of him who came

4. Philip H. Pfatteicher, *Journey into the Heart of God: Living the Liturgical Year* (New York: Oxford University Press, 2013), 182.

5. Pfatteicher, *Journey*, 183. See p. 200 for the sermon of John Chrysostom (fourth century) that celebrates Christ's victory with the theme of recapitulation.

6. See Vladimir Lossky, *The Mystical Theology of the Eastern Church* (Crestwood, NY: St. Vladimir's Seminary Press, 1997), 204. The study of Evagrius Ponticus (fourth century) offers a good introduction to this soteriological orientation.

to share our humanity, your Son Jesus Christ; who lives and reigns with you
and the Holy Spirit, one God, for ever and ever.[7]

There is much that is commendable in these Eastern Christian expressions
of what is involved in *theōsis*, especially its emphasis on the restoration of
the image of God in humanity. And God's elevation of humanity in union
with God is often, though not always, missing in Western thought. But there
is heavy Platonic and Neoplatonic influence in the early expressions of these
views, which has led to everything from a belief in immortal preexisting souls
to locating the human problem in ignorance to a shift in emphasis from the
cross to the incarnation.

Eastern Christian understandings have also emphasized the resurrection
in what is referred to as the classical view of the atonement. In recent times
Gustaf Aulén's *Christus Victor* has promoted this view. With a military metaphor, Christ is portrayed as victorious over Satan, sin, and the powers of evil.
The apostle Paul employs this image graphically in Colossians 2:15, using
the Roman practice of parading the conquered in a procession in front of the
victorious Roman army. At times the idea of ransom is applied to this view.
Christ paid the ransom that released us from the hold of Satan (see Mark
10:45; 1 Pet. 1:18–19). There is debate about the legitimacy of the ransom
and to whom it is paid, since Jesus's statement in Mark's Gospel does not
specify who receives the payment. Origen (third century) taught that Jesus
hung on the cross as "bait" for Satan, who thought he had defeated Christ,
until Satan was "reeled in," as it were, through the resurrection. This is why
fishing hooks are sometimes used to symbolize the saving work of Christ.
Either through a military victory or a ransom paid, Christ got us back and
delivered us from the enemy.

While this marvelous and biblical understanding of God's work to redeem
us is announced by the *Christ Pantocrator* (literally, "all power") image that is
often found painted on the interior ceiling of Eastern Orthodox churches, and
while the last word in this view is life risen from the dead, it tends to make the
atonement too objective. That is, humans become some kind of spectators
of a cosmic battle that leaves us moving from captives of one power to freed
servants of another power.

In the Western church the Latin view of the atonement has also been called
the satisfaction theory. Though we find variations of it as early as Tertullian
(third century), its iconic statement was articulated in Anselm's *Cur Deus
Homo* (Why God [Became] Man) (twelfth century). Anselm's cultural context

7. Cited in Pfatteicher, *Journey*, 88.

was medieval feudalism: the lord of a manor provided land to vassals who, in exchange, owed him honor and obedience. In this case, the "manor" is the universe, and from the Lord of *this* manor we robbed the honor due him because we did not maintain perfect obedience to God. Even if we committed only one act of disobedience, we can never make up for what is lacking in our obligation to have given obedience without exception. But in becoming one of us, the one who perfectly obeyed and honored God—who owed him nothing more—paid the honor we owed God, satisfying God's demands on our behalf and fulfilling God's original plan. And because this obedient one was God, his work of satisfaction has infinite value.

While there is some biblical basis for this view of the atonement (e.g., see Heb. 2:17, as well as chapters 8–10), it is interesting that Anselm does not appeal to Scripture but to logic to make his case. There is merit to his position: it takes sin seriously as honor depriving and to some extent could be illustrative of the kind of covenant arrangement into which God has called us. Nevertheless, it doesn't quite develop the notion that we have offended divine love. While we will elaborate this critique with the next view (and to some extent all the critical reflections regarding the next view will apply to the satisfaction theory), it is important to note that Anselm repeatedly finds what God did to be "fitting."

The atonement theory that has had the most popularity among evangelicals and others in the West is penal substitution. We find it in Luther and to some extent in Calvin. (Some argue that Luther espouses the classical view, and while there is some truth to that, penal substitution seems more prominent in his writings.) The metaphor in Anselm could be said to be a civil courtroom, but here the metaphor is definitely a criminal courtroom.

This view accentuates the biblical understanding of sacrifice or expiation (canceling or making up for sin by means of a sacrifice or payment). In taking on our humanity, Christ, who was without sin, *became* our sin and paid the penalty for it on the cross. Now when God looks at us, God no longer sees us but Christ in our place. Christ became what we are so that we might become what he is. Everything God intended us to be was accomplished and is now given to us as God's gift by faith in Jesus Christ. Luther called this the "happy exchange": our sin is imputed (transferred) to Christ, while Christ's righteousness is imputed to us.

Since this view has been the predominant atonement theory in Western Christianity, we need to examine it more in depth than some of the others. There are certainly biblical grounds for this position, especially 2 Corinthians 5:19–21. In addition, Paul's recurrent phrase "in Christ" appears to add support for something like Luther's exchange.

This view takes sin very seriously, since it requires the penalty of death. But that is where some have voiced criticisms or cautions. For one thing, proponents of penal substitution usually think of sin as law breaking, with God as the divine bookkeeper, yet the situation is much more than that. In our sin we also offend divine love. To illustrate the distinction, consider what would happen if someone killed a child through negligent driving. The court might find this person guilty of manslaughter and sentence him to prison for a couple of years. When the driver has served his time, he has paid the penalty for his actions as far as the law is concerned. But his act also offended the love of two parents, and before he is truly free he must be forgiven by and reconciled to those parents. As we alluded to in the case of the satisfaction theory, God has entered into a covenant of love with us, and though that covenant does involve legal obligations that we have broken (such as the Ten Commandments), breaking the covenant is also described in the Old Testament as adultery against the God who "married" Israel. (The book of Hosea captures this beautifully.) By extension, the church is to be the faithful bride of Christ in the New Testament. So we have not just broken divine law with our sin; we have been unfaithful to the divine Lover.

Another shortcoming of this theory is that the last word in penal substitution is death. Christ is left as the victim, but not the victor. This substantiates the claim that we need all of these theories of the atonement, since this position needs to be joined by the classical view of *Christus victor*.

Perhaps most significantly, this view can easily slip into the pagan notion of sacrificing to appease an angry God in order to get God to love us, setting the Father over against the Son as if the Father can only love us if the Son is first crucified. But the cross did not *change* God's mind about us; it *expressed* God's mind. It is God who initiates the process of reconciliation and provides God's self to atone for our sins. It is not a case of divine child abuse, as some criticize, but an act of a Triune God's love. This is beautifully expressed by Augustine as quoted by Calvin:

> God's love is incomprehensible and unchangeable. For it was not after we were reconciled to him through the blood of his Son that he began to love us. Rather, he has loved us before the world was created, that we also might be his sons along with his only-begotten Son—before we became anything at all. The fact that we were reconciled through Christ's death must not be understood as if his Son reconciled us to him that he might now begin to love those whom he had hated. Rather we have already been reconciled to him who loves us, with whom we were enemies on account of sin. . . . Therefore, he loved us even when we practiced enmity toward him and committed wickedness. Thus in a marvelous

and divine way he loved us even when he hated us. For he hated us for what we were that he had not made; yet because our wickedness had not entirely consumed his handiwork, he knew how, at the same time, to hate in each one of us what we had made, and to love what he had made.[8]

In the same century that Anselm wrote his treatise, another theologian—Abelard—was espousing a view that has been called moral influence or exemplarism. This position holds that Christ's life and death on the cross was the supreme demonstration of God's readiness to be made one with us, and such an expression of God's love should motivate us to live in a manner that exhibits the same kind of obedient love toward God and others.

Although this position correctly sees that there ought to be an emotional response to what God the Son did in taking on human flesh and suffering a cruel death—a response that is often expressed in hymns and praise songs during worship—this view by itself is insufficient, since it is weak on arguing for the necessity of the atonement. And that, in part, is due to its rather anemic view of the sinful human condition.

A recent position has been proposed in response to what is presumed by the satisfaction and penal substitution views of the atonement—namely, that salvation or reconciliation to God requires the killing of Jesus as an act that is necessary to satisfy divine justice. Labeling it a "Narrative Christus Victor" understanding of the atonement, Denny Weaver insists that these typical Western views are founded on the notion of retributive violence that assumes that divinely initiated or divinely sanctioned violence is necessary for restoring justice. Weaver's concern is that the older views provide no necessary role for the life or resurrection of Jesus, that they encourage church support for the violent interests of the state, and that they leave us with a soteriology that severs salvation through Jesus's death from living out the Christian life.[9]

Weaver insists that evil originates with humans, and *that* (not God) is what killed Jesus. "Satan" is the image or term that represents all the principalities and powers that have turned against God but are still redeemable (including us who are complicit in Jesus's death). God did not require Jesus's death as a compensatory retribution for the sins of his enemies and friends; his death resulted from fulfillment of his mission announcing and acting out the reign of God. His mission "invited" a violent response. What we call "sin" is bondage to the forces of evil; "salvation" is being freed from those evil forces and

8. John Calvin, *Institutes of the Christian Religion*, ed. John T. McNeill, trans. Ford Lewis Battles (Philadelphia: Westminster John Knox, 1960), 2.16.4, quoting Augustine's commentary on John's Gospel (110.6).
9. See Denny Weaver, *The Nonviolent Atonement*, 2nd ed. (Grand Rapids: Eerdmans, 2011).

being transformed by the reign of God, taking on a life shaped by the story of Jesus, whose mission was to make visible the reign of God by living in obedience to the Father's will. The bottom line is that Jesus came not to die, but to live—to witness to God's reign in history. (Weaver's biblical support begins with a reinterpretation of the book of Revelation.)

There is much to commend in Weaver's analysis. Even at the Christmas midnight Mass in the Gregorian Sacramentary (a set of liturgical books containing the text of the Eucharist and ascribed to the sixth-century Pope Gregory I), Psalm 2 is recited at the beginning: "Why do the nations conspire, / and the peoples plot in vain?" Philip Pfatteicher reflects that this is a "solemn reminder, even at the magical midnight Mass, of the hostility that the coming of Christ into the world generated. Herod was not the only ruler to feel threatened. The liturgical year and its appointments always reflect a realistic view of the way of the world and will not let us escape the truth."[10] Indeed, just three days after Christmas, on December 28, the church observes the "Feast of Holy Innocents"—a recognition of the infants and toddlers of Bethlehem who died as victims of Herod's paranoia and jealousy.

But there have also been some criticisms of Weaver's view. They can be posed as questions. Does the death of Christ become unnecessary? Is Weaver too close to Abelard's exemplarism? Does Weaver end up making "nonviolence" an imposition on the narrative rather than letting the biblical narrative take priority (including the Old Testament stories of a violent God)?

What should we make of all these models of the atonement? First, we should not reject them, but we do need to reinterpret them, since, as we have mentioned, some tend to be bound to time, place, and culture. Second, as we have said, since these are metaphors, no one soteriological model could express all the truth of Christ's atoning work. Third, however we articulate Christ's work, it must be faithful to the biblical text and to the Christian tradition while being relevant to the situation in which it is being explained. Fourth, what was decisive for the New Testament church was *that* the cross was necessary for salvation, not the explanation of *why* or *how*, so we must keep the main thing the main thing. Fifth, we need to keep in mind several biblical and theological details: the New Testament does not speak of "punishment" when referring to Christ's death; Jesus used a meal at *Passover* (not the Day of Atonement) to "explain" his death;[11] the New Testament understands the language of sacrifice to refer to God's mercy and self-giving

---

10. Pfatteicher, *Journey*, 81.

11. See N. T. Wright, *The Day the Revolution Began: Reconsidering the Meaning of Jesus's Crucifixion* (San Francisco: HarperOne, 2016), 178–94.

and not to appeasing God's wrath; forgiveness is not simply subtraction from count-keeping but involves restoration of relationships; and the Father is not the subject while the Son is the object, but the Father and the Son both act as subjects in agreement. Finally, we must reiterate a most important point—namely, that the life, death, and resurrection of Jesus *must* be contextualized within the entire biblical narrative.[12]

Salvation as Justification

The Greek word translated "justification" is *dikaiosyné*, which literally means "to be put in the right" or "to place someone in the right"—such as placing humans in a proper relation with God. In the Old Testament the corresponding Hebrew word *tsedaqah* refers to behavior that maintains a two-way covenant relationship between God and humans. In later rabbinic Judaism it connoted conformity to the law.

In other words, justification refers to "right-relatedness" rather than being ethically right. For the Christian, justification is the right-relatedness of Christ that we receive by grace and participate in by faith. For the apostle Paul, this meant that God the judge has exposed our guilt, but has also acquitted us and pronounced us rightly related by virtue of our relationship to the covenant-keeping Jesus Christ. In this way we are liberated to *become* righteous.

But all of this became fodder for debate in the late Middle Ages. Recalling what we have said about the distinction between objective and subjective soteriology, the late medieval debate specifically involved this question: What is the relationship between Christ's objective fulfillment of righteousness and the subjective righteousness of the faithful?

We mentioned in the previous chapter that semi-Pelagianism arose in the medieval West after the Council of Orange (529) had largely decided in favor of Augustine's position over against Pelagius. Though the understanding of justification was not monolithic by the late Middle Ages, a general description will help one understand Martin Luther's decisive break that, in part, launched the Protestant Reformation.[13]

---

12. Scot McKnight is right to point out that the sermons in Acts (chapters 2, 3, 4, 10, 11, 13, 14, and 17) originally had to do with the fulfillment of the Old Testament story in Jesus. He argues that only in a secondary way do they have to do with forgiveness of sins and justification: "To gospel is to tell the story that Jesus is Lord and that we are to repent and believe and get baptized to enter into that lordship story." Scot McKnight et al., *Church in the Present Tense: A Candid Look at What's Emerging* (Grand Rapids: Brazos, 2011), 139.

13. We have to say "in part" because it has been said that if there had not been a Protestant Reformation, there would have been a revolution. The social conditions in the sixteenth century were ripe for an upset.

What Luther inherited from his training in late medieval semi-Pelagianism was the teaching that God's grace *initiates* our salvation with forgiveness of original sin and the infusion of love that makes meriting God's acceptance possible. But we must *cooperate* with grace that keeps coming to us through sacraments (like penance and Eucharist) until we eventually receive eternal life. In other words, God's prevenient grace comes to us through the act of baptism, we grow in the habit of grace through sacraments, we obtain merit by doing the best we can in cooperation with the grace received, and then we are rewarded with God's full acceptance.

Steven Ozment provides a very good analogy to help us understand this.[14] A human being is a unique creature by virtue of his reason. But if a person wants to become a "tennis-playing man," he has to acquire the habit of play-ing tennis (and playing it at his best) through infused instruction *and* his own exercise and practice on the basis of that instruction. Similar to the way that the habit of playing tennis exists in a person, God's grace exists in the soul. By this means the person receives the essential foundation (like basic instruc-tion) needed to order his life in obedience to God. This essential foundation is the infusion of an initial disposition and the removal of the hindrance of original sin to do good works that God has committed himself to reward. He must still exercise this received grace in order to become an expert in the skill of loving God and fellow humans. But if he has done his very best in the state of grace, then God will welcome him into eternal life.

The Council of Trent (mid-sixteenth century) articulated this view as it responded to the rise of Lutheranism. In its canons on justification, it argued that the "free will of man, moved and aroused by God" (i.e., by prevenient grace), cooperates "by responding to the awakening call of God, so as to dispose and prepare itself for the acquisition of the grace of justification." It rejected the teaching that "the impious is justified by faith alone—if this means that nothing else is required by way of co-operation in the acquisition of the grace of justification."[15]

Though there is much more that is involved, including purgatory—the "realm" or process in which one is further purified and undergoes any remain-ing temporal punishment before entering paradise—what has been outlined is

14. Steven Ozment, *The Age of Reform, 1250–1550: An Intellectual and Religious History of Late Medieval and Reformation Europe* (New Haven: Yale University Press, 1981), 32–33. He is describing Thomas Aquinas's version of this medieval schema. Duns Scotus and the nominal-ist school had some significant differences with Thomas's realist account of all of this, and a popularized version of the nominalist position was influential in Luther's thinking. Ozment's book explains this further.

15. Henry Bettenson and Chris Maunder, eds., *Documents of the Christian Church*, 4th ed. (New York: Oxford University Press, 2011), 266.

sufficient to understand Luther's problem, which was this: How is it possible to be pleasing to God—to merit God's full acceptance—particularly when all we do before a just God is contaminated by our sinful self-interest?

After much agonizing introspection and study of Paul's Epistles, Luther finally came to the conclusion that he had misunderstood what Paul was saying in Romans 1:17—an iteration of Habakkuk 2:4, which says that "the just shall live by faith." Luther had interpreted this phrase along the lines of his theological training: we must *be* just in order live eternally. But his new understanding was that we are *made* just (or *declared* just—there is some debate among Lutheran scholars) by the faith we put in Christ. (Luther said it was by "faith *alone*," though the New Testament never uses the word "alone" with "faith.") The justice of God is not his judgment or punishment of us, but that by which he justifies us *even while* we are sinners. We are *simul justus et peccator*—simultaneously righteous and sinner.

God's verdict is *always* condemnation of us because of his justice, but what satisfied his justice is not our meritorious works, but his mercy in the substitution of Christ for us. (Recall the "happy exchange" we mentioned earlier in this chapter.) The baptized Christian is covered with Christ's righteousness such that God sees the person as righteous even though he is still a sinner. The following analogy captures nicely the point Luther expounds in comparison to the Roman Catholic Council of Trent, which clearly stated the late medieval view:

> The key question is whether or not something really happens to human nature through grace. Let's start with the premise that human nature is sinful to begin with (a dungheap): extrinsic justification [Luther's view] says that if you have faith, then even though you remain a dungheap, you smell like a bed of roses to God; nothing really changes you, but by virtue of the grace of Christ, God treats you as a garden. . . . Intrinsic justification [Trent's conception] starts with human nature as equally sinful, a dungheap, but it says that the sacraments of the church give you grace so that you will be changed into a rose garden. Something really happens to you, or, to put it in the religious language of the times, "grace transforms nature." Christians are being healed of sin, changed from sinners into saints. Luther did not believe this.[16]

So Luther would not say that "good works make a person good," but that "a good person does good works."[17] In other words, Christ's righteousness—an

---

16. Mary Jo Weaver and David Brakke, *Introduction to Christianity* (Belmont, CA: Wadsworth, 2008), 93.

17. See Martin Luther, "The Freedom of a Christian," in *Martin Luther's Basic Theological Writings*, ed. Timothy F. Lull (Minneapolis: Fortress, 1989), 613.

"alien righteousness"—is imputed to us, and *on that basis* we then live out our Christian lives. John Calvin largely agreed and said that this understanding of justification was that on which the church stands or falls; it is "the hinge on which religion turns," and all other doctrines are to be reassessed in its light.[18]

Actually, Calvin sought to restore a proper balance between justification and sanctification (the process of becoming holy). Trent had essentially equated justification with sanctification: "This disposition or preparation is followed by justification itself, which is not the remission of sins but the sanctification and renewal of the interior man through the voluntary reception of grace and of the gifts, whereby from unjust man becomes just, and from enemy a friend, that he may be 'an heir in hope of eternal life' (Titus 3:7)."[19] Luther had essentially separated the two, insisting that justification was an instantaneous "event" that was complete and that freed the person to do good works. Calvin put it a bit differently with his emphasis on our union with Christ: "Justification is received by faith alone, but since that faith unites us to Christ as sanctifier, justification and sanctification can no more be separated than Christ himself can be divided." Though we will unpack the doctrine of sanctification in the next chapter, it will be helpful at this point to begin to think about how justification and sanctification might be closely related as Calvin insisted.

Some recent discussions have attempted to reconnect what Luther purportedly separated. Of course, not all argue that Luther *did* separate justification from the lived Christian life. The Finnish school in the Lutheran camp takes a position that has been articulated by Robert Jenson that Luther is to be interpreted in a more Eastern sense in terms of *theōsis* (divinization) and participation in the divine life of Christ, rather than merely forensic imputation—the notion that God simply declares the believer righteous. This perspective—which is not shared by all Lutherans—argues that justification is both *forensic* and *effective* in the Christian's life.

Similarly, from the Reformed camp, Bruce McCormack has voiced Karl Barth's position that justification is both *judicial* and *transformative*. Justification takes place objectively in Christ and is appropriated subjectively as humans come to faith in him. The difference between believers and unbelievers is that the former consciously enjoy their justification and live it out.

Though it can seem somewhat complicated, an important reassessment of the apostle Paul's teaching on justification has been advocated by N. T.

---

18. Calvin, *Institutes*, 3.2.1.
19. William C. Placher and Derek R. Nelson, eds., *Readings in the History of Christian Thought*, vol. 2, *From the Reformation to the Present*, rev. ed. (Louisville: Westminster John Knox, 2017), 34.

Wright.[20] He prefers a more Reformed approach over what he perceives to be a Lutheran disconnect between justification and sanctification. He articulates Paul's doctrine of justification this way: "The new world has been inaugurated, God's promise to Abraham (to bless the whole world through his family) has been fulfilled, and Jesus has been vindicated—and so all those who belonged to Jesus were vindicated as well! . . . Justification is God's declaration that someone is in the right, is a member of the sin-forgiven covenant family." A key to Wright's reinterpretation is translating the Greek phrase *pistis Christou* not as "faith *in* Christ," as it is usually translated in the Bible, but as "faith *of* Christ." In other words, Wright argues that Paul taught we are not saved by *our* faith, but by the faithfulness of Christ, which we appropriate by faith.

One advantage of Wright's approach is that it anchors our salvation in the biblical story. In God's covenantal faithfulness, Israel's history required a faithful Israelite—Jesus Christ. It is not that the judge's status is imputed to create a moral fiction (that we are righteous or moral as defined by the law); instead, in the "court's" decision God creates or grants a status by declaration, and we thereby become members of God's true family. The Messiah's death under the curse of the law (Gal. 3:13) is more than a simplistic exchange. In Paul's logic, God's promises to Abraham were stuck in the Deuteronomic curse and could not go forward in history to their fulfillment. Jesus the Messiah came to bear the covenantal curse in himself, so that the new covenant blessings might flow out at last to the whole world.

Now justification so understood is connected to the life of the Christian: the covenant agreement always included the law (Torah), and it was to be kept not to *earn* membership (which Paul argues against), but in order to *express* and *maintain* membership as people identified with the faithful Israelite who kept the covenant—Jesus Christ.[21]

20. See N. T. Wright, *Justification: God's Plan and Paul's Vision* (Downers Grove, IL: InterVarsity, 2009), for what follows.

21. John Piper has taken issue with Wright's interpretation of Paul (as have others) in a rather heated exchange on the part of both parties. Piper argues for the more traditional penal substitutionary view of the atonement. See John Piper, *The Future of Justification: A Reponse to N. T. Wright* (Wheaton, IL: Crossway, 2007), and N. T. Wright's subsequent responses in *Justification: God's Plan and Paul's Vision* (2009; repr. with a new introduction, Downers Grove, IL: InterVarsity, 2016).

9

Who Is the Holy Spirit, and What Does the Holy Spirit Do? Pneumatology

We Pray the "Epiclesis" That Invokes the Holy Spirit's Active Presence in Communion

If we were in a liturgical service, at this point the person celebrating communion would pray what has been called the *epiclesis* (Greek for "called upon"). It is a request to the Father to send the Holy Spirit to consecrate (set apart) the bread and wine for this special use and, at the same time, to consecrate those who will be receiving this bread and wine. The practice goes far back in church history, though it fell out of use in the Western church during the Middle Ages, only to make a comeback in more recent times. It has always been part of the Eastern church's liturgy to mark the point at which the bread and wine become the body and blood of Christ. Those in the Western church who believe that something happens with the bread and wine during communion mark the change at the point when the words of institution (e.g., Matt. 26:26–29; 1 Cor. 11:23–26) are pronounced.

A typical epiclesis is this one used in the American Lutheran church:

> And we implore you mercifully to accept our praise and thanksgiving and, with your Word and Holy Spirit, to bless us, your servants, and these your own gifts of bread and wine; that we and all who share in the body and blood

of your Son may be filled with Heavenly peace and joy and, receiving the forgiveness of sin, may be sanctified in soul and body, and have our portion with all your saints.[1]

Simon Chan has made a profound observation about the significance of the epiclesis in the communion liturgy: "The Eucharist is where the past and future are effectively brought together in the present through the epiclesis. . . . The epiclesis represents the most distinctive mark of ecclesial existence between the ascension and the parousia."[2] What Chan means is that when we celebrate the Eucharist we are not only remembering a past event—the Last Supper that Jesus had with his disciples—but we are also reliving that meal in the present and, in a proleptic way, experiencing the coming Banquet of the Lamb, when Jesus once again drinks the wine with all of us in the Father's kingdom (Matt. 26:29). But the present time in which we celebrate this is the time between Christ's ascension (forty days after the resurrection) and Christ's parousia (the future "return" or appearance of Christ), and it is the interval between the past and the future when Christ is present to us *through the Holy Spirit*—the same divine person who is requested to be present in the epiclesis and who Jesus said *would* be present to us in this in-between time (John 7:39; 14:25–26; 16:4–15). The answer to the question about the Third Article of the Apostles' Creed (i.e., the last paragraph, which begins "I believe in the Holy Spirit") in Martin Luther's Small Catechism beautifully articulates the role of the Holy Spirit in this interim:

> I believe that by my own understanding or strength I cannot believe in Jesus Christ my Lord or come to him, but instead the Holy Spirit has called me through the gospel, enlightened me with gifts, made me holy and kept me in the true faith, just as he calls, gathers, enlightens, and makes holy the whole Christian church on earth and keeps it with Jesus Christ in the one common, true faith. Daily in this Christian church the Holy Spirit abundantly forgives all sins—mine and those of all believers. On the Last Day the Holy Spirit will raise me and all the dead and will give to me and all believers in Christ eternal life. This is most certainly true.[3]

1. See Paul F. Bradshaw and Maxwell E. Johnson, *The Eucharistic Liturgies: Their Evolution and Interpretation* (Collegeville, MN: Pueblo Books, 2012), 328. The early history and evolution of the epiclesis is discussed on pp. 38–44 and 121–23. This is a case in which the *orandi* followed the *credendi*.

2. Simon Chan, *Liturgical Theology* (Downers Grove, IL: InterVarsity, 2006), 37.

3. "The Small Catechism," in *The Book of Concord: The Confessions of the Evangelical Lutheran Church*, ed. Robert Kolb and Timothy J. Wengert, trans. Charles Arand, Eric Gritsch, Robert Kolb, William Russell, James Schaaf, Jane Strohl, and Timothy J. Wengert (Minneapolis: Fortress, 2000), 355–56.

All that we have said so far reminds us that when it comes to the liturgy and prayers such as the epiclesis, we are not just going through the motions of ritual, but we are asking the Spirit to use liturgical practices to enrich our Christ-infused lives so that the church will be built up to serve the world that God is in the process of redeeming. And so we turn our attention to the Third Person of the Trinity—the Holy Spirit.

Who Is the Holy Spirit?

In some ways and for various reasons we sense more mystery attached to the Holy Spirit than to the Father and the Son, yet the Holy Spirit has been active since the beginning. The Spirit was present at the creation (Gen. 1:2). The Spirit empowered Israel's leaders in the time of the judges (e.g., Gideon in Judg. 6:34). Kings such as David were anointed with the Spirit (e.g., 1 Sam. 16:13). The Spirit spoke through the prophets (e.g., Isa. 61:1; 2 Pet. 1:21). The Spirit came upon Mary at the conception of Jesus (Luke 1:35), and it was the Spirit who anointed Jesus at his baptism (John 1:32–33) and then guided Jesus into the wilderness to be tempted (Luke 4:1). Believers begin their Christian lives by the Spirit (John 3:5–8; Acts 2:38) and can call God "Father" because of the Spirit (Rom. 8:15–16; Gal. 4:6). The Christian church came to life through the Spirit's descent on the day of Pentecost (Acts 2:1–33), an event on the liturgical calendar fifty days after Easter that has been celebrated as a feast day since at least the third century.

The deity of the Holy Spirit was contested in the early church but was settled on the heels of the debates about the divinity of Jesus that we discussed in chapter 5. Just as Athanasius argued against an Arian Christ who was a creature, so Basil the Great argued against the semi-Arian Pneumatomachians or "Spirit-fighters" who denied the deity of the Spirit.[4] Much of his late-fourth-century argument was based on the church's use of prepositions in its worship when referring to the Holy Spirit. Early in his treatise he wrote: "Lately when I pray with the people, some of those present observed that I render the glory due to God in both ways, namely, *to* the Father, *with* the Son together *with* the Holy Spirit, and *to* the Father, *through* the Son, *in* the Holy Spirit."[5] And he concluded: "Therefore, in worship the Holy Spirit is inseparable from the Father and the Son, for if you are outside of him, you

---

4. See Basil the Great, *On the Holy Spirit*, trans. Stephen M. Hildebrand (Crestwood, NY: St. Vladimir's Seminary Press, 2011).

5. Basil the Great, *On the Holy Spirit*, 29 (1, 3) (italics added). He argues on the basis of other prepositions used in worship as well—*in* and *from*.

will not worship at all while if you are *in* him, you will in no way separate him from God—at least no more than you will remove light from the objects of sight. For it is impossible to see the Image of the invisible God, except in the illumination of the Spirit, and it is impossible for him who fixes his eyes on the image to separate the light from the image."[6]

Just as we saw in the battle against Arianism, so here liturgical practices such as prayers and baptism in the name of the Father, Son, and Holy Spirit demanded recognition that the Spirit was fully God; otherwise, the church was baptizing in the name of God and a creature. Basil made this clear in his treatise: "For he who does not believe the Spirit does not believe the Son, and he who does not believe the Son, does not believe the Father. 'For he cannot say "Jesus is Lord" except in the Holy Spirit' (1 Cor. 12.3). . . . Such a person is bereft of true worship, for he cannot worship the Son except in the Holy Spirit, and he cannot call upon the Father, except in the Spirit of adopted sonship."[7]

This divine parity was then made clear in the Nicene Creed as revised at Constantinople (381)—the creed as we have it today, confessing belief in the Holy Spirit who is "worshiped and glorified together with the Father and the Son."

It should be obvious that the issue at stake in establishing the deity of the Son—our salvation—was equally the issue at stake in establishing the deity of the Spirit.

We can infer the Spirit's deity from New Testament references. The apostles Peter and Paul seem to equate the Spirit with deity in Acts 5:3–4 and 1 Corinthians 3:16–17. Various Scriptures ascribe to the Holy Spirit certain attributes and actions associated with deity (e.g., Luke 1:35; John 3:5–8; Rom. 8:11; 1 Cor. 2:10–11; Titus 3:5; Heb. 9:14).

The establishment of the Spirit's deity brings us back to our confession that God is one being in three persons. There is a theological formula that goes by a fancy Latin phrase: *opera Trinitatis ad extra indivisa sunt*, "the external works of the Trinity are undivided." It reminds us that even though we appropriate to one of the triune persons certain works of God in relation to the world, they are never really separate in these works. Even in the creed we appropriate creation to the Father, redemption to the Son, and our sanctification to the Spirit.

---

6. Basil the Great, *On the Holy Spirit*, 103 (26, 64) (italics added). Note that Basil admits that the Bible nowhere attests to the worship of the Holy Spirit (107–8 [27, 68]), but his argument is based on giving equal status to written Scriptures and the unwritten tradition of the apostles *and* nonbiblical customs, such as the sign of the cross, facing east in worship, the epiclesis, threefold baptism for each person of the Trinity, and anointing with oil (see 104–5 [27, 66] and 111 [29, 71]). This appeal to language and traditions outside the Bible makes sense here since the canon was just coming into its final form when he wrote his treatise.

7. Basil the Great, *On the Holy Spirit*, 59 (11, 27). Cf. 107 (27, 68).

But as we saw in chapter 4, the inner life of the Trinity involves a perichoretic unity in which the three cannot be severed. And so, we express this worship of the three mutually indwelling persons simultaneously, even if we are praying to the Father or praising the Son. (There are no prayers or worship of the Holy Spirit in the Bible, but they begin to appear as early as the third century.)

The confession of God's triune existence as three persons in one God has been denied by some fringe groups with regard to the Holy Spirit. Groups like the Way International deny the personhood of the Spirit, wanting only to refer to "it" as a gift or power. But biblical references suggest that the Holy Spirit is to be thought of as a person. Personal pronouns are used in referring to the *pneuma* (Spirit) in John 16:13–14, and in John 14:16, which associates the Spirit with personal works, such as glorifying Jesus and acting as an Advocate or Comforter (depending on the translation). The Spirit engages in personal behaviors and responses, such as being lied to, being grieved, teaching, reminding, and interceding (see John 14:26; Acts 5:3–4; 15:28; Rom. 8:26; 1 Cor. 12:11; Eph. 4:30). And all of this reinforces the title given to the Holy Spirit in the Nicene Creed: Lord!

An Introduction to the Doctrine of Sanctification

As we pointed out in the previous chapter, justification and sanctification are like two sides of the same coin. They are inseparable yet distinct moments of grace in the Christian life. If justification has to do with our identification with Christ that makes us acceptable to God, sanctification has to do with the relation between God's sovereign work in our lives and the believer's participation in that work.

This raises a bundle of questions: How are we to understand the believer's conquest of sin? What *is* sin in the *believer's* life? How seriously are we to take God's call to be "perfect"? What is the relationship between the "old nature" and the "new nature"? What is the function of the law in the believer's life? And just what *is* the role of the Holy Spirit in all of this?

With regard to this doctrine the key biblical passage is Romans 6–8, where the apostle Paul says that we have died to sin and should not live in sin any longer, yet he admits that he does what he should not and does not do what he should, so he ends up praising God that everything will work out in the end.[8]

Much of what we have to say about sanctification in the Roman Catholic tradition and to some extent in the Orthodox tradition will be taken up in our

---

8. Other significant passages having to do with sanctification include 2 Cor. 7:1; Phil. 3:12–14; Heb. 12:14; and 1 Pet. 1:15–16.

discussion of the sacraments in chapter 11. In this chapter we will discuss sanctification in the context of three Protestant traditions: Lutheran, Reformed, and Holiness/Pentecostal. There are subtle differences between the first two, but significant theological differences lie between the first two and the third.

The Lutheran View of Sanctification

One Lutheran theologian has defined sanctification as "the art of getting used to justification."[9] It is our being grasped by the fact that God alone justifies us by his unconditional promise. In other words, sanctification *is* the justified life, not something added to justification. The term refers to our being captivated more and more by the fullness and unconditionality of God's grace.

Another way to put this would be to emphasize the opposite: self-justification. An apocryphal story about Martin Luther has the devil tempting Luther with the accusation, "Luther, you're a sinner!" The hope is that Martin would revert to self-justification with a comeback such as, "No, I am pretty good." But Martin did not take the bait, and instead responded, "I know, and Jesus Christ came to die for sinners like me." The Christian life is simply a life lived not in self-confidence, but in the confidence that we have been made fully acceptable to God through the work of Christ.

The Spirit nourishes our faith through the Word and the sacraments, but in other ways we might not even be fully aware of how God is working in our inner life. For Luther our conquest of sin is a victory based on God's work alone, and, as such, it is a hidden work. (Luther often talked about the *deus absconditus*—the hidden God, which only the eyes of faith can see, even on the cross.) The Spirit's work is often quiet and secretive in the Christian's life. We may not even recognize it. Luther even claimed that outwardly there might not be much difference between a Christian and a decent honest person.[10]

The old nature is dead—that which attempted to exist and act under the law, producing good works to justify the self (see 2 Cor. 5:17). We have made a radical break with that nature. In other words, sanctification is not merely a repair of the old self, but the death of the old self and resurrection to a new life—living as a new creation. And so, as we mentioned in the previous chapter, the Christian experiences the simultaneity of the dead old self and the raised

9. For this definition and what follows in this paragraph, see Gerhard O. Forde's contribution in *Christian Spirituality: Five Views of Sanctification*, ed. Donald Alexander (Downers Grove, IL: InterVarsity, 1989).

10. See Luther's commentary on Galatians 4:6 in Martin Luther, *Galatians*, Crossway Classic Commentaries, series eds. Alister McGrath and J. I. Packer (Wheaton, IL: Crossway, 1998), 203–9.

new self—*simul justus et peccator*. Still, sanctification is a lifelong process: "This life, therefore, is not righteousness, but growth in righteousness; not health, but healing; not being, but becoming; not rest, but exercise. We are not yet what we shall be, but we are growing toward it."[11]

What role does the law play then? It does not lead to holiness, since it is part of the old nature's attempts to justify self by trying to keep the law. Thus, the law can only lead to repentance and drive us to grace, demonstrating that we are in need of salvation that we cannot provide for ourselves (Rom. 7:7; 8:1–4; Gal. 2:16–21). For humanity the law does have a civic function in the present age. So for Luther the law has two functions: it convicts of sin and it restrains evil in civil society.

The Reformed View of Sanctification

The key phrase in the Reformed understanding of sanctification—indeed, in Paul and in John Calvin—is "in Christ" or "union with Christ."[12] Sanctification involves living out the reality of our union with Christ. What is essential in relation to sin and to God is not the believer's past, but Christ's past (and present and future). The Christian is dead to sin and alive to God *in union with* Jesus Christ (see Rom. 6:1–14; Col. 3:1–3). The Christian is to become like Jesus Christ (John 13:15; 1 Pet. 2:21), and, in doing so, she is transformed into her true humanity. For Calvin, sanctification is becoming fully human again.[13]

So the conquest of sin happens through our union with Christ that takes place through the Spirit and is exercised by faith. But the conquest is not instantaneous. The new nature exists along with the old nature: "death to sin" means we are freed from the power of sin, but not from its presence and influence in our lives. So we *reckon* ourselves dead to sin, and we *act* accordingly (Rom. 6:3–11).

This reality means that the Christian life will always include tension (Rom. 7). The presence of the Holy Spirit does not raise us *above* spiritual conflict; it *produces* spiritual conflict. It is because we have the first fruits of the Spirit that we groan for our redemption (Rom. 8:22–23). In fact, Calvin might even say that the more closely one recognizes his union with Christ, the more sensitive he will be to the presence of sin in his life. As Calvin puts it, "The

11. Luther, quoted in Philip H. Pfatteicher, *Journey into the Heart of God: Living the Liturgical Year* (New York: Oxford University Press, 2013), 325.

12. A good introduction to the Reformed view is found in Todd Billings, *Union with Christ: Reframing Theology and Ministry for the Church* (Grand Rapids: Baker Academic, 2011).

13. John Calvin, *Institutes of the Christian Religion*, ed. John T. McNeill, trans. Ford Lewis Battles (Philadelphia: Westminster John Knox, 1960), 1.15.4.

life of a Christian man is a continual effort and exercise in the mortification of the flesh, till it is utterly slain, and God's Spirit reigns in us. Therefore, I think he has profited greatly who . . . having been engrated into the life and death of Christ, he may give attention to continual repentance. Truly, they who are held by a real loathing of sin cannot do otherwise. For no one ever hates sin unless he has previously been seized with a love of righteousness."[14]

The Reformed tradition differs from the Lutheran regarding the function of the law in the believer's life. Calvin agreed with Luther that the law convicts us of sin and restrains evil in civic life. But whereas conviction of sin was the primary use of the law for Luther, for Calvin the primary function was a third use in the believer's life: the law gives form or shape to the gospel and defines what a human being should be.[15] The law is one of the ways that God graciously provides for our sanctification (along with the sacraments, the church, and God's providence). The concrete imperatives arise out of the indicatives of grace (see the "therefore" links in Rom. 12:1–2; Eph. 4:1–3). In fact, when Calvin discusses the Ten Commandments in his *Institutes*, he does not begin with the first commandment, but he begins where the biblical text begins—with the identification of the Lawgiver as the One who redeemed Israel out of bondage in Egypt (Exod. 20:1–2). In other words, the Lawgiver is the Redeemer, and if Israel wants to remain free from bondage, she will keep God's commands. This is why the twentieth-century Reformed theologian Karl Barth can discuss the Ten Commandments as "permissions" in volume III/2 of his *Church Dogmatics*. "Thou shalt not kill" means the Christian has permission to protect life.

The Wesleyan-Holiness and Pentecostal Views of Sanctification

We include in this section both the Wesleyan-Holiness and Pentecostal traditions because they emphasize the Spirit-filled life and personal experience in ways that differ from the Lutheran and Reformed traditions. One might say that they distinguish "levels" of the sanctified life, though these two related traditions differ when it comes to the issue of *glossolalia* ("speaking in tongues") as a legitimate variety of Christian experience.[16] There are even differences in how sanctification is understood *within* each of these two

14. Calvin, *Institutes*, 3.3.20. This is why, for Calvin, faith comes before repentance.
15. Calvin, *Institutes*, 2.7.12.
16. In some respects the Pentecostal movement evolved out of the Holiness tradition. Pentecostalism gave birth to the charismatic movement (those who emphasize the contemporary relevance of the Holy Spirit's gifts and who use more expressive forms of worship), but the latter now embraces more than just Pentecostals.

A Hymn by Charles Wesley, May 21, 1738

Granted is the Saviour's prayer,
Sent the gracious Comforter;
Promise of our parting Lord,
Jesus now to heaven restored.

Christ, who now gone up on high
Captive leads captivity;
While his foes from him receive
Grace, that God with man may live.

Never will he thence depart,
Inmate of an humble heart;

Carrying on his work within,
Striving till he casts out sin.

Come, divine and peaceful Guest,
Enter our devoted breast;
Holy Ghost, our hearts inspire,
Kindle there the Gospel-fire.

Now descend, and shake the earth;
Wake us into second birth;
Life divine in us renew,
Thou the gift and giver too!

From John Lawson, *A Thousand Tongues: The Wesley Hymns as a Guide to Scriptural Teaching* (Atlanta: Paternoster, 1987), 76.

traditions, but we will describe something like the lowest common denominator in what follows.

John Wesley (1703–1791) drew a distinction between sanctification and "entire sanctification," referencing 1 Thessalonians 5:23. All justified believers are "sanctified"; sanctification begins at one's spiritual birth and involves a lifelong process. These are the children of God in the "lowest sense"—those who have been forgiven of their sins. Those believers who later experience an instantaneous gift of God's grace of being made perfect in love (*wholly* committed to Jesus Christ; loving God with *all* their heart) are "entirely sanctified." These are children of God in the "highest sense"—those who have freedom from sin. This is what Wesley called "Christian Perfection," something that is attainable in this life.[17]

Some in the Holiness tradition have used biblical typology to make this distinction between the initial stages of the Christian life and higher levels of sanctification, such as the difference between the exodus and the conquest of Canaan, or the difference between Easter and Pentecost. Entire sanctification is based on a "second work of grace" or "second blessing," which purifies (circumcises) the heart from the sinful "flesh" through the fullness of the Holy Spirit. This involves a postconversion cleansing action of the Spirit that enhances the believer's holiness and radically removes the bent to sin. This later came to be referred to as "being filled with the Spirit," which is

---

17. See John Wesley, *A Plain Account of Christian Perfection*, available in many editions.

sometimes equated with the "baptism of the Holy Spirit" (see Acts 15:8–9; Rom. 2:28–29).

We could talk about this as a difference between receiving Christ and receiving the Holy Spirit. There is evidence of this distinction in the New Testament: John 14:5–20 and Acts 2:4 (Christ's disciples and the first Jewish believers); Acts 8:14–17 (the Samaritans); and Acts 19:1–7 (the Ephesian Gentiles). Those in the Holiness tradition (especially in Pentecostal circles) insist that this second work of grace, when the Holy Spirit comes upon believers, is normative for all Christians. In contrast, those especially in the Reformed tradition have argued that these are onetime events in the New Testament church's experience that confirmed for each group (Jews, Samaritan half-Jews, and non-Jewish Gentiles) that their inclusion in the Christian church is as legitimate as any other group. Once all were assured that they were equally part of the body of Christ, a separate reception of the Holy Spirit subsequent to conversion was not to be expected. This view might appeal to the postbaptismal imposition of hands related to the gift of the Holy Spirit in the Western church since the second century and the postbaptismal chrismation for the gift or seal of the Holy Spirit in the Eastern church since the fourth century.[18]

Wesley believed that "entire sanctification" roots out what remains of the "old self" so that one is empowered with a perfect love for God. What counts is intent or will or motives. Wesley did not think that "entire sanctification" meant we are flawless in our behavior or free from the consequences of sin. Christian perfection refers to the quality and purity of our love for God and others. It refers only to voluntary transgressions, not to involuntary immoral acts due to psychological motivations beyond our control, ignorance, mistaken judgment, and the like. But both types of transgressions (voluntary and involuntary) need the atoning work of Christ. (Precedent for this distinction is found in 1 John 3:4–8 and in the difference between witting and unwitting sins found in Leviticus; regarding the latter, the Day of Atonement took care of both, while the former alone were dealt with through daily sacrifices.) How does one arrive at "entire sanctification"? Wesley taught that a Christian must desire it and pray for it with a repentant heart. The Holy Spirit makes it a reality in an instant, but it can also be taken away.

The law has a positive function in the believer's life in much of the Holiness tradition. Works of piety and a disciplined life are typical. The Reformed tradition would never allow that perfection can be attained in this life; all are to be making progress, whether crawling or running. But the Reformed and

---

18. See Maxwell E. Johnson, *Praying and Believing in Early Christianity: The Interplay between Christian Worship and Doctrine* (Collegeville, MN: Liturgical Press, 2013), 55.

Holiness traditions have not considered the law an enemy of the Christian, as Luther often taught. As a result, those who follow in Calvin's or Wesley's wake sometimes tend toward legalism, while those who follow in Luther's steps have sometimes been accused of antinomianism (lawlessness).

We have mentioned previously that maturity in the Christian life—sanctification—can only happen in communion with the body of Christ. To that doctrine we now turn.

10

What Is the Church? Ecclesiology

We Continue the "Liturgy of the Table" with the "Passing of the Peace of Christ"

Typically, before the eucharistic prayers the pastor or priest will say the words of assurance of pardon or pronounce the absolution, which we previously referred to, and then invite the people to share with each other the peace of Christ that they have just experienced in God's gracious act of forgiveness. According to John's Gospel account (John 20:19), the words come from Jesus's first declaration to his disciples after his resurrection: We say to each other, "The peace of the Lord be with you."

William Dyrness points out that passing the peace is not simply saying "Good morning" to our fellow churchgoers:

> The act suggests that we do more than simply forget their slights and trespasses against us; we actually reach out to them in love and communion. . . . Though I often do not feel like greeting people, the very act of doing so reminds me of my relationship to them and of our mutual responsibilities. And carrying out this act frequently brings with it feelings of love and unity. Here we model God's action in which God reaches out and embraces us in Christ and calls us to the ministry of reconciliation. We embrace each other on behalf of God.[1]

1. William A. Dyrness, "Confession and Assurance: Sin and Grace," in *A More Profound Alleluia: Theology and Worship in Harmony*, ed. Leanne Van Dyk (Grand Rapids: Eerdmans, 2005), 49.

The fact that we need and extend reconciliation reminds us of this: we do not profess faith *in* the church. To do so would be to put our faith in ourselves, since we broken humans *are* the church. And if we put our faith in the church, we will eventually be disappointed. As someone said, if you find a perfect church, don't join it, because you will spoil it. We believe in Christ to whom the church witnesses—the Lord of the church. Many who have misplaced their faith in the church have been disillusioned and have rejected both church *and* Lord in the process.

Instead, the church is the community *within* which the Christian professes her faith. It is the community that has passed on the faith and transmitted the Scriptures for generations. It is the community in which faith is born, nourished, lived out, and proclaimed. Simon Chan puts it so well: "The church is our nourishing Mother, and we are entirely dependent on her for our existence as Christians. We are not saved as individuals first and then incorporated into the church; rather, to be a Christian is to be incorporated into the church by baptism and nourished with the spiritual food of the body and blood of Christ in the Eucharist. Failure to understand this fact has led to a reduction of the church's role to a largely sociological one of a service provider catering to individual believers' spiritual needs."[2]

Said differently, it is impossible to *become* and to *be* a Christian apart from the church. To be a Christian is to be part of Christ's body. There is no individual Christianity. Even most of the occurrences of the pronoun *you* in the Greek New Testament are plural.

Biblical Images of the Church

Strangely, the Gospel accounts speak of the church only twice. In Matthew 16:18 Jesus responds to Peter that "on this rock" the church will be built.[3] In Matthew 18:17 Jesus gives instructions about conflict resolution within the church. What is odd is that, as far as we know, Jesus gave no further instructions about the church.

Actually, the New Testament word we translate as "church" is the Greek word *ekklēsia*, derived from the verb *kalein* (to call) and literally meaning "to call out."[4] Or, in a more idiomatic translation, it simply means "assembly."

2. Simon Chan, *Liturgical Theology* (Downers Grove, IL: InterVarsity, 2006), 24.

3. Protestants and Roman Catholics disagree about what Jesus was referring to when he spoke of "this rock" (which is *petros* in Greek). The former insist that this had to do with Peter's *confession* of Christ as the Messiah, while the latter insist that Jesus was referring to Peter's *person*.

4. The English word *church* actually derives from the Scottish *kirk* and the German *kirche*, which find their origins in the Greek *kyriakon* and, ultimately, *kyrios* (Lord), so that the origin of our word technically means "belonging to the Lord."

In secular circles this Greek word referred to an assembly of citizens who had been summoned by a herald. (See Acts 19:32, 41; 19:39. One reference is to a "mob," while the other is to a "lawful assembly.") So if we had only this to go on, "church" would simply be an assembly of people meeting for a particular purpose. Fortunately, we have more to help us.

The Septuagint (the Greek translation of the Hebrew Bible, abbreviated LXX) always translates the Hebrew *qahal* as *ekklēsia*. While *qahal* can refer to an assembly of any type, the Hebrew Bible often used the phrase *qahal Yahweh*, meaning "community of God." So the LXX's use of *ekklēsia* for a worshiping community, especially in the Psalms, made it the most suitable biblical word for the early meetings of New Testament believers.[5] In fact, the word refers to the Christian community 109 times in the New Testament.

Sometimes it is used of the *local* assembly to designate all those who profess their allegiance to Christ in a particular locale (e.g., 1 Cor. 4:17; 7:17; 2 Cor. 11:8; Gal. 1:22; 1 Thess. 1:1). At other times it refers to the *universal* church—the spiritual unity of all believers in Christ (e.g., Acts 8:1–3; 9:31; 1 Cor. 12:28; 15:9; Eph. 1:22–23; Col. 1:18).

But note this: the universal church is always the universal fellowship of believers who meet visibly in local assemblies. It is not that the universal church is the sum total of many individual churches. It is the universal church manifested in or made visible in a particular locality. Notice Paul's language: "to the church of God that is *in* Corinth" (1 Cor. 1:2; 2 Cor. 1:1). The local church fully manifests or represents the assembly of Christ. It is not a subdivision of the "real" church, nor does it merely belong to the "church." The local church *is* the church in that it participates in the undivided grace of God and in the life of the Triune God.

This point is significant because it means that when a local church baptizes someone it is doing so on behalf of the entire church, such that when a person moves to another local church she is not rebaptized if she has already been baptized with water in the name of the Father, Son, and Holy Spirit. (There are, of course, issues that come up with infant baptism in churches that baptize only adult believers. We will discuss that in the next chapter.) For instance, if a Protestant who has been baptized decides to enter the Roman Catholic Church, he is not rebaptized, but is welcomed through a rite of reconciliation. In addition, when we participate in a local church's communion service, we are participating with far more than just those whom we can see in the building.

---

5. See Scott W. Hahn, *The Kingdom of God as Liturgical Empire: A Theological Commentary on 1–2 Chronicles* (Grand Rapids: Baker Academic, 2012), 64–65.

Figure 4
Paul's Ecclesiology

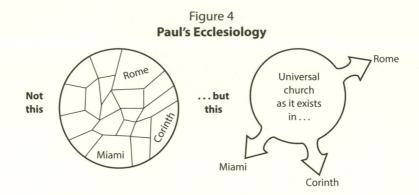

Speaking of the building, we should point out that the New Testament never uses *ekklēsia* to refer to a church's building. Today we often speak as if we are "going *to* church," when, technically, we ought to be saying that the church is going to the building where it will worship before leaving that building to infiltrate society with the gospel. In other words, the church exists 24/7 wherever its members are. Accordingly, Paul Bradshaw traced the early development of the church's designation of Sunday as the day it assembled for worship, pointing out that Sunday, then, became the day for the manifestation or epiphany of the church, revealed in the celebration of the Eucharist, while during the rest of the week the church was dispersed and "hidden."[6]

Beyond what is conjured up in our imagination when we see the phrase *qahal Yahweh*, the New Testament contains many images of the church, including these:

Temple/building of God	1 Corinthians 3:16; Ephesians 2:20–22; 1 Peter 2:5
Fellowship of saints	Romans 1:17
Royal priesthood	1 Peter 2:9
Bride of Christ	Ephesians 5:22–32
New creation	2 Corinthians 5:13; Galatians 6:15
Family	Ephesians 2:19
Vineyard	Colossians 1:13
Kingdom of Christ	Colossians 1:13
Flock	John 10:1–15, 26–30

While each deserves explanation, two other biblical images are particularly important.

6. Paul F. Bradshaw, *Early Christian Worship: A Basic Introduction to Ideas and Practices*, 2nd ed. (Collegeville, MN: Liturgical Press, 2010), 85.

First, the church is referred to as the "people of God" (*laos theou* in Greek).[7] This is beautifully expressed in 1 Peter 2:9–10 and in Romans 9:25–26. Those who were not a people have been made a people by God's grace. This became one of the two major images of the church that were unpacked in Vatican Council II's "Constitution on the Church."[8]

We notice first that in this image "people" does not refer to humanity in general, but to a *particular* people. (In fact, in the King James Version of 1 Peter 2:9 the phrase is translated "God's peculiar people"!) This is a people that is distinguished from all other people. And what distinguishes this people is that it is "of God."

As God's own people, the church is an assembly of people summoned only by God's call (see Eph. 1:4–5, 11; 1 Pet. 2:9–10). It is a covenant community that has been elected or chosen by God. In other words, it is a people whose existence derives only from God's own action, not human ingenuity. It is God's purposes, promises, and covenant that have formed this people—a people who were not a people until God's gracious act. So this people belongs to God, not to any nation, tribe, race, or political party. "Of God" transcends all human distinctions. And because this people is formed only by God's grace, God's chosen can make no prideful or egotistical claims. In fact, as God is open, so this people must be radically open to the world. It can claim no exclusive privileges for itself.

This title, "people of God," links the New Testament church to Israel (see Exod. 6:6–7; Lev. 26:9, 11–12; Rom. 11:2, 26–29). It conveys the historical continuity of God's redemption program, relating the contemporary Christian generation to the historic community whose origin stemmed from God's covenant promises and whose pilgrimage has been sustained by God's call and faithfulness (recall the biblical story we outlined in chapter 1). In fact, in proclamations of the New Testament church, the "God of our ancestors"—namely, Abraham, Isaac, and Jacob—is the one who set all of this in motion with Jesus (Acts 3:13; 5:30; 7:32; 13:16–33; 22:14). The God who chose those ancestors is the very same God who has elected the church; they are all God's people. The New Testament associates the church with Old Testament Israel, and the "old" covenant is related to the "new" covenant (Eph. 2:11–22; Heb.

7. The Greek word *laos*, which means "people," is the word from which we get "laity," referring to the people in the church who are not ordained.

8. Vatican Council II (1962–65) was a Roman Catholic council that was called by Pope John XXIII and continued by Pope Paul VI. The other major image of the church in this document (also referred to as *Lumen Gentium*, the first two words of the document: "light of the nations") is "archsacrament to the world." As we will see in the next chapter, a sacrament is a visible sign of invisible grace, so the church is to be the most significant visible manifestation of God's grace.

8:8–13). Furthermore, as the people of God, the church is described in the New Testament as a new temple and a new kingdom, founded on a rock, built on the Son of God—all Davidic images found in Chronicles, so it portrays the church as a restoration of the kingdom of David and as the temple of Solomon. Recalling what we said above, it is even more profound, then, that the disciples appropriate to themselves the title of the Old Testament congregation of God—the *qahal Yahweh*.[9]

And just as the people of Israel began with the pilgrim journey of Abraham and all of his descendants—"strangers and pilgrims" (Heb. 11:13) looking for a home—so the church is a people on pilgrimage that began with a turn in a new direction (repentance) to head home to a place we've not yet been. As Philip Pfatteicher discusses, this pilgrimage is the "principal organizing image" for Lent as the church makes its journey "to a specific holy place, Jesus's cross and tomb and to the life that lies beyond."[10]

One major difference between the New Testament people of God and Old Testament Israel is that the former are referred to as the "new race in Christ" (Rom. 5:14–15). They are set apart from the masses by the action of God in Christ, completed by the Holy Spirit as the Spirit takes up residence in the church and works Christ's holiness into the lives of believers. Hence, such folks are called "saints"—a "holy nation" sanctified (set apart) in Christ (1 Cor. 1:2; 1 Pet. 2:9).

A second prominent image of the church is the "body of Christ." This may be *the* New Testament image of the church, and it is certainly Paul's favored description of the church. In fact, it is exclusively Pauline (see Rom. 12:4–8; 1 Cor. 12:12–31; Eph. 4:1–16; Col. 1:18).

This image captures several characteristics of the church. There is unity yet diversity: the body has many different members that have various functions, gifts, strengths, and even honor, yet each of them serves the common good and supports the confession of Christ's lordship as head of the body. As with the human body, in which each part is organically connected to the others, so with Christ's church; as Paul puts it, we are "members one of another." As an organic whole, growth ensues as the parts work together toward the common goal of maturity. The head of the body is Christ, and as head Christ is sovereign over the body, the source of the church's life, and the sustainer of its life through individual members who serve as channels of nourishment.

9. See Hahn, *Kingdom of God*, 101–2.
10. Philip H. Pfatteicher, *Journey into the Heart of God: Living the Liturgical Year* (New York: Oxford University Press, 2013), 146–48.

Paul's elaboration of this image includes everything that has been said. Beyond that, this image of the church reminds us that the church continues what Jesus began to do and teach (Acts 1:1–8), and though Christ's presence in the world is not exhausted by the church, still, the church is to be the visible sign to the world of God's grace that has come to us in Christ (1 Cor. 3:16–17).

The Marks of the Church

The Protestant Reformers (Martin Luther, John Calvin, and others) were accused of breaking away from the true church, so they had to make the case that *they* were the "true" church.[11] In doing so, it should be noted that Calvin believed that some local Catholic churches were true churches[12] because they shared the true "marks" or characteristics that identify for us where the church is to be found. These marks are twofold: (1) where the Word is rightly preached and heard and (2) where the sacraments are properly administered and received (i.e., as Christ intended).[13] We noted in chapter 3 that Calvin insisted that the main purpose of Scripture is to "show forth Christ"; he also made the same point about the sacraments (in this case, baptism and the Lord's Supper): "Therefore, let it be regarded as a settled principle that the sacraments have the same office as the Word of God: to offer and set forth Christ to us, and in him the treasures of heavenly grace."[14] So, the bottom line is that the Reformers were insisting that the marks of a true church identify a church that makes Christ heard in its proclamation and visible in its practice of the sacraments.

Common to the confession of all three major branches of the Christian church (Roman Catholic, Eastern Orthodox, and Protestant) is the Nicene Creed, and it lists four marks of the church: one, holy, catholic, and apostolic.[15] This presents us with another way of determining where the true church is to be found.

We must recognize at the outset that when we speak of the church as one or holy, we are referring to the spiritual realities of the church that exist as the church lives out its tension between what it *is* and what it *should* be—the

11. For example, Zwingli's successor in Zurich, Heinrich Bullinger, wrote *Das Alt Glaub* (The Old Faith) to argue that the Protestants never left the church that had begun with Adam and Eve.

12. John Calvin, *Institutes of the Christian Religion*, ed. John T. McNeill, trans. Ford Lewis Battles (Philadelphia: Westminster John Knox, 1960), 4.2.12.

13. Calvin, *Institutes*, 4.1.9.

14. Calvin, *Institutes*, 4.14.17.

15. This was added to the original creed at Constantinople in 381.

"already" and "not yet" of what God is up to in the cosmos. The church's nature determines her task. What she is by nature—a Spirit-created and Spirit-united community—must become what she is in fact, in her visible organization and missionary activity. We get a sense of this logic in the very structure of Paul's letters, such as in Ephesians, where he follows up the indicative in chapters 1–3 (what the church is from God's point of view) with the imperative in chapters 4–6 ("therefore," how the church should be living out the indicative in its everyday life). So these four marks are not meant for self-congratulation or for self-justification, but for self-*examination*. The church must always be reforming itself to become in visible reality what it is in essence.

In fact, these marks do not identify the place where such characteristics are exhibited as much as they indicate the tasks that the church must exercise. Charles Van Engen suggests that these marks should be thought of as adverbs rather than as adjectives—the church's unifying, reconciling, sanctifying, and proclaiming force. They describe the missionary action of the church's life in the world—a mission work that is essential to its existence as church much as fire exists by burning.[16]

So, the church is one (Eph. 4:4–6) because if it were not, that would imply a plurality of lords and spirits and gods. But this Spirit-created unity must be maintained over against our proclivities toward individualism and demands for uniformity. (Individuality is not the same thing as individualism, and unity is not the same thing as uniformity.) The church is catholic (Eph. 1:15–23) insofar as its mission is to *all*. The church is holy (Eph. 1:1–14; 4:15–5:1) in that it is set apart to take direction from its head. And the church is apostolic, minimally because it is faithful to the life and teachings of the original apostles.[17]

Authority in the Church

To a large extent the development of authority in the church has been a response to heresies such as gnosticism, which made claims antithetical to the teachings of the apostles. Agreement with what was found in the canon became one of the ways the church could ensure orthodoxy. We have seen that

16. Charles E. Van Engen, *God's Missionary People: Rethinking the Purpose of the Local Church* (Grand Rapids: Baker, 1991), 68. The analogy of fire and burning comes from Emil Brunner's *The Word and the World* (London: Student Christian Movement Press, 1931), 108.

17. There is disagreement about the meaning of this fourth mark. What we have identified as "minimal" is true of all church bodies; what would be "maximal" is Rome's claim that it is apostolic because it can trace the lineage of the bishop of Rome—the pope—back to the apostle Peter.

even though the canon was established by 367, its basic shape was already in place as early as 200. But even the canon was not enough to refute the heretics, since they could twist Scripture to their own use and could claim, as gnostics did, that they had received secret teachings from Christ and the apostles in addition to what was found in the Scriptures.

To refute these heretics, the church relied upon an evolving hierarchy. The New Testament church was loosely structured, with different forms of administration that became more established as it moved into its second century. It is true that all members of the church are "ministers" (Eph. 4:7, 12)—a truth expressed in the "priesthood of all believers." Martin Luther argued that the priesthood of all believers is the law of the church's life, since it flows from Christ's priestly office, in which we all have a share (Heb. 7:25; 1 Pet. 2:5). Luther declared, "God has been so gracious to us that he has stuffed every corner of the world full of God's words" in the form of brothers and sisters.[18] We are priests to and for each other.

But Luther and others recognized we still need offices and servants of the church who administer the sacraments and preach publicly. These proceed from the "priesthood of believers," and we need them to avoid confusion. Of course, this was nothing new; the early church recognized that there are distinctions within the body of believers, not in terms of holiness or prestige, but in terms of gifts, functions, and spheres of ministry. We see at least two tiers of church office or hierarchy in the New Testament: deacons and elders (*presbyteroi*). The latter were also referred to as bishops (*episkopoi*), as we can see in Paul's use of both terms in reference to the same office (Titus 1:5–7).[19]

The early church ordained those who would hold these offices. This practice did not "make" them qualified to take up the mantle. Rather, it recognized that they had already been gifted and called to these ministries by the Holy Spirit. In the ordination liturgy, the church asked the Spirit to empower those whom God had chosen. For instance, these instructions and prayer were recorded in a document from the early third century:

> When a presbyter [elder] is ordained the bishop will lay a hand upon his head, the presbyters [who have already been ordained] likewise touching him, and he shall speak as we said above, as we said before concerning the bishop, praying and saying:

18. Cited in Paul Althaus, *The Theology of Martin Luther*, trans. Robert C. Schultz (Philadelphia: Fortress, 1966), 318.
19. Some scholars do see a distinct role for bishops in the New Testament; see Alistair C. Stewart, *The Original Bishops: Office and Order in the First Christian Communities* (Grand Rapids: Baker Academic, 2014).

God and Father of our Lord Jesus Christ, look upon this your servant and impart the Spirit of grace and counsel of presbyterate so that he might assist and guide your people with a pure heart, as you looked upon the people of your choice and directed Moses to choose presbyters whom you filled with your spirit which you gave to your servant. And now Lord, grant that the Spirit of your grace may be preserved unceasingly in us, filling us and making us worthy to minister to you in simplicity of heart, praising you through your child Jesus Christ, through whom be glory and might to you, with the Holy Spirit in the holy church both now, and to the ages of the ages. Amen.[20]

Early on, the concept of apostolic succession also began to take hold. This is the idea that bishops should be able to trace their appointment back to the original apostles through a sequence of bishops. Here is the way Clement of Rome affirmed it in the year 95 when he was writing to Corinth to argue for the legitimacy of duly appointed church leaders whose position had been challenged by young interlopers:

The Apostles for our sakes received the gospel from the Lord Jesus Christ; Jesus Christ was sent from God. Christ then is from God, and the Apostles from Christ. Both therefore came in due order from the will of God. Having therefore received his instructions and being fully assured through the Resurrection of our Lord Jesus Christ, they went forth with confidence in the word of God and with full assurance of the Holy Spirit, preaching the gospel that the Kingdom of God was about to come. And so, as they preached in the country and in the towns, they appointed their firstfruits (having proved them by the Spirit) to be *bishops and deacons* of them that should believe. . . .

Our Apostles knew also, through our Lord Jesus Christ, that there would be strife over the dignity of the bishop's office. For this reason therefore, having received complete foreknowledge, they *appointed* the aforesaid, and after a time made provision that on their death other approved men should *succeed* to their ministry.[21]

In the second century we begin to see a definite demarcation between elders and bishops (though the words still get used interchangeably from time to time). The transition is not entirely clear, but some evidence of it appears in the letter to the Smyrnaeans from Ignatius, bishop of Syrian Antioch. And

---

20. This comes from the "Apostolic Tradition," which is traditionally ascribed to Hippolytus, probably written ca. 215 in Rome. See Hippolytus, *On the Apostolic Tradition*, trans. with introduction and commentary by Alistair Stewart (Crestwood, NY: St. Vladimir's Seminary Press, 2001), 81–82.

21. Henry Bettenson and Chris Maunder, eds., *Documents of the Christian Church*, 4th ed. (New York: Oxford University Press, 2011), 67 (italics added).

we can see a growing emphasis on the role of the bishop in preserving purity of belief and practice in order to maintain the unity of the church:

> Avoid divisions as the beginning of evils. All of you follow the bishop as Jesus Christ followed the Father, and follow the presbytery as the Apostles; and respect the deacons as the commandment of God. Let no man perform anything pertaining to the church without the bishop. Let that be considered a valid Eucharist over which the bishop presides, or one to whom he commits it. *Wherever the bishop appears, there let the people be, just as, wheresoever Christ Jesus is, there is the Catholic Church.* It is not permitted either to baptize or hold a love-feast [a meal associated with the Lord's Supper] apart from the bishop. But whatever he may approve, that is well-pleasing to God, that everything which you do may be sound and valid.[22]

Finally, in the mid-second century, Bishop Irenaeus wrote a treatise against heretics explicitly teaching apostolic succession with a list of the sequence in Rome, whose bishop is already given primacy:

> When they [heretics] are refuted out of the Scriptures they betake them to accusing the Scriptures themselves as if there were something amiss with them and they carried not authority, because the Scriptures, they say, contain diverse utterances, and because the truth cannot be found in them by those that know not the tradition. For that, they say, has been handed down not by means of writings but by means of the living voice. . . . And this wisdom each one of them claims to be that which he has found by himself, that is, a thing invented. . . .
>
> Yet when we appeal again to that tradition which is derived from the Apostles, and which is *safeguarded in the churches through the successions of presbyters*, they then are adversaries of tradition, claiming to be wiser not only than the presbyters but even than the Apostles, and to have discovered the truth undefiled. . . . Thus it comes about that they now agree neither with the Scriptures nor with tradition. . . .
>
> Those that wish to discern the truth may observe the apostolic tradition made manifest in every church through the world. We can enumerate [list] those who were appointed bishops in the churches by the Apostles, and their successors down to our own day, who never taught, and never knew, absurdities such as these men produce. . . . But as it would be very tedious, in a book of this sort, to enumerate the successions in all the churches, we confound all those [heretics] . . . by pointing to the apostolic tradition and the faith that is preached to men, which has come down to us through the successions of bishops; the tradition and creed of the greatest, the most ancient church, the church known to all men, which was founded and set up at Rome by the two most

22. Bettenson and Maunder, *Documents*, 67 (italics added).

glorious Apostles, Peter and Paul. For with this church, because of its position of leadership and authority, must needs agree every church, that is, the faithful everywhere; for in her the apostolic tradition has always been preserved by the faithful from all parts. [Enumeration follows.][23]

In the late second century these positions were further set in stone by the church's reaction to Montanism. Montanus claimed to be a prophet, along with two women, Prisca and Maximilla, who claimed similar gifts. Maintaining that they received direct revelations that they delivered in a kind of ecstatic utterance as the mouthpiece of the Holy Spirit, they espoused a rigorous lifestyle in light of the imminent return of Jesus and insisted that rejection of what they said amounted to blasphemy against the Holy Spirit. The church held this movement in check, arguing against the manner in which such revelations were received and delivered, as well as the extent of such revelations that went beyond the apostolic era.

It wasn't just the church hierarchy determining who was in and who was out. Creeds served this purpose as well. Creeds (from the Latin *credo*, meaning "I believe") function as contemporary interpretations of Scripture. Consider the Apostles' Creed: it begins with creation and ends with the ultimate destiny of the resurrected—essentially the biblical story from start to finish. Creeds also guard against heresy as summaries of the Faith—a "crash course" in the essentials of Christianity. For this reason creeds have been associated with the "Rule of Faith" (*regula fidei*).

There are two kinds of creeds. Some are known as baptismal creeds. The Apostles' Creed was taken apart and taught to those who were to be baptized on Holy Saturday (the day before Easter Sunday) so that when they were baptized in the name of the Father, Son, and Holy Spirit (Matt. 28:19), they knew exactly what they were affirming when the celebrant asked them, "Do you believe in God the Father Almighty, maker of heaven and earth?" and so on.[24] Other creeds are conciliary; that is, they are the result of councils, as is the case with the Nicene Creed.

These creeds have helped the church to determine who is in and who is out. They are like passwords. Those who can affirm the essentials of the Faith that these creeds articulate are identifying themselves as members of a group of people who share these beliefs.

23. Bettenson and Maunder, *Documents*, 72 (italics added).
24. Maxwell Johnson argues that the Apostles' Creed was originally generated out of the West's practice of using the three creedal questions and answers regarding the Father, Son, and Holy Spirit in the context of conferring baptism. See *The Rites of Christian Initiation: Their Evolution and Interpretation*, rev. ed. (Collegeville, MN: Pueblo Books, 2007), 105–6.

The Apostles' Creed

I believe in God, the Father almighty, creator of heaven and earth.

I believe in Jesus Christ, God's only Son, our Lord, who was conceived by the Holy Spirit, born of the Virgin Mary, suffered under Pontius Pilate, was crucified, died, and was buried; he descended to the dead [or, some read, to hell]. On the third day he rose again; he ascended into heaven, he is seated at the right hand of the Father, and he will come to judge the living and the dead.

I believe in the Holy Spirit, the holy catholic Church, the communion of saints, the forgiveness of sins, the resurrection of the body, and the life everlasting. Amen.

From *Day by Day: The Notre Dame Prayer Book for Students*, ed. Thomas McNally and William G. Storey (Notre Dame, IN: Ave Maria Press, 2004), 52.

Excommunication was one way that the church guarded the gate. This involved literally being ex-communioned, unable to participate in the sacraments of the church, especially the Lord's Supper. Initially three especially grievous sins warranted a person's dismissal from the fellowship: apostasy (denial of Christ), sexual sin, and murder.[25] Knowing who determined excommunication, on what basis, and the terms of readmission needed clarification, however.

Early on some thought that the Lord would grant forgiveness and a second chance at least once to a repentant sinner.[26] But not all agreed with this at first. For instance, Bishop Callistus of Rome (ca. 217) insisted that the church would forgive and readmit those guilty of sexual offense, but this upset moral rigorists like Tertullian. Callistus defended his stance on the grounds that he was the successor of Peter, to whom Jesus had committed the keys of the kingdom with authority to bind or loose on earth what will then be bound or loosed in heaven (Matt. 16:19). Tertullian argued that Jesus said this only to Peter, and that the bishop's job was not to forgive but to administer discipline. Significantly, Callistus responded that the church was not a society of saints, but an ark and a school for sinners; those who are thrown overboard

---

25. It is evident in Scripture that some sins are worse than others. In the Old Testament, for instance, transgressions were punished to various degrees depending on whether they were committed wittingly or unwittingly. In the New Testament, Jesus also asserts there will be degrees of punishment, as when he speaks about Tyre and Sidon in Matthew 11:22–24. Cornelius Plantinga wisely says that, while all sins are equally wrong, not all sins are equally bad. See *Not the Way It's Supposed to Be: A Breviary of Sin* (Grand Rapids: Eerdmans, 1996), 21.

26. There is evidence of this in the first- or second-century text the Shepherd of Hermas.

have no chance for salvation. (He also appealed to Jesus's parable about the wheat and the tares.) Eventually, the view of Callistus and Rome won out with regard to sexual offenders.

The Christian church soon suffered empire-wide persecution under two emperors—Decius around 250 and Diocletian around 305. In both cases many Christians fell away (committed apostasy) but later desired readmittance to the church. Many who had been imprisoned and survived (the "confessors") advocated liberal forgiveness. But it was not theirs to offer. During the Decian persecution, Bishop Cyprian of Carthage was not ready to readmit the "lapsed" at first, even though he shared Callistus's view of the church. He argued that no human had the power to forgive apostasy; the guilty would have to await God's judgment.[27] But, in part owing to his withdrawal during the persecution, he changed his position, claiming that the powers of the keys *were* invested in the bishop to forgive the lapsed after some delay and on a graded scale of penance. But the bishop's forgiveness was absolutely necessary for readmission to the church—to the ark that was essential for salvation. In his argument he made two assertions that continue to be reasserted today even though they admit various interpretations. Cyprian claimed, "Outside the church there is no salvation," and "He cannot have God for his Father who has not the church for his mother." In addition, Cyprian insisted that the focus of the church's unity is the bishop, so that to forsake the bishop is to forsake the church.[28] The church had come a long way in a relatively short time from centering church membership on acceptance of apostolic teaching as taught by the bishop to submission to the bishop himself.

An issue arises at this point that will be helpful to recall when we discuss baptism in the next chapter. One of those who objected to Cyprian's tolerance was Novatian, an educated elder in Rome who gathered a large following. He took the position that the church was less like an ark and more like a city set on a hill to give light to the world by its holy example. The church could only intercede for the sinner at the last judgment; it had no power or authority to grant forgiveness of the three major sins. Novatian wanted to be bishop, but he lost to Cornelius, who said that the bishop *could* remit (forgive) these sins. So the Novatians left the church. But eventually some of his followers applied for readmission to communion. They had been baptized by Novatian, so Cyprian of Carthage insisted that such a baptism administered outside the bounds of the Spirit-filled church is not baptism. This was contested by a

27. See St. Cyprian of Carthage, "On the Lapsed," trans. Allen Brent, in *On the Church: Select Treatises* (Crestwood, NY: St. Vladimir's Seminary Press, 2006).
28. See Cyprian, "On the Unity of the Catholic Church," trans. Allen Brent, in *On the Church*.

new bishop of Rome, Stephen, who said that baptism administered in water in the name of the Trinity was valid wherever it was done. Those baptized outside the recognized church should not be rebaptized but simply reconciled by the laying on of hands. The sacraments do not belong to the church, but to Christ, so that the sacraments depend on the correctness of their administration, not on the correctness of the one who administers them. The issue was not settled by the time that both bishops died, but it reared its head again fifty-five years later under the Diocletian persecution when a group similar to the Novatians—the Donatists—separated and claimed that only clergy who were free from grave sins could administer the sacraments validly. This time Carthage sided with Rome, and years later Augustine argued that the validity of the sacraments does not depend on the holiness of the priest: "Baptism belongs to Christ regardless of who may give it"—even if the administrator is a heretic. This position is known by the Latin phrase *ex opere operato*, which is translated "on the basis of the work performed" (as opposed to *ex opere operantis*, "on the basis of the one who performs the work").

Church Polity: The Basic Options

Like the word *politics*, polity refers to the government or organizational structure of churches. There are three basic options, all with New Testament precedent, but none are usually found in their pure state. Implicit in each option are commitments regarding how the Holy Spirit guides the church and wherein authority lies.

Episcopal polity is a system of government overseen by bishops (*episkopoi* in Greek). In some cases the bishops are understood to stand in some sense of apostolic succession (as is the case with Roman Catholic, Eastern Orthodox, and Anglican churches). In other cases bishops are simply recognized as having precedent in the New Testament (as is the case with Lutherans, Methodists, and the Church of the Nazarene). (The latter grouping does not always use the word "bishop," but instead might use labels such as "district superintendent.") The Holy Spirit's authority rests for the most part on bishops in this polity. And their authority works its way down through priests (or pastors), deacons, and, finally, to the laity. Essentially it can be portrayed as a pyramid structure.

The bishop's chair is called a *cathedra* (deriving ultimately from the Greek word for "chair"), so that the bishop's church is a *cathedral*. The bishop oversees the churches that are located in a geographical region that is usually referred to as a *diocese*. In many cases it is the bishop's prerogative to ordain priests and to administer the sacrament of confirmation. Priests can celebrate the Eucharist and pronounce absolution (forgiveness of sins), as well as preach and baptize. Deacons serve, ultimately, at the behest of the bishop and are primarily concerned with meeting the administrative and material needs of the parish (local church).

Congregational polity lies at the other end of the spectrum—a system of government run by the local congregation. It can be portrayed as a circular structure, with the Holy Spirit's guidance flowing within and through the members of the congregation. In many cases the pastors and in all cases the officers come from within the congregation.

There are two types of congregational polity. One is pure or independent congregationalism, wherein the local church decides its own theological orientation and practices. So-called nondenominational churches fall into this category. Another type is associational congregationalism. In this case the local church has autonomy, but it relates to a larger body of believers, so each church belongs to a group larger than itself. The group shares certain theological commitments, and they might pool some of their resources to support missionaries, educational curricula, outreach opportunities, and so forth. No association has any *legal* power over a congregation, and there is no obligation to join or participate in the association. Baptist denominations, United Church of Christ, Brethren, Mennonites, and Quakers are typical examples of this polity.

Historically, many congregationalist churches began in protest against episcopal and presbyterian polities in places such as England, Germany, and Scandinavia, seeking freedom from creedal uniformity and from interference in the life of the local congregation by the church hierarchy or by the state.

Presbyterian polity falls between the episcopal and congregational forms, looking something like a trapezoid when pictured (see figure 5). It is a circulating system of church government by a group of elected elders (*presbyteroi* in Greek), not overseen by a single figure (bishop) nor localized within a congregation. Authority and the Spirit's guidance move up and down through specified levels of organization, something much like US constitutional government (due to historical, colonial linkages between the two). Elders selected by local church members represent the local church in a geographical region of churches that is much like a diocese, but is usually called a presbytery or a synod. Representatives from those regions then constitute a national assembly, often referred to as a General Assembly or a General Synod. Decisions made by the national body have been issues generated by the lower bodies, but may still have to be ratified by those lower bodies before they become "law."

Obviously this polity is characteristic of Presbyterian churches, as well as any denomination that has "Reformed" in its title (such as the Christian Reformed Church).

Figure 5
Types of Church Polity

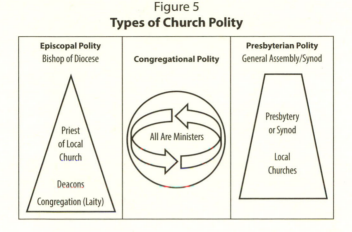

The Church's Relation to the World

Jesus told his disciples that they were being sent into the world as he was sent into the world by the Father (John 20:21). And we are also instructed to do so in the liturgy when the pastor gives the benediction or when the deacon stands at the back and sends us out. We gather from the world into the worship service and then, having been reminded of the story we are in, return to the world to live out our discipleship wherever God plants us.

The church's relation to the world has been cast in numerous ways—categorizations that help us to see the variety. In modern times one of the significant classifications was articulated by Ernst Troeltsch. Troeltsch used two categories: "*Sect*-type Christianity" and "*Church*-type Christianity."[29] The former views church as a voluntary association, usually a small group of believers whose values differ from those of the culture and who are hostile toward and suspicious of the world. These stress radical obedience to Christian ethics, don't expect their views to be adopted by society in general, are not inclined to see the church as an institution, and emphasize individual religious experience. The latter views church as a large institution whose values contribute to society as a whole, with expectations of social acceptability and views that should be sanctioned by the larger society.

29. See Troeltsch's discussion of these categories in *The Social Teaching of the Christian Churches*, trans. Olive Wyon (Chicago: University of Chicago Press, 1976), 1:331–43.

Later, in the 1950s, H. Richard Niebuhr penned his classic *Christ and Culture*. His five categories are somewhat self-explanatory given his titles and examples: Christ *against* Culture (Tertullian, monasticism); Christ the *Transformer* of Culture (Augustine, Calvin); Christ and Culture in *Paradox* (Luther); Christ *above* Culture (Aquinas and the medieval synthesis); and Christ *of* Culture (nineteenth-century liberal Protestants, such as Schleiermacher and Ritschl).[30]

More recently, Mary Jo Weaver and David Brakke suggested four positions that lie on a spectrum from church to culture.[31] *Withdrawal* from culture can mean physical withdrawal from a distracting world (monasticism), psychological withdrawal from an evil world (e.g., some fundamentalists), or cultural withdrawal from a threatening world (e.g., Amish). At the other end of the spectrum is *Domination*. Whereas those who withdraw get out, those who seek to dominate culture position themselves to stay in and convert, motivated by a desire to impose a Christian viewpoint on all members of society. These might have a negative view of the world (as some on the Religious Right) or an optimistic evaluation of human potential (as nineteenth-century Protestant liberals). Two positions experience tension between church and culture. One takes a posture of *Nonconformity*, motivated by a desire to distinguish the values of the gospel from the culture to which and against which the church seeks to witness; these do not assume that Christian values and beliefs are compatible with those of society or government policies, but they do not reject culture as irrelevant or entirely evil, even though they may express themselves in protest and confrontation. They are represented by groups like the recent neomonastic movement, Sojourners Fellowship, the Catholic Workers Movement, and the Mennonite Central Committee. Finally, within the tension is *Adaptation*, motivated by a desire to achieve aims through cooperation with government whose own aims are more often than not coextensive with the church's. Tactics include conforming, modifying, compromising, and accommodating in order to influence society. They place confidence in social structures, such as voting, supporting candidates for office, and lobbying efforts. Mainline denominations (such as the Presbyterian Church USA, the Evangelical Lutheran Church of America, and the United Methodist Church) typically take this approach.

If the church is sent into the world as the Son was sent into the world, then in the end there can be no bifurcation between the personal and the social, the sacred and the secular, the private and the political.

---

30. See Niebuhr's *Christ and Culture* (New York: Harper Collins, 1951).

31. See Mary Jo Weaver and David Brakke, *Introduction to Christianity* (Belmont, CA: Wadsworth, 2008), part 4.

Though Christians are more likely to stress the personal, sacred, and private, we must recognize the political character of our worship. We see this clearly in the Revelation to John, such as in Revelation 7:9–17. Stanley Saunders and Charles Campbell help us understand this truth:

> What we have come to know as religious language of the Christian faith [e.g., *kyrios*, Greek for "Lord"] was in fact the political language of the reigning powers of the empire. Christians like John took the words being spoken about Caesar and the empire and related them instead to Jesus.
>
> These Christians believed real power lay not in the hands of the emperors . . . but with the Lamb who was slain. . . . The cry of those gathered around the throne of God in verse 10—"Salvation belongs to our God, who is seated on the throne, and to the Lamb"—is not church talk, but a social and political claim about the real ruler of the world. "Blessing and glory and wisdom and thanksgiving and honor and power and might belong to our God forever and ever" (v. 12) is not empty doxology, but powerful and provocative praise in the face of the contrary claims of the Roman Empire.[32]

We must keep this in mind when we sing hymns and "praise songs" in our worship!

32. Stanley Saunders and Charles Campbell, *The Word on the Street: Performing the Scriptures in the Urban Context* (Eugene, OR: Wipf and Stock, 2006), 57–58.

11

The Sacraments

We Practice "Baptism" and Celebrate "Eucharist"

The most significant actions of the Christian church are baptism and the Lord's Supper: the former because it is the rite of initiation into the church community; the latter because it is the celebration that sustains church members as one body. Perhaps because these are such important ecclesiastical events, the understanding and practice of baptism and communion have seen both development and significant differences.

Churches even disagree about what to call these practices. Traditionally they have been referred to as *sacraments*, derived from the Latin *sacramentum* and the Greek *mysterion* (because these are "mysteries" that go beyond perceived space, time, and divine presence).[1] The classical definition of a sacrament is "a visible sign of an invisible grace (or reality)." Augustine compared them to the way language works. Here is the word *horse*. Unless you are reading this near a pasture, corral, or racetrack, chances are no actual horse stands within range of eyesight. But the word is a sign that has conjured up in your mind what it signifies. It points to the thing itself—to the reality. More than merely "pointing" to or "signifying," as Paul Bradshaw reminds us, in the world of the early church "a sign or symbol was not thought of as being

---

1. The early church instituted *post*baptismal instruction about some aspects of the Faith and about what the newly baptized had just experienced, since the baptized were not told much beforehand about what baptism involved. This postbaptismal instruction was called "mystagogy."

something quite different from the reality which it represented, but on the contrary was understood as participating in some way in that reality itself."[2]

Besides words there are nonlinguistic signs as well. Some are natural, such as smoke—a sign that there is fire. Some are conventional, such as a red traffic light that signifies "Stop!" In the same way, some sacraments are natural signs, such as the water of baptism that represents the grace that washes away the past. But sacraments are also conventional signs, such as Jesus's command to baptize, since there are many other ways to signify cleansing and initiation into a community.

Some churches prefer the word *ordinances* rather than sacraments. This is typical, for instance, of Baptist churches that understand baptism and communion to be outward rites that symbolize the inner spiritual experiences of participants. The word *ordinance* refers to the fact that Jesus himself ordained these symbolic actions.

Some churches do not use any word at all to describe these events, and some reinterpret them to be spiritual activities, such as Quakers (Society of Friends), who practice communion with God's Spirit in their hearts.

Disagreements over the Relation between Sacraments and Divine Grace

The sacraments or ordinances have been related to the reception of God's grace in various ways—from the tightest connection to no real relation at all.

The Roman Catholic position (which is similar to the Orthodox position) teaches that sacraments give grace (*ex opere operato*) to those who receive them with the right disposition (repentance, faith), when administered and received with the right intentions, using the right form (words) and right matter (elements or actions). There have been debates whether grace comes *with* the sacraments or *in* the sacraments. In either case, the sacrament makes what it signifies a reality.

A case in point helps to see how this works out in practice. If a marriage ceremony takes place (Roman Catholics and Orthodox see marriage as a sacrament) and the priest pronounces the couple husband and wife, what was not true a second before that pronouncement has now become a reality. The sacrament effects what it signifies. But if the bride or groom or both had no intention of keeping the vows by their free consent, an annulment could be granted in the future if the couple eventually divorced, meaning that the *sacrament* never really occurred, even though there was a ceremony.

2. Paul F. Bradshaw, *Early Christian Worship: A Basic Introduction to Ideas and Practices*, 2nd ed. (Collegeville, MN: Liturgical Press, 2010), 58.

The Lutheran and the Reformed traditions understand sacraments as channels of grace—the means through which God can make divine grace a reality, though they do not *give* grace themselves. They must be received in faith, but grace is not restricted to the sacraments. In fact, even though Luther believed the sacraments were necessary for the nurture of our faith, he was adamant that it is the grace *of the Word of God* (the gospel itself) that comes *through* the sacrament that saves us. The sacrament is God's chosen means for our receiving this grace. An analogy might be this: pipes deliver water for drinking; it is the water, not the pipes, that quenches our thirst, but the pipes are necessary for delivering the water tó us.

John Calvin said that the sacraments confirm, proclaim, and seal the promise of God's grace, announcing, showing, and ratifying the good news of the gospel. It is helpful to appeal to Calvin's use of "seal" here. In his day, if an emissary of a person in authority brought a written message, its authenticity was confirmed by a wax seal with the imprint of the authority's ring. If the paper had nothing written on it, the seal would have been useless, but if the written message did not have the seal, then one could not be certain he could believe the message. Similarly, if there is no good news, then merely having the seal of baptism or the Lord's Supper communicates nothing, but having those sacraments confirms the good news that they communicate. That is, in part, why Calvin insisted that a sacrament must always be accompanied by a sermon in worship, though a sermon without a sacrament was permissible.

The Baptist and Anabaptist[3] position holds that these ordinances are merely symbols of God's goodness toward us that are in no way involved in the transmission of God's grace.

Disagreements over the Proper Number of Sacraments

The early church did not think in terms of a specified number of distinct sacraments. All holy actions of the church could be considered sacramental—visible manifestations of God's grace. Augustine taught that the church was the place where grace is encountered. The sacramental activity of the church—its ministries—simply provided the context in which we expect to experience God's grace. And this experience included activities of the church such as

3. *Anabaptist* literally refers to the "rebaptism" that some were accused of performing who protested against the continued use of infant baptism in the Reformed churches (such as Huldrych Zwingli's in Zurich). They claimed that they were not *re*baptizing, because they rejected the legitimacy of the baptism of infants. Most Baptists are not historically connected to Anabaptists, since many Baptist groups emerged in reaction to Lutheran, Reformed, and Anglican churches.

baptism and the Lord's Supper. But the number of sacraments was undetermined and could include a list as large as thirty, largely based on medieval numerology and symbolism. (Numbers such as 3, 4, 7, and 10 were filled with symbolic significance and were used in liturgy and art.) A slow, barely traceable development resulted in seven sacraments, defined by Peter Lombard[4] in the twelfth century, followed in the next century by Thomas Aquinas's systematic reflections on the seven.

In essence, natural life parallels the supernatural life in the sacramental system. Sacraments become the means for moving up to our supernatural end in life. The table below illustrates the parallelism:

Baptism	Birth/rebirth
Confirmation	Growing up
Eucharist	Daily nourishment
Penance (now Rite of Reconciliation)	Healing, restoration
Extreme unction (now Anointing of the Sick)	The entrance to eternal life upon physical death

And one of the following:

Marriage	Providing the basis on which the supernatural life can be lived by procreating biological life
Ordination/Holy Orders	Ensuring the continuing existence of a dispensation of grace

This life-cycle approach to the sacraments forms the *habit* of grace as we grow spiritually. The grace of God becomes all-embracing throughout our entire life.

Though some Protestants (such as Anglicans) might recognize confirmation, marriage, and ordination as sacraments, the Protestant Reformers claimed that only two sacraments had explicit biblical sanction—baptism and the Lord's Supper. (Reformers also saw this reduction as a way to reduce the power of the priesthood in what had become "sacerdotalism.")

Baptism

Baptism is a ritual of initiation into the Christian Faith and into the body of Christ. The New Testament would regard "an unbaptized Christian" as an

4. Peter Lombard's *Four Books of Sentences* was *the* theological textbook of the late medieval period in Western Europe.

oxymoron. While not *necessary* for salvation (even in the Roman Catholic tradition, which has an allowance called "baptism of desire" for those who have no opportunity to be baptized), baptism is *essential* for salvation (see Acts 2:37–41). The Great Commission that Jesus gave to his disciples in Matthew 28:19–20 was to *make* disciples *by baptizing* and by teaching what Jesus taught (following the grammatical construction of the Greek in this passage).

Baptism also signifies that we share in the divine life. In Romans 6 Paul reminds his readers that they have been baptized into the death and resurrection of Jesus. Indeed, since the Greek word *baptizō* literally means "I immerse," immersion into the waters of baptism is a drowning from which we are suddenly delivered as we are brought up out of the water. We have died to the old self by being buried with Christ, and we have been raised to new life by participation in Christ's resurrection. (Some believe that John 3:5 may be referring to our spiritual rebirth through baptismal water.)

The early church had no standardized baptismal theology, and it is possible that not all baptisms were done by immersion. Baptism could be said to indicate illumination (Heb. 6:4; 10:32), repentance (Acts 2:38), death and resurrection with Christ (Rom. 6:2–11), being sealed as God's people (2 Cor. 1:22), being clothed in a new garment (Gal. 3:27), being anointed with the Holy Spirit and chosen by God (1 Tim. 2:20, 27), rebirth (John 3:5), or washing. Approaching the fourth century, the church came to insist upon practices that had already been taking place—prebaptismal instruction in doctrine and ethics, fasting, prayer, and repentance—all preceding baptism. In addition, by the fourth century it was also an almost universal custom to baptize on Easter with the forty-day season of Lent serving as a time of preparation for those being baptized. Paul's theological understanding of baptism as participation in Christ's death and resurrection also became more prominent (Rom. 6). As Paul Bradshaw cleverly states, "The baptismal font was now portrayed as both womb and tomb"—as both rebirth in the Christian life and participation in the death of Christ.[5] What we call confirmation today was also closely associated with baptism as the giving of the Holy Spirit—one of the postbaptismal acts, along with the newly baptized's first communion. An interesting side note is

5. For the material in this paragraph, see Bradshaw, *Early Christian Worship*, 23–26, 30–32. For the idea of the baptismal font as "the womb of Mother Church from which her children are born" and the parallel to the immaculate womb of Mary, especially as portrayed in the Easter Vigil, see Herbert McCabe, *The New Creation* (New York: Continuum, 2010), 40–41. Ambrose (fourth century) gives early church evidence of this connection when he writes: "If then, the Holy Spirit coming upon the virgin brought about the conception and performed the work of generation, there should be no doubt that the Spirit, coming upon the font or upon those who present themselves for baptism, has truly brought about rebirth." Lawrence J. Johnson, *Worship in the Early Church: An Anthology of Historical Sources* (Collegeville, MN: Liturgical Press, 2009), 2:40.

that Sunday's early significance as the "eighth day"—the celebration of the Lord's resurrection and thus the beginning of the *new* creation—carried over to baptismal fonts that are frequently octagonal to symbolize that the newly baptized has risen with Christ and been raised into the new creation.[6]

Disagreements over baptism have been virulent at times. In Huldrych Zwingli's Zurich, Anabaptists were drowned or burned at the stake for rejecting infant baptism, though it was not so much the mode of baptism that led to the executions as it was the implication that the parents were traitors who did not allow their children's existence to be recorded with the state for future military service and taxation to defeat the Turks who were threatening Western Europe. While churches and towns do not execute people today for having a different point of view about baptism, the arguments can still get quite heated.

Those who practice believer's baptism and reject infant baptism (or pedobaptism) argue that infant baptism is not explicitly recognized in the New Testament. They argue that baptism always followed belief and that it signifies that one has become a disciple of Jesus. Most churches that practice only believer's baptism also practice baby dedication (though that is not recognized in the New Testament as a Christian practice).

Those who practice pedobaptism (and will also practice believer's baptism for adult converts) argue that it is the New Testament equivalent of circumcision in the Old Testament—a sign that the infant is a member of the covenant community. They also appeal to the New Testament references to household baptisms (Acts 10:44–48; 18:8; 1 Cor. 1:16; cf. Acts 2:39), arguing that infants and toddlers must have been present in those cases. Jesus's words about children are often cited as well (Matt. 18:1–10; 19:13–15).

Some who were baptized as infants seek to be baptized as adults because their baptism "didn't mean anything to them" and they "don't remember it." (Of course, they don't remember inoculations as infants, but that does not mean that those were not significant events that have had an impact on their lives.) This is important to those who profess believer's baptism, since the primary actor in the event is the one being baptized. Those who practice pedobaptism argue that the primary actor is God and that it is more important that God remembers it.

6. Philip H. Pfatteicher, *Journey into the Heart of God: Living the Liturgical Year* (New York: Oxford University Press, 2013), 20. A sermon of Jerome's (fifth century) on Easter Sunday articulated the importance of Sunday as the eighth day: "Just as Mary, the Virgin Mother of God, holds first place among all women, so today is the mother of all days. This is something new, and yet it is confirmed by the Scriptures; this day is both one from seven as well as one beyond seven." He follows this with citations of many occurrences of eight in Scripture (L. Johnson, *Worship in the Early Church*, 3:358).

There is also contention about the role that faith plays in baptism. Believer's baptism allows only the baptized person's faith to play the determining role. Pedobaptism finds precedent in the New Testament (e.g., Luke 5:17–26) for the faith of others to stand in for the individual's, as it were, such as the faith of the parents who bring the child for baptism.

The baptism of infants had become standard practice by the fifth century, though its evolution is not easily discerned, and the doctrine of infant baptism was not formalized until a few centuries after the practice had become the norm.[7] As the practice continued, it was thought that baptism had the power to convey sanctifying or habitual grace by removing the stain and guilt of original sin, making it possible for the baptized to experience God's sustaining grace throughout life.

Though some Lutherans and some Anglicans hold to this view, Protestants during the Reformation largely rejected it due to their conviction that justification comes by faith alone. True, the Lutherans and the Reformed continued to practice infant baptism, but it awakened faith only because of the Word of God that accompanied it. Though Luther sometimes did argue that baptism was necessary for salvation and that the Holy Spirit effects regeneration through baptism, Calvin consistently argued that infant baptism is God's way of sealing the child into the covenant community such that the children of believers are sanctified by their parents. But both Luther and Calvin believed that baptism initiated a process that continues throughout life.

Should baptism be done by immersion or by sprinkling or pouring? As we have noted, the Greek word literally refers to immersion, and most likely that was originally the usual mode of baptism. In fact, the Eastern Orthodox typically immerse a child three times! The image in Romans 6 lends itself to immersion. The first recorded sprinkling is of Novatian on his deathbed ("clinical" baptism) around 250, though some see possibilities earlier, even in the Gospel accounts.

We have already discussed different points of view about what baptism "does." It removes sin or makes one a member of the covenant community or signifies belief and discipleship . . . or a combination of these.

Eucharist

The Greek word *eucharistō* means "I give thanks." We are told in Paul's letter to the Corinthians that on the night Jesus was betrayed he "took a loaf of bread, and when he had given thanks, he broke it and said, 'This is my

7. Bradshaw, *Early Christian Worship*, 34–35.

body that is for you. Do this in remembrance of me'" (1 Cor. 11:23–24). So Eucharist has become the way we refer to the Lord's Supper, the account of which is referred to as the "narrative of institution" (of the Lord's Supper). In fact, many churches simply refer to it as the Lord's Supper (referring to what was recorded in Luke 24:30–33, for instance). The Roman Catholic Church often uses the label Holy Communion, while the Orthodox Church refers to it as the Divine Liturgy.

In any case the ritual remembers the life, death, and resurrection of Christ, and it anticipates his return, "for," wrote Paul, "as often as you eat this bread and drink the cup, you proclaim the Lord's death until he comes" (1 Cor. 11:26). Indeed, in the Eucharist, past, present, and future are brought together at the table.

Disagreements revolve around the meaning of Jesus's words about the bread when he said, "This is my body." Is that to be taken literally or figuratively? During the Protestant Reformation, Luther and Zwingli debated this question at the Marburg Colloquy in 1529. At issue were also these questions: How should we conceive of Christ's presence when participating in the Eucharist—as bodily or spiritual? And how should we conceive of the benefit of this sacrament?

In part, the Protestants were reacting to the Roman Catholic doctrine of transubstantiation.[8] Aristotelian distinctions between accidents (changeable properties or characteristics) and substance (or essence, the underlying reality) form the background to this doctrine. To illustrate, human beings are *substantially* just that—human—but they come in all different sizes, shapes, eye and hair and skin color, with or without all appendages, and so on. These differences are "accidents." In the same way, bread is *essentially* bread even though it comes in all shapes, textures, ingredients, tastes, and so on. So, in the celebration of the Eucharist it is the *substance* of the bread that is *trans*formed, not the accidents. It still tastes, feels, and smells like bread, but essentially or substantially it has become something else—the body of Christ. The same is true of the wine. This happens when the priest administers the sacrament and comes to the words "this is my body" (*hoc est corpus meum* in Latin). Of course, only by faith can this be discerned.

During the Middle Ages this understanding took on magical aspects: laity were restricted from taking the wine; much was done behind the curtain with bells indicating what was happening; the Mass (from *missa*, meaning

8. Luther did not completely reject transubstantiation; he just believed it was not necessary to go to such lengths to explain what is happening. See "The Babylonian Captivity of the Church," in *Martin Luther's Basic Theological Writings*, ed. Timothy F. Lull (Minneapolis: Fortress, 1989), 286.

dismissal) was conducted in Latin,[9] incomprehensible to the laity; adoration of the consecrated host (bread) was emphasized. The Protestant Reformers attempted to restore New Testament practices as they saw them, rejected the explanations of medieval theologians, and restored both "kinds" (i.e., the bread and the wine) to the laity. Yet the question remained: Exactly how is Christ present in the Eucharist if transubstantiation is not embraced?

The Lutheran position is sometimes known as *consubstantiation*, though Lutherans typically prefer not to use that word. As Luther taught, they believe the body of Christ is "in, with, and under" the elements, though no inner or substantial change takes place in the elements. In other words, the real *bodily* presence of Christ is affirmed in the Eucharist.

The Reformed position did not deny that Christ was *really* present when a communicant consumed the bread and wine, but it was the *spiritual* presence of Christ, not the bodily presence. It is the Spirit who connects us to the localized risen body of Christ. An analogy might help. If you are connecting with someone on the computer using FaceTime or Skype, the person at the other end is not bodily present in the same room, yet they *are* really present to you through all that goes on in the wireless ("spiritual") connection. Calvin rejected the notion that a human body—even the risen body of Christ—could be everywhere present, since that is not a characteristic of human bodies. Christ is present bodily at the right hand of the Father. In that sense, Calvin's position was closer to the Antiochene view that we discussed in chapter 5. On the other hand, Luther's view was sympathetic to the *communicatio idiomatum* that typified the Alexandrian position, such that a human body could have communicated to it the divine characteristic of omnipresence.

Both Zwingli and the Anabaptists viewed the bread and wine as mere commemorations of Christ's death and resurrection that nonetheless strengthen the believer's faith. Christ is not more present in the elements than he is in any other context. If anything, the bread and wine act as symbols of Christ's death and Christian unity, much like a national flag can symbolize a people's history and allegiance.

9. Some have suggested that *hocus pocus* comes from the laity's misunderstanding of the Latin *hoc est corpus*, the point at which the bread "magically" becomes the body of Christ.

12

What Is the Future of God, Humans, and the World? Eschatology

The "Dismissal" That Sends Us Out into the World from Which We Gathered

As we have mentioned, in some liturgies a deacon might remain at the back of the church after all the other clergy and attendants have processed out and say something like, "Let us go forth into the world, rejoicing in the power of the Holy Spirit." This is the dismissal. Given what the congregation has heard and seen and tasted, it is now ready to return to the world from which it came and infiltrate God's creation to spread good news of the coming kingdom and serve others in the name of Christ until he comes again.

So this introduces us to the concept of eschatology. The word comes from the Greek *eschaton*, meaning "end things" or "last things." Eschatology, then, is the study of the end—the end of our individual lives and the end of the cosmos as we know it. Specifically, it deals with questions about death, resurrection, Christ's return, heaven and hell, the final judgment, the kingdom of God, and other related topics.

Of all the topics in theology, this is the one that has generated the most speculation, sometimes with elaborate charts and detailed analyses of biblical passages and words intended to help us see where we are now and where we will be in the near future in the grand scheme of things. But eschatology was never meant for speculation. We are given information about the end or goal in order to know how to order our lives now. As we discussed in an earlier chapter, Christians are to live their lives on the basis of what is coming. Even the prophets in the Old Testament foretold what was going to happen in order for the recipients of their message to straighten up or else. The story of Jonah is a good example.

Traditionally, eschatology has been divided between personal eschatology and general or cosmic eschatology.

Personal Eschatology: Who Will Be Saved?

A perennial question has to do with the extent of salvation, especially since there are many who will never have the opportunity to hear the gospel before they die. Three positions have typically addressed this issue.

The first is universalism or *apokatastasis*—the doctrine that eventually all will be saved. One hears echoes of this even in the New Testament, when Paul declares that *all* things will be reconciled in Christ (Col. 1:20) and that God desires *everyone* to be saved (1 Tim. 2:4). There will be punishment for sin; that is not denied. But it is not eternal, and it is more a fire of purification than anything else. Significant church leaders and theologians have held this position. Among them are Clement (second century), Origen (third century), Gregory of Nyssa (fourth century), and Theodore of Mopsuestia (fifth century). More recently, Schleiermacher advocated this view in the nineteenth century, and the logic of Barth's theology seemed to lead in this direction in the twentieth century, though he would not pontificate one way or the other. In fact, at one point Barth warned against panic over the word *universalism* before some careful investigation and then added this admonition: "We have no theological right to set any sort of limits to the loving-kindness of God which has appeared in Jesus Christ. Our theological duty is to see and understand it as being still greater than we had seen before."[1] This makes sense when we emphasize God's love and omnipotence: if God *does* desire that none perish but *all* be saved, and if God *is* all-powerful, then universalism seems to follow. As someone has said, we should at least be "*hopeful* universalists."

At the other extreme is exclusivism or particularism. This view emphasizes New Testament judgment passages such as the division between sheep and goats (Matt. 25:31–46), the condemnation of those who do not believe in the Son (John 3:16–18), and the insistence that only those who proclaim Christ's lordship are saved (Rom. 10:9–15). Despite slight variations within

---

1. Karl Barth, "The Humanity of God," in *The Humanity of God*, trans. Thomas Wieser (Louisville: Westminster John Knox, 1996), 61–62.

this camp, essentially the conviction is that only those who explicitly acknowledge Christ's lordship during an unrepeatable life will be saved. Others will be condemned to the irrevocable state of hell. In one sense or another, this has been the majority position throughout the history of the Christian church. Some might admit agnosticism when it comes to those who never have a chance to hear the gospel, while others are adamant that having heard it or not, those who do not believe are eternally condemned.[2]

A mitigating position between the two extremes has been labeled inclusivism. This position again appeals to 1 Timothy 2:4 and also to Hebrews 11:6, which teaches that God rewards those who seek him. Biblical examples of Melchizedek and Cornelius (both outsiders) are mentioned. This view holds that God's mercy is wide enough to save those who seek God, even if they are seeking him in other religions. They are saved only *through* Christ, but they do not necessarily have to *know* Christ. A recent advocate of this view was the twentieth-century Roman Catholic theologian Karl Rahner, who said that a Buddhist, for example, might be an "anonymous Christian" who has "implicit faith" in Christ. The Protestant theologian Clark Pinnock articulated a very similar view, even allowing for postmortem conversions of those who had not heard the gospel before death but who, in the afterlife, might meet the Christ they had sought all along.

Personal Eschatology: How Will They Be Saved?

Another way of asking this question is, What happens when we die? What do we know about our deaths and the afterlife for individuals? On the one hand, we must not want to know too much (see 1 John 3:2 and Mark 13:32). We have a limited ability to understand and express what is known about death, and the Bible does not give us a single message concerning death, though we can find some common denominators.

Death is spoken of as natural—a condition of weak, frail human nature (e.g., Ps. 39:4–6). Yet death is also portrayed as unnatural, contrary to our innermost being, and something having an ethical significance—our enemy (1 Cor. 15:54–57). But we affirm that Christ has decisively, if not yet finally, conquered death, and it will be no more in the new heaven and new earth (Rev. 21:4).

We can say with certainty that there is no series of incarnations or transmigrations of the soul (Heb. 9:27). There is no absorption into an impersonal

---

2. On this division of opinion, see the positions of Alistair McGrath vis-à-vis R. Douglas Geivett and W. Gary Phillips in *Four Views on Salvation in a Pluralistic World*, ed. Dennis Okholm and Timothy Phillips, rev. ed. (Grand Rapids: Zondervan, 1996).

whole; we retain our personal identities (e.g., Matt. 17:1–4; 22:23–32; also 1 Sam. 28:13–14). And death is not annihilation: at the least, it is "sleep"; at the most, it is a conscious awareness of the soul awaiting the resurrection of the body.

When we examine the Old Testament, we do not find much about resurrection or coming back to life after death. Notions of the afterlife developed more in the intertestamental and New Testament periods.

In the Old Testament, Sheol (Hebrew for "pit"; from "to demand, demanding") is the place of the shades to which we are inexorably summoned—the lowest level of Hebrew cosmology. It is the place to which *all* the dead go: the wicked (Pss. 9:17; 31:17; 49:14; Isa. 5:14) and the righteous (Job 3:11–19; 14:13; 17:16; Pss. 6:15; 16:10; 88:3), though the emphasis is especially on the place for the unrighteous (Prov. 2:18; 5:5; 7:27; 9:18). It is not hell, but it is usually portrayed as a place of absolute silence, inactivity, and no remembrance, cut off from God, completely separate from life (see Ps. 88:3–6, 11–12; Eccles. 9:5–6, 10). Still, the possibility of a degree of consciousness does appear (Isa. 14:9–11, 15–17), and God is not entirely cut off from Sheol; we even find expressions here and there of being delivered from Sheol by God (1 Sam. 2:6; Job 14:13–15; 26:6; 38:17; Pss. 16:10; 49:15; Prov. 15:11; Isa. 26:19; Amos 9:2).

By the time we get to the New Testament, we see a brighter picture in some respects. The parallel to Sheol is the Greek Hades, though its portrayal differs somewhat. As with Sheol, Hades seems to be the place to which all the dead go (Rev. 6:8). Even Christ is said to have gone there (Acts 2:27, 31, and the Apostles' Creed). Some say it includes "paradise" and gehenna, separated by a chasm.[3] And over against Sheol, while apparently there can be no communication between those in Hades and the living, there does seem to be communication and some consciousness in Hades (Luke 16:19–31; Rev. 6:7–11). Furthermore, God has access; Christ has the keys to Hades and to death (Rev. 1:18).

Though there had been no single picture or consistent use of terminology regarding the afterlife, by the time of Jesus, the Jewish understanding seemed to look something like this: death is followed by an intermediate state that involves sorting into temporary locations in a divided Hades, waiting for one's final destination in paradise or gehenna. So the question becomes: What is the status of our existence between physical death and the final resurrection?[4]

3. "Paradise" and "gehenna" seem to be basically the equivalent of heaven and hell. "Paradise" is the heavenly Eden that comes to be the residence of the blessed and the elect where they dwell with the Lord, but its location and duration are various. "Gehenna" (the valley of Hinnom) was literally the garbage dump just south of Jerusalem and the place where the Israelites had sacrificed their children to Moloch. Figuratively, it designates the place of eternal fiery torment of the damned.

4. One good resource for all of this is John Cooper's *Body, Soul, and Life Everlasting: Biblical Anthropology and the Monism-Dualism Debate* (Grand Rapids: Eerdmans, 2000).

Whatever one answers, two biblical emphases must be taken into account. First, the New Testament asserts that immediately at death we may expect to be with Christ (Luke 23:43; Phil. 1:23; also see 2 Cor. 5:1–10; Luke 16:23). Second, the New Testament suggests that there is something like a waiting "sleep" of all the dead until they are raised on the "last day" (1 Thess. 4:13–18; also see Matt. 27:52; John 11:11–13; 1 Cor. 11:30; 15:20, 51; 1 Thess. 5:10; Rev. 6:11).

Beyond these emphases, some argue that upon death the "soul" will be with the Lord in Hades while the body remains in the grave. On the "last day" the body is raised, reunited with the soul, and faces final judgment. This view would account for the claim that Christ visited the dead before he was raised on the third day (see Luke 16:22–31; 23:43; 2 Cor. 5:1–8; Phil. 1:23–24).

Others argue that the separation of the soul and body is not biblical. Instead, the whole person dies—soul and body, though there is an unbroken and immediate presence with Christ. According to this view, Christ was totally dead in the grave before the Father raised him (Heb. 2:17; 1 John 2:2; 4:10). The intermediate state is a time of sleep, and when awakened one has a sense that no time has elapsed (see John 5:25–29; 1 Thess. 4:13–18). Some Lutherans have held this idea, along with Seventh-day Adventists.[5]

The Eastern Orthodox and Roman Catholic traditions have included the notion of purgatory—a state or place or process for those who will be saved. Though the teaching is found in developed form as far back as Gregory the Great in the sixth century, it was further enunciated by the Catholic Church at the Councils of Lyon (1274), Florence (1439), and Trent (1545–63), which stressed the need for further purification before meeting a holy God and for temporal punishment for the satisfaction (expiation) of sins insufficiently satisfied and of unrepented, unforgiven venial (i.e., not mortal or deadly) sins. Current Catholic teaching emphasizes only the need for purification in the sense that it defines a process by which one's basic love of God, which becomes immutable at death, penetrates the resistant elements in the personality: it purges the aftereffects of sin, integrates character, and purifies one of sin since nothing impure can enter heaven (Rev. 21:27). The alleged biblical basis comes from Matthew 12:31–32 and 1 Corinthians 3:11–15, but primarily from the Apocrypha in 2 Maccabees 12:42. Protestant Reformers rejected the doctrine on two counts: first, they rejected the need for temporal punishment, insisting that the atoning work of Christ took care of *all* punishment for sin, and second, they argued that the doctrine really did not have any biblical basis.

Before we look at general or cosmic eschatology, we must emphasize that the Christian concept of the afterlife is *not* that of disembodied souls hovering

---

5. This view is also held by Jehovah's Witnesses and by Mormons.

somewhere in outer space. The influence of Platonism has been so prevalent in Christian history that salvation is popularly portrayed as the soul's eternal separation from the body and from the material world. Nothing could be further from the truth. We will be raised *bodily* to inhabit a renewed earth.

General Eschatology

Christian theology insists that the cosmos is headed somewhere under the guidance of God toward a new world of justice, healing, and hope. In fact, Christians believe that the future has already begun to come toward us who dwell in the present—between the "old age" and the "new age."

Traditionally, there have been four views about this future, and in one way or another, everyone's eschatology seems to fit into one of these categories.[6] That said, all four do have common emphases. They have in common these convictions:

- God is sovereign, and Jesus Christ is the Lord of history.
- We live between the "already" and the "not yet" reality of the kingdom of God.
- The church does not exist to serve itself, but to be a witness to Jesus's kingdom (Matt. 28:18–20; Luke 24:44–48; Acts 1:8).
- Christ will "come again" (though we may need to speak of it as Christ's "second appearance").
- The end will include the final defeat of Christ's enemies (1 Cor. 15:25; Rev. 19:11–16).
- All humanity will be raised to answer to Christ (Matt. 25:31–46; John 5:24–29).
- The kingdom of God in its fullness will involve a "new heaven and a new earth" (though we may need to more carefully understand the word *new* as "*renewed*"—a difference in quality, not quantity).

Historically, differences have arisen because of controversies about the timing of Jesus's second coming (the *parousia* in Greek) and the nature of the millennium. Often these views have been associated with various times in history, since prevailing social conditions have appeared to corroborate one view over the others.

6. E.g., see Stanley Grenz, *The Millennial Maze: Sorting Out Evangelical Options* (Downers Grove, IL: InterVarsity, 1992).

Many attitudes about society, the church's role in the world, the value of education, involvement in the culture, and interest in political processes reflect Christians' eschatological views.

The traditional discussion of eschatology focuses on the issue of the second coming of Christ, which is mentioned in twenty-three of the twenty-seven books of the New Testament (described in Revelation only in Rev. 19). (Revelation 19–20 forms a continuous narrative announcing the marriage of the Lamb, the victorious return of Christ, and Christ's victory over his enemies.)

The *millennium* (the word around which all these views revolve) refers to the period explicitly mentioned only in Revelation 20:1–6 when Christ reigns for a thousand years—the promised messianic kingdom. This period occurs after Satan has been thrown into the abyss and is unable to deceive the nations. Thus, the millennium is usually conceived of as a time of unparalleled righteousness, peace, and prosperity for the earth. At the end of this period, though, Satan will be released. Once again he deceives the nations in a period of tribulation—a time of intense persecution—and is defeated and thrown into the "lake of fire," which finally seals his fate.

The labels for the three prominent positions arise from the question: When will Jesus's second coming occur? There are three answers:

1. *Premillennialism*: Jesus's second coming will occur before the millennium and after the tribulation (*posttribulational*) or before the tribulation (*pretribulational*). (There is a midtribulational view as well.)

2. *Postmillennialism*: Jesus's second coming will occur after the millennium.

3. *Amillennialism*: There is not a specific millennial period per se.

General Eschatology: Premillennialism

The general position of premillennialism with its two variations argues that Christ's second coming (when the godly are raised) will occur *before* the millennial (literal 1,000-year) reign of Christ over the earth, after which will come the completion of God's plan when the ungodly will be raised to judgment and a new heaven and new earth are created.

Posttribulational (or *historic*) *premillennialism*: Following a straightforward—some would say "literal"—reading of Revelation 20, this position understands Christ's second coming as a *single* event that occurs after the tribulation. So, the "rapture of the church" (the event in which believers are transported to be with Christ) also occurs after the tribulation. At this time Christ destroys the antichrist and his forces at Armageddon. All believers are then raised to reign with Jesus during the millennium. With the end of the millennium God's plan reaches completion with the final judgment and the creation of a new heaven and new earth.

A major question facing this position concerns the purpose of the millennium, since it will be occupied by nonbelievers and believers reigning with Christ. These advocates note that the millennium represents a new advance for the kingdom from its status during the "church age." In some way Satan will be less active than he was previously during the church age, and Jesus will now be reigning visibly instead of invisibly in heaven. During this period, when Satan is locked up and unable to deceive the nations, this sinful world is as perfect as possible.

This view tends to be less sympathetic to modern-day Israel, denying that there are two covenants (one for Jews and one for the church) and that the Jews have a special place of privilege in the millennium (though it is willing to admit that Israel remains the elect people of God and that "all Israel" will be saved à la Rom. 11:26). In fact, this view (similar in this regard to amillennialism) concludes that the New Testament applies Old Testament prophecies to the New Testament church, identifying the church as the spiritual Israel. This view criticizes dispensationalism for taking a literal interpretation of the Old Testament and fitting the New Testament into it, rather than vice versa.

This position was the historic position of the early church fathers until about AD 400. Its strengths, along with the next view, include the seriousness with which it treats Scripture, as well as its recognition of sin's depth that only Christ can reverse.

Pretribulational premillennialism (or *dispensationalism*): This view divides Christ's second coming into two phases, one for the church that occurs before the tribulation and a second for Israel that occurs during the tribulation. Jesus's return begins with the rapture of the church prior to the tribulation. That means that the present church age (in which we live) leads up to the rapture of the entire church (the first phase). Just before the rapture of the church there will be signs, including the preaching of the gospel to all nations and increasing wickedness (such as apostasy, wars, famines, earthquakes, and the appearance of the antichrist). Christ's return is therefore *imminent* (i.e., soon, at any moment), and when it begins the dead believers will be raised and living Christians will meet Christ in the air and triumphantly go to heaven. This spectacular event prompts Jews to recognize Christ as their Messiah, and many are converted during the subsequent period.

The tribulation follows this, when the antichrist attacks Israel. This world ruler will be defeated at Armageddon by Jesus Christ and his heavenly forces (Rev. 19:11–21) during the second phase of his second coming. At that time the dead saints and the tribulation martyrs will be raised, and Christ will reign for a thousand years on earth with Jerusalem as the capital of his kingdom. This will be a time of peace and righteousness, with evil held in check. The purpose of this millennial period is to fulfill the Old Testament promises given to Israel. God had promised to Abraham that his descendants would possess the land of Canaan (Gen. 12:1–7); that they would have a privileged and prosperous place in the world (Ps. 72); and that one of David's descendants, the Messiah, would rule over the Israelites (Isa. 11). Then Satan will be loosed, and there will be wars on Jerusalem. This is followed by the "Great White Throne" judgment and the creation of the new heaven and new earth.

Closely tied to dispensationalism, this view dominated evangelicalism during much of the twentieth century, and more recently with the *Left Behind* book series and movies. It was widely disseminated through the teaching of John Nelson Darby (nineteenth century) and the Scofield Reference Bible (twentieth century). The predominance of this view among evangelicals has had the effect of stimulating financial assistance for modern-day Israel, since those who hold this view believe that the current nation-state is to be the recipient of God's Old Testament promises. (The perhaps unintentional side effect has been the near neglect of Palestinian Christian brothers and sisters in the same region.)

Premillennial dispensationalism has also been indicted for its pessimism about the church's ability to transform society on political, economic, and social levels (especially in its earlier classical form). If our only hope is the rapture at the second coming, then a person may not be eager to get involved in social action. The only purpose of the church is to "save souls," as was portrayed in the movie *A Thief in the Night*, in which the sole concern of Christians in the film is that people not be left behind when Jesus comes back unexpectedly. (A corrective needs mentioning at this point, since the phrase "left behind," found in Matt. 24:36–44, is wrongly attributed to those who are unbelievers. Jesus compares the "coming of the Son of Man" with the "days of Noah": the flood swept away all but Noah and his family, so, "as it was . . . so it will be" at "the coming of the Son of Man" those who will be taken away are like those who were swept away in the flood, while those who are "left behind" are like Noah and his family.)[7]

Still, premillennialism provided much of the motivation for the worldwide missionary initiative in modern times, even in evangelizing and providing social help to those the political establishment had already discarded, such as

---

7. This point is made by Brian J. Walsh and Richard Middleton in *The Transforming Vision: Shaping a Christian Worldview* (Downers Grove, IL: InterVarsity, 1984), 104.

the homeless, alcoholics, and prostitutes. Dwight Moody in Chicago is a good example. The dispensationalist W. E. Blackstone (1841–1935) was a political visionary at a time when the United States was isolationist, vigorously working for a land for persecuted Russian Jews and advocating an international court of justice where national disputes could be settled justly; his advocacy significantly aided the Zionist movement in America, as well as President Wilson's promotion of a World Court.

But has premillennialism adopted a wooden interpretation of the Bible in ways that leave little room to be surprised at how prophecy might be fulfilled in unexpected ways, similar to serious mistakes in the misreading of Jesus's first coming? Moreover, a key issue questions whether the Old Testament promises can be so sharply disconnected from the realities that the church experiences. The New Testament appears to insist that the Old Testament promises are now being fulfilled within the church (1 Pet. 2:9).

The next two views stress the church's role in evangelism *and* the transformation of society (the two going hand in hand), and they encourage Christians to work through normal political and social means to transform society.

General Eschatology: Postmillennialism

Postmillennialists teach that Jesus's second coming will occur after the millennium. Jesus bound Satan during his earthly life (Rev. 20:2–3; cf. Matt. 12:29; Luke 10:18). As a result, Jesus has not only commanded the church to extend his rule throughout the whole world (Matt. 28:18–20), but he even promised that nothing will resist the church's onward march (Matt. 16:18). Consequently, there will be an unprecedented revival in the church preceding Christ's return. Through its preaching of the Word and acts of self-sacrificial love, which bring social justice and improved living conditions, the Spirit-empowered church is already extending the kingdom of God. Christian values are pervading the world, transforming the problems that plague society (such as slavery, injustice, disease), and progressively bringing the world under the rule of God. The whole world will experience peace and improving social conditions until Christ returns, though not everyone will become a Christian.

So the millennium is not a visible reign of Christ on earth, but an invisible spiritual reign of Jesus through the power of the church that comes in gradually during a time that may or may not be a literal thousand years. *The church brings about the millennium*, not the visible presence of Jesus Christ! At the end of the millennium Satan will be unleashed for a little while (Rev. 20:7–8) and the tribulation will occur (1 Tim. 4:1; Matt. 24:14–27), though believers will survive. Then, at Christ's second coming, as he comes back to a Christianized world, the dead will be raised and the final judgment will take place. The world will finally be under the complete uncontested reign of Christ.

Postmillennialism was the dominant view of some conservative Protestants in the nineteenth century, such as the nineteenth-century abolitionists and revivalists Charles Finney and Jonathan Blanchard, the first president of Wheaton College. Affirming God's goal to restore creation to its original perfect state through evangelism and social action, it motivated many to take up the cause of abolition, women's rights, and care for the poor. The best summary of the position comes perhaps from Blanchard in one of his addresses, "A Perfect State of Society": "Society is Perfect where what is right in theory exists in fact; where Practice coincides with Principle, and the Law of God is the Law of the Land."[8]

The strength of this position is that it affirms the goodness of the world that God has created and the activity of God in working out his plan to restore his creation to its original perfect state. Thus, it provides a strong encouragement in both evangelism and social action.

In recent times, with the perception of worsening conditions in the world, postmillennialism has fallen out of favor. Opponents also charge that it fails to do justice to Scripture's pessimism about the human condition (Mark 13), empirical evidence of the pervasiveness of sin, and some biblical prophecies (Rev. 20).

General Eschatology: Amillennialism

Amillennialism is not as unduly optimistic about the future as postmillennialism or as pessimistic as premillennialism. This position insists that we are *now* in the so-called millennium since Christ bound Satan, established the kingdom in part, and now reigns in the church and the hearts of the redeemed. (Those believers who have died are living and reigning with Christ in heaven.) Simply put, we are in the "last days." As we get nearer the final end, there will be increasing wickedness (tribulations). The church, however, eagerly looks forward to Christ's second coming, which comes after, not before, the millennium. At that time, all living believers will welcome the return of Christ. Then the world will be under the complete reign of Christ; that is to say, the consummated kingdom will finally exist. Thus, the kingdom of God is both a present reality (that began with the first advent—"inaugurated eschatology"—Luke 17:20–21) and a future hope (that will be realized with the second advent of Christ—"future

8. Jonathan Blanchard, "A Perfect State of Society" (address, Society of Inquiry, Oberlin College, Oberlin, OH, 1839).

eschatology"—Matt. 7:21–23; 8:11–12). The "thousand" years is symbolic (ten stands for "completeness," and this is ten to the third power).[9]

This view has been popular from the fourth century on, especially after Constantine was converted and made Christianity a legal religion in the Roman Empire. Christianity subsequently gained popularity and ascendancy, and the church viewed itself as making the kingdom present. It has been especially popular with many in the Reformed tradition, which stresses the transformation of the present world until Christ comes again.

A strength of this view is perhaps its track record. It has been a persistent eschatological view that has been maintained respectably by a great number of theologians over a long period of time.

But the position has also been criticized for a weakness in that it interprets Scripture figuratively to fit its schema (e.g., the millennium is not literally one thousand years). Critics also suggest that amillennialism diminishes evil's destructive power. This view usually denies that the end of time involves a destruction of the creation and its re-creation. Rather it envisions creation being released from the perverting powers of evil.

General Eschatology: Recent Discussions

Though they can be located within the four positions just described, it is worthwhile to indicate discussions of eschatology that have taken place in the last two centuries, at least in the West.

What brought eschatology back to the attention of theologians in the modern period was perhaps Johannes Weiss's *Jesus' Proclamation of the Kingdom of God* (1892). He was reacting against some of nineteenth-century Protestant liberalism that had focused on the quest for the real historical Jesus purportedly beneath layers of myth. Significant figures such as Adolf von Harnack and Albrecht Ritschl viewed the kingdom of God as something that should be constructed through human effort, believing that God is our Father and

9. A paraphrase of Revelation 20:1–3 by Anthony Hoekema is instructive: "During the gospel era which has now been ushered in, Satan will not be able to continue deceiving the nations the way he did in the past [i.e., the "Abyss"], for he has been bound. During this entire period, therefore, you, Christ's disciples, will be able to preach the gospel and make disciples of all nations" (Matt. 12:28–29; Luke 10:17–18; John 12:31–32). He continues: "There is no indication in these verses [Rev. 20:1–6] that John is describing an earthly millennial reign. The scene . . . is set in heaven. Nothing is said in verses 4–6 about the earth, about Palestine as the center of this reign or about the Jews. The thousand-year reign of Revelation 20:4 is a reign with Christ in heaven of the souls of believers who have died. This reign is not something looked for in the future; it is going on now, and will be until Christ returns." *The Bible and the Future* (Grand Rapids: Eerdmans, 1979), 235.

Jesus is our exemplary brother and teacher. Weiss argued that Jesus's vision of the kingdom was not something that humans could put in place now, but was a future work of God.

At the beginning of the twentieth century, Albert Schweitzer criticized the nineteenth-century "lives of Jesus" in his book *The Quest for the Historical Jesus*, arguing that all the questers had looked down the long well of history only to see their own reflection. In other words, they had read their own modern assumptions into the story and teachings of Jesus. Schweitzer argued that Jesus taught a radical eschatology about a future kingdom that was supernatural and would come suddenly following a cosmic cataclysm. Jesus not only taught this during his lifetime, but he tried to engineer the kingdom's coming through popular apocalyptic and messianic expectations. But Jesus died prematurely before he could make the kingdom a reality, dying a disillusioned man who cried out to God on the cross.

Schweitzer's contention that eschatology was a major theme in Jesus's teaching was affirmed during the first half of the twentieth century by C. H. Dodd, but Dodd insisted that Jesus did not teach a future kingdom, but a kingdom that had been foretold in the Old Testament and had already arrived. In this "realized eschatology," the "day of the Lord" has come, fulfilling Old Testament prophecies of God's triumph, judgment, and eternal life that is now ours. All the New Testament accounts of Jesus's teaching a future coming of the kingdom were fabricated by the early church using Jewish apocalyptic literature. God's kingdom is a reality that goes beyond space and time.

Not so, countered Oscar Cullmann, a twentieth-century Lutheran theologian. The kingdom of God becomes reality in our linear time. Jesus's crucifixion, resurrection, and ascension are the midpoint between creation and Jesus's second coming. The kingdom has "already" come—Jesus decisively defeated Satan on the cross (like D-Day in World War II)—but it is still "not yet" because all the evil that remains must be dealt with (like V-Day in World War II). So now we live in the tension between the "already" and the "not yet," an understanding that brings together the present and the future dimensions of the kingdom.

Though his school is no longer prominent, Rudolf Bultmann challenged positions such as Cullmann's that viewed God's plan worked out in linear time and historical space. Working from the philosophical perspective of existentialism, Bultmann argued that the eschatological symbols in the Bible simply reflected the mythology of the people at that time as they considered their present existential experiences. If we strip away or "demythologize" the myth in Scripture, we can reinterpret or "remythologize" eschatology for our modern times. What the Bible really refers to is not some future sequence of events, but the present experiences of all people when they are confronted by the Word of God and forced to respond with a decision, to come to a new self-understanding, and to become radically open to the future. And God continues to meet us as God confronts us in the "eschatological moment."

More recently, Protestant theologians such as Jürgen Moltmann and Wolfhart Pannenberg and Roman Catholic theologians such as Johann Metz have stressed the future aspect of Christianity. It can be said that Moltmann has made eschatology the most prominent of the loci in Christian theology, beginning with the 1965 publication of *A Theology of Hope*, in which he taught that God is the God of the future, and Jesus Christ is only known to us as he comes to us from the future. The church is the community that waits for God to fulfill God's promises in history—in the kingdom of God, which is present now only as the horizon of a promise and a hope that stands in contradiction to the present. This disjunction draws the church into conflict as it takes ethical and political stands as a way of making what is coming in the future something of a present reality now.

Eschatology: Final Assessments

Eschatology is not as central as other branches of doctrine such as Christology, the Trinity, sin, and salvation. But, as we have pointed out, much of the Christian's attitudes regarding society, the church's role in the world, and the interpretation of history are affected by her eschatology. Our vision of the future is essential for the way we live as Christians. We are even commanded to give reasons for the hope that we have (1 Pet. 3:15). Those who dismiss eschatology and the various points of view as mere theological quibbles that don't matter much are simply misguided in their thinking.

Not only that, but eschatology has been a significant theme in the church's liturgy and calendar for centuries. It seems that the Western church calendar has begun with the first Sunday of Advent (from the Latin *adventus*, meaning "arrival" or "coming")—at least since the beginning of the seventh century.[10] Since early in the church's history, the liturgy of the four Sundays of Advent not only reminds us of God's coming to us in Jesus Christ but also focuses our attention on the future return of the risen Lord. So Advent becomes a time when we not only reenter the story of Israel's long wait for its Messiah, but also prepare our lives for the future advent of Jesus. Similarly, Christmas

---

10. Philip H. Pfatteicher, *Journey into the Heart of God: Living the Liturgical Year* (New York: Oxford University Press, 2013), 27. The Eastern Orthodox calendar begins the church year on September 1, the beginning of the tax year in the Byzantine Empire; see p. 25.

looks backward at the event of Jesus's first appearance, but also forward to the future event of Jesus's second appearance—the *parousia*. In fact, when Isaac Watts (an eighteenth-century minister known as the "Father of English Hymnody") wrote the well-known hymn "Joy to the World," he was not thinking of Christmas, as we have appropriated it. It was a song about the second coming of Christ:

> Joy to the world, the Lord is come!
> Let earth receive her King;
> Let every heart prepare Him room,
> And heav'n and nature sing.
>
> Joy to the earth, the Savior reigns!
> Let men their songs employ;
> While fields and floods, rocks, hills, and plains
> Repeat the sounding joy.
>
> No more let sins and sorrows grow,
> Nor thorns infest the ground;
> He comes to make His blessings flow
> Far as the curse is found.
>
> He rules the world with truth and grace,
> And makes the nations prove
> The glories of His righteousness,
> And wonders of His love.

Watts treats the future event as if it had already happened: the king has come to reclaim what is his; creation rejoices (see Rom. 8:18–23); the devastating effects of the fall are undone (see Gen. 3:17–18); and his truth, grace, justice, and love rule in all nations.

This brings personal and general eschatology together as N. T. Wright has done in his writings.[11] This also brings it back to where we started this book—the biblical story into which we have been baptized. The promised final future is *not* that immortal souls will leave behind their mortal bodies. If so, then death wins! To believe that salvation is the death of the body so that the soul can escape to heaven is way off the mark; in fact, it is to join forces with death. There is very little in the Bible about "going to heaven when you die." We have misconstrued Christian eschatology because of a residual Platonism

---

11. See N. T. Wright, *Surprised by Hope* (San Francisco: HarperCollins, 2008), for what follows. Also see J. Richard Middleton, *A New Heaven and a New Earth: Reclaiming Biblical Eschatology* (Grand Rapids: Baker Academic, 2014).

that envisions salvation as disembodied souls, an overemphasis on the individual at the expense of the larger picture of God's creation, a dismissal of the significance of the bodily resurrection of Jesus, and misunderstandings of biblical texts and phrases.

The Bible's message proclaims God's sovereign rule—the kingdom of God "on earth as it is in heaven," for which we plead every time we pray the Lord's Prayer in the liturgy. As we have mentioned, God's sovereign rule has already broken into the present world. It was seen in Jesus's healings and exorcisms (e.g., Luke 4:17–21). This fulfills the hope of Israel (Isa. 52:7–12). Yet this in-breaking is also the purpose for which God called Israel in the first place—to cooperate with God in reestablishing God's sovereignty over the whole creation as a great act of healing and rescue, not *from* creation, but to be a light to the Gentiles so that humans could be rescued to be God's rescuing stewards or priests over all creation. Jesus launched a whole new state of affairs in which the power of evil is decisively defeated and the new creation is decisively inaugurated. Jesus's followers are commissioned and equipped to put that victory and that inaugurated new world into practice. So if we want to benefit from Jesus's saving death, we must become part of his kingdom project. This is a salvation for humans, through God's elect, for the wider world. It forms the basis of the church's mission.[12]

Debates will continue based on hermeneutical issues, and people will disagree about the exact ways in which we go about cooperating with God's kingdom agenda and about the nation-state of Israel today. But we have learned that such is the ongoing project of theology—getting to know more and more about a God we love and the relationship God intends to have with the creation God loves. And so, it is into that world that the deacon dismisses us as we go forth, rejoicing in the power of the Holy Spirit, who gives the church strength and courage to love and serve God in every good thing we say and do.

12. Wright, *Surprised by Hope*, 204–5.

The Benediction

As the liturgy ends and we are sent into the world with a vision that has been once again reshaped and reinforced by the biblical story, the shepherd of the flock speaks words that wish us well (literally, a *benediction*) on our journey:

> May the Lord bless you: May he cause you to prosper richly in every good spiritual gift there is in Christ Jesus.
>
> May he watch over you, guard and protect you and all whom you love.
>
> May his countenance be upon you, his face turned toward you such that you would see in Jesus how very much he loves you, accepts you right where you are, and invites you to follow him.
>
> May he be gracious unto you: May you sense his favor, mercy, and goodness as you walk with him.
>
> May the Lord grant you peace: May you be at rest and centered in Jesus, who is our Lord, and through whom we ask all these things.[1]

---

1. Benediction used with permission of Todd Hunter, bishop in the Anglican Church in North America.

Appendix

Examples of Assignments to Be Used with This Book

At appropriate places in the reading, these assignments, or ones stimulated by these examples, will help bring what has been read in this book in touch with real-life situations. Their purpose is to demonstrate understanding of the doctrinal or liturgical issues involved and wrestle with the ways in which those issues intersect with day-to-day life.

Analyze Liturgies and Rituals

Attend and analyze two "liturgies." In his book *Desiring the Kingdom*, James K. A. Smith discusses "rituals of ultimate concern"—that is, "rituals that are formative of our identity, that inculcate particular visions of the good life, and do so in a way that means to trump other ritual formations."[1]

> Part 1: Attend a *Christian* worship service (preferably an Episcopal/Anglican service, Roman Catholic Mass, or Eastern Orthodox Divine Liturgy). Analyze the liturgy using the set of nine questions below.
>
> Part 2: Go to a *major* shopping mall. Spend the same amount of time you spend in the liturgy in part 1 (preferably on the same day), and analyze the "liturgy" that is going on there using the same nine questions below.

1. James K. A. Smith, *Desiring the Kingdom: Worship, Worldview, and Cultural Formation* (Grand Rapids: Baker Academic, 2009), 93.

1. Where did you go? (specific church and mall)
2. When did you go?
3. How were you "drawn in"? (consider parking, architecture, entrance, etc.)
4. Once you were inside the building, what was the relationship to the "outside" world?
5. How were you made aware of the season/time of year/calendar?
6. What did artwork, statues, symbols, images communicate?
7. What were you made to think about yourself: what you are now, what you ought to be, and what you should become?
8. How did people act? Were they led? Were they acting out of habit? Did they know what to do? Did they act like a community or act independently?
9. Were you given a sense that there was something that transcended—went beyond—our present reality?

Analyze "rituals." As mentioned in the previous assignment, in *Desiring the Kingdom*, James K. A. Smith discusses "rituals of ultimate concern"—that is, "rituals that are formative of our identity, that inculcate particular visions of the good life, and do so in a way that means to trump other ritual formations."[2] We engage in ritual practices every day. Some are highly significant, and some are not. Examples are mentioned in chapter 1. Your assignment is to investigate *one* of the following rituals:

- putting a hand over the left breast when saying the pledge of allegiance or when singing the national anthem
- a bride's throwing her bouquet over her shoulder for a female wedding guest to catch
- blowing out birthday candles on a birthday cake
- putting hands together (i.e., applauding) to show appreciation

In brief responses to the following, analyze the ritual you chose. First, identify which ritual you are discussing, and then answer:

1. What is the origin of this ritual practice? (cite your sources)
2. Why is this ritual engaged in? Why is it practiced? (cite your sources)

2. Smith, *Desiring the Kingdom*, 93.

3. How does this ritual practice shape us, or what is its significance (consciously realized or not) for our lives?

Questions

Address one of the following using what you have learned from your reading, as well as Scripture, your church tradition, reason, and experience. You can write this up as an essay, an imaginary dialogue, or the outline of a presentation.

Options:

1. Did God create the universe in six twenty-four-hour days, or did he use evolution, or did he do it in some other way? Should what scientists say have an effect on the way we read Genesis 1?
2. Does everything [including 9/11 and the Nazi Holocaust] happen because God wills it?
3. Does God predestine people to be saved? If so, why are the ones not predestined born? If not, why wouldn't God save everyone, since God desires that none should perish?
4. Are people "saved" because *God* decides they will be or because *they* decide they will be? What about someone in, say, Sudan who grows up Muslim and never hears the Christian story about Jesus—can God simply choose that this person will be saved, or is he saved as long as he lives a good life, or does he need to hear the gospel to be "saved"? If he can be rescued by God without hearing the gospel, why do we even need missionaries?
5. If your church decided to call a woman to be the head pastor, what would be your reaction? What would you say to encourage the folks who agree with your position, and what would you say to those who disagree with your position? Could the church avoid a split over this issue, or should some people leave if they think this is a wrong decision?
6. Should we baptize infants?

Case Studies

In an essay, address the issues raised by one of the four case studies regarding a particular doctrine. Use what you have read, as well as Scripture and reason.

1. *The doctrine of revelation*: You were at Starbucks the other day and struck up a conversation with a Muslim student. She is devout and was respectful of your Christian orientation. But she encouraged you to accept her belief that the Qur'an is inspired and the result of a miracle, and she believes that your Christian Scriptures have been compromised and corrupted. What do you say in response?

   Another possibility: You were at Starbucks the other day and struck up a conversation with two Mormon missionaries who were taking a break. (They were drinking water, but thought Starbucks would be a good place to encounter non-Mormons in their mission work.) They talk to you about the Book of Mormon, but you've been studying Christian theology and believe that Scripture consists of only the Old Testament and the New Testament. They suggest you read the Book of Mormon, asking God the Father, in the name of Christ and by the power of the Spirit, to convince you that it is *indeed* the truth (Moroni 10:3–4). How will you respond to their arguments about Scripture that go beyond the Bible?

2. *The doctrine of providence*: A friend just lost his mother in a mass shooting back home. Several people were killed and more were injured. You go to the funeral with your friend because you want to offer some comfort. The pastor of their home church preaches at the funeral and says that we Christians can take some comfort in the fact that this was God's timing and all in God's plan, even if it was not in ours. This was all in God's providence, even though it was an evil action that led to her death. Your friend isn't sure he agrees with the pastor, but he knows you are taking this theology class and wants to know what you think about what the pastor said. What do you tell your friend?

   Another possibility: In conversation with a friend about why he refuses to visit a church or Bible study, he blurts out that his uncle was killed in the 9/11 attack on the World Trade Center. Some people in his church said God knew that 9/11 would happen. They said, "God took him home. It was his time." He even heard a TV preacher say God *wanted* 9/11 to happen! He asks if you think God knew it would happen. How do you answer? Explain whether you think God ever wills for evil to happen and for people to die at a specific time, even if it is three thousand individuals at the same time. What would you have said to comfort him when his uncle was killed?

3. *The doctrine of the atonement*: You are on a church committee that is putting together their own book of hymns and praise songs for worship

on Sundays. One of the contemporary hymns being considered is by Getty/Townend, entitled "In Christ Alone." You remember singing this in chapel and in church, but now an argument ensues. A few people on the committee want to include the hymn, but a couple of people object to its inclusion because they do not think the line "On that cross as Jesus died, the wrath of God was satisfied" is good theology. They will accept the hymn's inclusion if that line is changed. Explain the position you take in the committee's discussion about this.

Another possibility: In your studies this semester you have learned about models of the atonement that are forensic (e.g., satisfaction and penal substitution theories). In fact, you have heard these explanations of how we are saved by Jesus in your church and in some of your classes. But your roommate recently heard a sermon during a church worship service on the parable of the prodigal son that spoke of salvation as restoration of relationships. He/she comes to you confused because that sounds so different from the forensic views about which you've been telling your roommate. How can you help deal with your roommate's confusion? How do you make sense of the fact that reconciliation takes place in this parable without any sacrifice? (Keep in mind the religious context of the parables when Jesus told them.)

4. *The doctrine of the sacraments*: You started going to a Presbyterian church because you like the pastor. After you've gone for a while, you adopt an infant child. The pastor counsels you to have the infant baptized as soon as possible. How will you respond? What will you say to your parents who are Baptists and reared you to be a Baptist, especially since they believe baptizing infants is something Roman Catholics do, which they, as Baptists, find unacceptable?

Another possibility: You were baptized as a Presbyterian when you were an infant. You have attended a Presbyterian church all of your life, and, frankly, you like the Presbyterian denomination. But you also need to eat, and you just heard of a new paid position for youth director that opened up at a large Baptist church in the area. You have a successful interview and they want to hire you, but, knowing of your Presbyterian infant baptism, they insist that you must be baptized in their church. Write a letter to the Baptist Church personnel committee explaining what your decision will be, supporting it with good theology and Scripture.

Another possibility: You've been asked to attend the baptism of your infant nephew. Are you going to go with enthusiasm, celebrating the baptism of your nephew, or are you going to go with a bad feeling about this because you think only believers should be baptized? What will be your attitude and (theological) thoughts as you watch your nephew being baptized? Or are you going to avoid going altogether because this is just wrong (having to explain to your sister and brother-in-law at a later date why you didn't show up)? How will you explain it if you do not attend?

Theologically Analyzing Story

1. Watch the movie *Stranger than Fiction* (starring Will Ferrell). Write an essay engaging in some theological reflection about this movie. Background: Emma Thompson's character is a God-figure (note the glimmering white loft high in the sky where she writes her novel), and Will Ferrell's character is a kind of Christ-figure (with a required death written into the script, a kind of Gethsemane wrestling with his fate while riding a bus all night, a sacrificial death, and a kind of resurrection). (*Do not take these characters literally. They are merely types or figures. God is probably not a chain smoker!*) If the novelist is a bit like God determining history—and particularly Harold Crick's history—discuss how the movie illustrates the theological issue of God's story, witnessed to in Scripture (as discussed in chapter 1), and our participation in God's story. Include in your discussion the extent to which we are free to disengage from or change the plans God has for the world and for us as individuals.

2. Read *one* of the following short stories by Flannery O'Connor: "Revelation," "The River," "A Good Man Is Hard to Find," "The Artificial Nigger," "The Displaced Person," "A Temple of the Holy Ghost," or "Parker's Back." Identify the doctrinal or liturgical issue that O'Connor is focusing on. Analyze how she treats it in the story and what she is trying to communicate. In your analysis, use what you have read as well as Scripture. Include succinct and poignant quotes from the story (but do *not* simply summarize the story).

Scripture Index

Subject Index